T0211439

# Beginning PowerShell for SharePoint 2016

## A Guide for Administrators, Developers, and DevOps Engineers

### Second Edition

Nikolas Charlebois-Laprade

John Edward Naguib

Apress®

*Beginning PowerShell for SharePoint 2016: A Guide for Administrators, Developers, and DevOps Engineers*

Nikolas Charlebois-Laprade
Gatineau, Québec, Canada

John Edward Naguib
Cairo, Egypt

ISBN-13 (pbk): 978-1-4842-2883-8
DOI 10.1007/978-1-4842-2884-5

ISBN-13 (electronic): 978-1-4842-2884-5

Library of Congress Control Number: 2017942718

Cover image designed by Freepik

Managing Director: Welmoed Spahr
Editorial Director: Todd Green
Acquisitions Editor: Gwenan Spearing
Development Editor: Laura Berendson
Technical Reviewer: Adam Driscoll
Coordinating Editor: Nancy Chen
Copy Editor: James A. Compton, Compton Editorial Services
Compositor: SPi Global
Indexer: SPi Global
Artist: SPi Global

Distributed to the book trade worldwide by Springer Science+Business Media New York, 233 Spring Street, 6th Floor, New York, NY 10013. Phone 1-800-SPRINGER, fax (201) 348-4505, e-mail orders-ny@springer-sbm.com, or visit www.springeronline.com. Apress Media, LLC is a California LLC and the sole member (owner) is Springer Science + Business Media Finance Inc (SSBM Finance Inc). SSBM Finance Inc is a **Delaware** corporation.

For information on translations, please e-mail rights@apress.com, or visit http://www.apress.com/rights-permissions.

Apress titles may be purchased in bulk for academic, corporate, or promotional use. eBook versions and licenses are also available for most titles. For more information, reference our Print and eBook Bulk Sales web page at http://www.apress.com/bulk-sales.

Any source code or other supplementary material referenced by the author in this book is available to readers on GitHub via the book's product page, located at www.apress.com/9781484228838. For more detailed information, please visit http://www.apress.com/source-code.

Printed on acid-free paper

*Thanks to my parents for raising, helping, and support.*
*Thanks to my wife and my daughter for understanding and support.*
*Thanks to my whole family. I love you so much.*

*—John Naguib*

*To my beautiful kids Eloïk & Emy, and wife Krystel.*
*Thanks for allowing me to always reach my goals in life and*
*set even bigger ones once I reach them.*

*—Nik*

# Contents at a Glance

# Contents

# About the Authors

**Nikolas Charlebois-Laprade** is a Microsoft Premier Field Engineer in Gatineau, Canada. His background as a Software Engineer and as a Technical Program Manager makes him a well-rounded web technologies expert. Nik is always looking to fill up gaps between two technology stacks by coming up with innovative solutions that help empower the users. He is currently involved in helping various PowerShell Desired State Configuration (DSC) open-source projects reach their next level of maturity. His wife and kids are what motivates him to always push the boundaries of what's possible to achieve.

**John Edward Naguib** is a Microsoft MVP in Office Servers and Services, an experienced collaboration & senior consultant and solution architect with deep knowledge of SharePoint. In addition to being a consultant and architect he has a strong application development background in .NET. John also has experience with several other Microsoft products, including Office 365 and Azure, and holds MCP, MCTS, MCITP, MCPD, MCT, and TOGAF 9 Foundation certificates. John is a recognized SharePoint expert within the industry, speaker, event organizer, and Wiki Ninja blogger, and has published several gold award articles on Microsoft TechNet. You can find John on Twitter @johnnaguib.

# About the Technical Reviewer

**Adam Driscoll** is an experienced software developer and a Cloud and Datacenter MVP based out of Madison, WI, USA. He has experience working with a range of Microsoft technologies and programming languages. Adam is the author of the open-source project *PowerShell Tools for Visual Studio*. This extension is used by thousands of developers around the world and currently ships as part of the Visual Studio installation package.

# Acknowledgments

Whilst writing this book I have had the help and support of many people. First I would like to thank my Microsoft MVP colleague Chendrayan Venkatesan for his recommendations; it is appreciated.

Then I need to thank the fantastic team at Apress: Gwenan Spearing, Acquisitions Editor; Nancy Chen, Coordinating Editor; and Laura Berendson, Development Editor.

I would like also to thank my Microosft MVP colleague Adam Driscoll for being the Technical Reviewer.

I would also like to thank Microsoft Corporation and whole Microsoft MVP program for all the things you are doing for MVPs.

Last but not least, I would like to thank my colleague Nikolas Charlebois-Laprade. It was an honor for me to work with him on this book and I hope we work on another project soon.

—John Naguib

# CHAPTER 1

■ ■ ■

# Introduction

PowerShell brings the best of both worlds: the world of administrators and the world of developers, allowing administrators to view in clear text what is being executed as part of a script, and developers to reuse their knowledge of the SharePoint object model by writing reusable modules and methods. It doesn't require users to compile any code, and it leverages all of the power of the Microsoft .NET framework. The goal of this book is to try to bridge the gap that exists between SharePoint IT pros and developers by giving users tools enabling them to deploy, manage, and monitor their SharePoint environment themselves. By the end of the book, you will be able to perform most operations that are available through the Central Administration interface or through the SharePoint object model, by developing your own flexible and reusable PowerShell scripts.

## The SharePoint Challenges

In IT organizations it is common to find a clear distinction between the developers and the administrators. Developers create new modules and functionalities for systems, and administrators are responsible for implementing and deploying them to production environments. Administrators are also normally in charge of configuring and maintaining the environments where these solutions have been deployed. In many cases, developers create solutions without really grasping what their solution will imply for configuration. They give the administrators the instructions to implement their product, and off they go. Even in the SharePoint world, this is often the case.

We've worked in several IT organizations that have been dealing with the technology, and we've seen many cases in which administrators have to perform hours of manual intervention to configure solutions properly across all sites in a SharePoint environment. To give you a concrete example, think of a typical scenario in which a development team creates a new web part that needs to be added to all existing webs in an environment. What if the environment includes 10,000 web pages spread across multiple site collections? To think that someone is going to go through each of these and manually add the web part is pure craziness. This type of situation highlights the need for a solution that would let the administrators responsible for implementing solutions automate tasks in a repeatable fashion.

Before PowerShell was available, we had to create .exe applications using .NET console applications or .NET windows applications, or even develop extra ASP.NET pages or web parts to apply what is needed to the SharePoint farm. When PowerShell came around, near the end of SharePoint 2007's life, it was like a revelation. Now, we could have the same repetitive configuration tasks being executed against the server, but they were no longer contained in these black boxes that were the console applications. They were now stored as plain-text PowerShell scripts that administrators could open to peek at the logic they contained. For the record, PowerShell scripts are stored as .ps1 files and can be edited using any text editor software. We personally use Notepad++ for all our scripts, but there are some other good free alternatives that offer

© Nikolas Charlebois-Laprade and John Edward Naguib 2017
N. Charlebois-Laprade and J. E. Naguib, *Beginning PowerShell for SharePoint 2016*,
DOI 10.1007/978-1-4842-2884-5_1

advanced features such as the automatic completion of command names after a few characters to help speed the writing process. The problem, however, was that if you didn't know your way around the .NET programming world, chances were that you would be totally lost in the code. SharePoint 2007 did not provide any PowerShell methods to interact with its components. You had to load the SharePoint assemblies into your PowerShell sessions and interact with the .NET objects directly. It was basically the same as writing your code in Visual Studio.

SharePoint 2010 then came to the rescue. It offered what we can call shortcut methods, or cmdlets (pronounced "command-lets"), that allowed users to interact with various SharePoint artifacts in a very straightforward and easy way. For example, assume that you are trying to get the title of a specific SharePoint web in your environment. In the SharePoint 2007 world, this had to be achieved using the something similar to the following lines of PowerShell:

```
[System.Reflection.Assembly]::LoadWithPartialName("Microsoft.SharePoint")
$site = New-Object Microsoft.SharePoint.SPSite("http://localhost")
$web = $site.RootWeb
$title = $web.Title
```

Using PowerShell with SharePoint, the same operation can now be achieved using the following two lines of PowerShell:

```
$web = Get-SPWeb http://localhost
$title = $web.Title
```

---

■ **Note**  It is best practice when including a URL to add the `-identity` parameter, as shown here:

```
Get-SPWeb -Identity http://localhost
```

but for simplicity we will not use the `-identity` parameter in this book.

---

This new way of using PowerShell to interact with SharePoint not only made scripts simpler, it also made them more readable. Administrators wanting to write scripts no longer had to know the SharePoint object model inside-out in order to build powerful PowerShell scripts (although it definitively helped).

PowerShell is not just for administrators, however. Complex scripts might still require some level of programming skill in order to be completed. In many organizations, developers are still responsible for writing the PowerShell scripts for maintenance tasks. This is an interesting paradigm, because it forces them to be aware of how the administration modules of SharePoint actually work. If you want to have a PowerShell script developed for your organization that automates the creation of hundreds of crawled properties for your SharePoint search engine, the developer writing the script will need to understand the various search administrative components to develop the script. This means that, on one end of the spectrum, we need administrators to start understanding some high-level programming concepts and understand the SharePoint object model to some level, and, on the other end, we have developers who need to be more open-minded about the administration aspect and learn how to configure the administrative components of SharePoint properly. Figure 1-1 illustrates this concept.

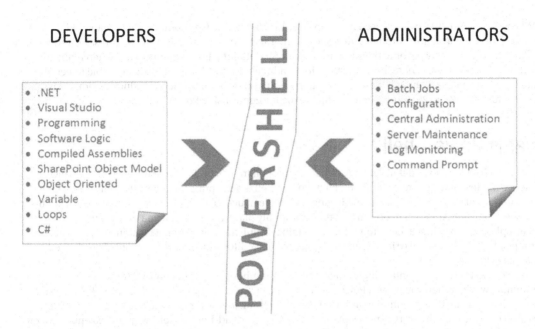

*Figure 1-1.  Traditional developers versus traditional administrators*

Throughout this book, we will cover material that in a traditional mind-set would be specific to SharePoint administrators, such as timer jobs, health monitors, and backups, but we will also touch on topics that developers would normally be more familiar with, such as lists and list items. In writing this book, our goal was to try to bring traditional SharePoint developers to learn more about the administration aspect of the product, and for administrators to learn more about how the various artifacts are organized in the SharePoint object model. Therefore, by the time you finish reading this book, we hope to bring you out of your comfort zone by opening your horizons and making you understand the possibilities to bring as many developers and administrators on par with regard to their SharePoint skillsets.

# History of PowerShell

Microsoft's latest scripting language, PowerShell, was first released in the Fall of 2006, just a few months before the release of SharePoint 2007. Because of the parallel development schedule for the two products, SharePoint 2007 never really had any integration points with PowerShell. You could interact with your environment using PowerShell and by making direct calls to objects inside the SharePoint assemblies, but that was never really publicized or even recommended by Microsoft as an official way of managing your systems. SharePoint administrators had to manage their environments using a legacy command-line tool called Stsadm that was first introduced with the original release of SharePoint, then called SharePoint Team Sites (STS).

A few years later came SharePoint 2010, and the story changed completely. Microsoft finally came out and announced that PowerShell was now an official contender on the SharePoint administration scene. In this version, administrators were now officially allowed to choose between the old Stsadm way of managing SharePoint environments or using this new technology called PowerShell and being one of the cool kids. Microsoft also announced it was investing a lot in the technology, and that it was making over 400 methods available to administrators to help them better manage their farms. Not only is PowerShell more powerful in terms of the type of scripts you can produce using it, but it also performs better in most cases than its Stsadm equivalent. The technology allows you to interact directly with any .NET entity and to declare custom ones if need be, placing PowerShell somewhere between a pure development language and a traditional sequential scripting one.

When SharePoint 2013 was released in the spring of 2013, Microsoft announced that it had made several new methods available through PowerShell to interact with the new platform's features. Nowadays, PowerShell has definitively become the standard tool for SharePoint administrators to use when managing their farms. It is important to note, however, that the Stsadm command-line tool is still available to people that are feeling nostalgic. Although it exists to support compatibility with previous product versions, it is deprecated for SharePoint 2016 and Microsoft highly recommends using PowerShell instead.

# What Is PowerShell?

Without going into too much detail yet about what PowerShell truly is under the hood, we will try to give a 1,000-foot overview of what it really is about. First, PowerShell is a scripting language. It is not a tool, nor is it a framework; it's just a plain human-readable language you can use to write your scripts. PowerShell scripts are in many ways similar to batch jobs, in that they are simply plain-text files that you execute through a console application to achieve the automation of certain administrative tasks on a machine. The scripts are not compiled, and they can be written using any good old text editor software. We write all of our PowerShell scripts using Notepad++.

A PowerShell script can contain logic loops, variables, methods, and other entities from the programming world. When you write a PowerShell script, you normally save it as a plain-text file having a .ps1 extension. You are then required to initiate a PowerShell console session to execute your script. The PowerShell console looks in every aspect similar to the old command-line console, with the exception that it has a blue background with white text. Everything that you can do in a command-line console can be done in a PowerShell console session—and more. You do not even need to write scripts in PowerShell to execute a sequence of logical operations. The console keeps the various variable declarations in memory for the entire duration of the PowerShell session. Figure 1-2 shows you a fairly simple PowerShell session in which variables have been declared and are remembered throughout the execution of the various commands. It starts by declaring two variables, variableA and variableB, whose values will later be reused to perform mathematical operations. The script continues by changing the value of one of the two variables already declared and rerunning the same addition operation to get a different result based on the new value entered.

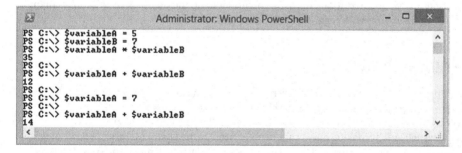

***Figure 1-2.*** *Using variables in a PowerShell console session*

PowerShell scripts can also make use of external .NET assemblies, which, to us, is what really brings the scripting tool to the next level. Imagine that developers in your organization have developed a .NET utility that exposes a bunch of methods that are to be used by various .NET applications and services in your organization. If the methods contained in the resulting assemblies are publicly exposed, meaning that any external process can access them, then PowerShell can leverage the functionality inside these utilities for scripting purpose.

Take the following example, in which you have developed a .NET application that has a graphical interface that lets the users view and interact with an interactive bedtime story, say Snow White (yes, I have a young daughter). Now, pretend that your developers have exposed a method called MirrorMirror that, when called by the graphical interface, returns the name of the person who's the fairest of them all. Well, you could use PowerShell to import a reference to this functionality and have it used in your script for other purposes. Figure 1-3 shows that this scenario is easily achievable with the PowerShell technology.

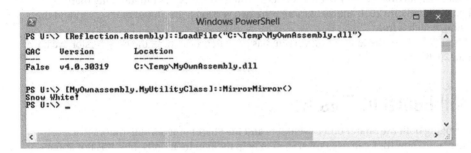

***Figure 1-3.*** *Using PowerShell to interact with external .NET assemblies*

Another very interesting thing to note about PowerShell is that because it is built on top of the Microsoft .NET stack, it can also reuse any graphical interface component that .NET has to offer. Although you could argue that you would realistically never need to build a graphical user interface using PowerShell, this example highlights the fundamentals of reusing various building blocks that are made available through existing components to come up with interesting solutions. For instance, you could reuse a combination of .NET libraries and the SharePoint Client Object Model to build interactive graphical applications that can interact remotely with a SharePoint environment Figure 1-4 shows a graphical interface generated by PowerShell.

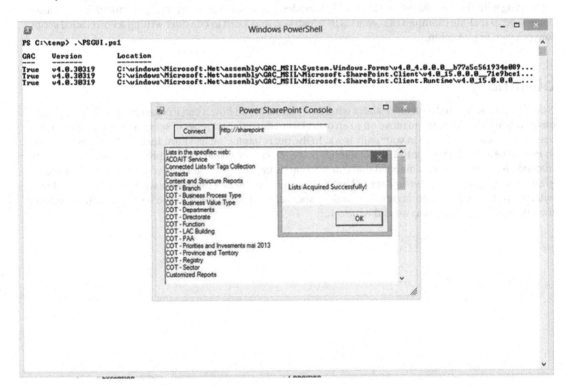

***Figure 1-4.*** *A graphical interface generated by PowerShell*

# SharePoint Foundation versus SharePoint Server

It has been a while since Microsoft released SharePoint Server 2007, known as MOSS 2007. It was followed by another free version, called Windows SharePoint Services, which contains less functionality than MOSS 2007; and then in SharePoint 2010 and 2013 there were two versions: the SharePoint server; and the SharePoint Foundation, which is free.

But now with SharePoint 2016 the foundation version has been deprecated, so the only version we have now is the SharePoint 2016 Server.

# What You Will Learn in This Book

This book is about bringing both the SharePoint developers and the SharePoint administrators to a level where they both understand how they can use PowerShell to help them in their daily jobs. It is not about teaching the internals of SharePoint, although we will take a brief look under the hood. We will assume throughout this book that readers have had some exposure to SharePoint but no exposure to the PowerShell technology whatsoever. We will cover the basic concepts of PowerShell, and will slowly dive into the various aspects of SharePoint administration. There's one thing that readers need to keep in mind throughout this book: we are developers, and our background is purely development. The ultimate goal of this book is to allow developers to slowly make a move toward the dark side of SharePoint administration, and for administrators to improve their development skills by developing dynamic PowerShell scripts.

Throughout this book, you will learn how to configure your environment to use PowerShell, how to interact with the various components of SharePoint 2016 both on-premises and in the cloud, and how to facilitate your SharePoint 2013 to 2016 migration using PowerShell. Special attention will be given to interacting with the new SharePoint 2016 add-in model, previously known as the Apps model. We will also cover several real-life examples of scenarios in which you may want to consider writing a PowerShell script for your own organization.

# Summary

Now that you've learned a bit more about what PowerShell is and how it can interact with your SharePoint environment, you are ready to move on to an overview of the different types of scenarios in which you can use PowerShell to assist you in your daily work. In the next chapter, we will introduce you to the new features in PowerShell with SharePoint 2016. Remember that each chapter builds on the previous one to deliver new material. It is strongly recommended that you read carefully through each chapter to make sure that you grasp every concept. Whether you are a SharePoint administrator or a developer, we truly believe this book will help you grow as an Information Technology specialist, and we hope that you have as much fun reading the information it contains as we had writing it.

# CHAPTER 2

■ ■ ■

# What's New in SharePoint 2016

SharePoint 2016 was first announced at the Microsoft Ignite 2015 conference in May, 2015. It was the very first time that Microsoft went public with details about what the next major version of its on-premises version of the software was going to include. At that time, several exclusive participants from the Microsoft Most Valuable Professional (MVP) community had already been selected, one of the authors included, to participate in what the software company calls a Technical Assessment Program (TAP). This very limited program granted access to Alpha versions of what would eventually become SharePoint 2016 to its members. For months we've tested the new features and those that have been updated, reporting bugs and making suggestions back to the product team.

In this chapter, we will highlight what the nice new features are, and will quickly describe how PowerShell can be used to interact with, configure, and enable them.

## New Features

In this section of the chapter, we will give an overview of the new software features introduced in SharePoint 2016. While this chapter won't list every single new feature, those covered in the following are those that we believe most users will look for when migrating to SharePoint 2016.

### Zero Downtime Patching

This is going to be very cheering news if you manage large environments; the size and number of the packages are reduced. The developers have also removed the downtime previously required to update SharePoint servers.

### OneDrive Redirection

Although this feature has been available in SharePoint 2013 since SP1, with SharePoint 2016 you can redirect your My Sites to your Office 365 subscription's OneDrive for Business host. If a user clicks OneDrive, they will be redirected to their Office 365 My Site and no longer to their On-Premises.

### File Size

Microsoft has increased the maximum file size allowed to 10 GB. This means that users can now upload bigger files in their document libraries. In SharePoint 2013, the maximum was set to 2GB for a file. This setting is set at the web application level, and is represented in the SharePoint Object Model by the property `MaximumFileSize`, which sets the maximum size allowed for a single file in megabytes.

© Nikolas Charlebois-Laprade and John Edward Naguib 2017
N. Charlebois-Laprade and J. E. Naguib, *Beginning PowerShell for SharePoint 2016*,
DOI 10.1007/978-1-4842-2884-5_2

To specify this setting, we need to start by obtaining a reference to the web application object. This can be achieved by calling the Get-SPWebApplication PowerShell cmdlet and passing it the URL of any site collection contained within the web application in question. In our case, we only have one web application configured locally on port 80, so in order to get a reference to this web application, we need to call the following line of PowerShell code using the SharePoint 2016 Management Shell:

```
$webApp = Get-SPWebApplication http://localhost
```

This line will retrieve a SPWebApplication object representing our SharePoint web application on port 80 and assign it to a PowerShell variable named $webApp. Now that we have a reference to our web application, all that is left is to modify its MaximumFileSize property. The following line of PowerShell will reuse the variable we have just obtained and will set the maximum size for a file we are trying to upload to a document library to 5,000 MB (roughly 5GB):

```
$webApp.MaximumFileSize = 5000
```

After assigning the value, in order to make sure we commit our changes back to the SharePoint configuration database, we need to call the Update() method on our web application object (see Figure 2-1):

```
$webApp.Update()
```

```
Administrator: SharePoint 2016 Management Shell                _ □ x
PS C:\> $webApp = Get-SPWebApplication
PS C:\> $webApp.MaximumFileSize = 5000
PS C:\> $webApp.Update()
PS C:\> _
```

*Figure 2-1.* *Changing a SharePoint 2016 web application's maximum file size using PowerShell*

To verify that our changes have taken effect, we can navigate to SharePoint Central Administration and verify whether the new value took effect via the graphical user interface. On the main page, under the Application Management heading, click Manage Web Application (see Figure 2-2). This will bring you to the list of all existing web applications in your SharePoint 2016 farm.

*Figure 2-2.* *Manage web applications option from SharePoint 2016 Central Administration*

Select your web application from the list. In our case we will be selecting the web application running on port 80. Clicking on your web application should automatically enable several buttons in the ribbon menu. From the ribbon, click the General Setting button (the icon, not the expandable menu, as shown in Figure 2-3).

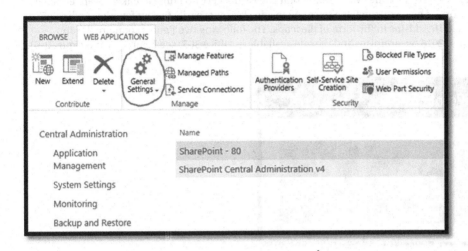

***Figure 2-3.*** *General Settings option from the Manage Web Applications adminsitrative page*

When you click the General Settings button, a dialog window will appear, displaying all of the common properties for your web application. If you scroll down, near the bottom of the dialog window you will see a property named *Maximum Upload Size*. This property should reflect the 5,000 MB value we set previously with PowerShell (see Figure 2-4).

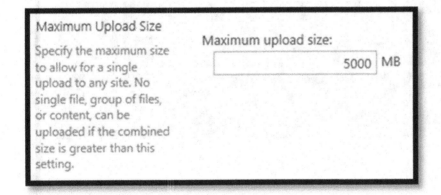

***Figure 2-4.*** *Viewing the Mazimum Upload Size property from SharePoint 2016 Central Administration*

# Durable Links

In SharePoint 2016, Microsoft has introduced a very useful feature for everyone who works extensively with multiple documents. This feature is called *durable links*, and it allows a user to move a document around in different libraries, sites, and site collections, to rename the document, and to still be able to access it using a "universal" URL. Upon activating this feature, documents will be accessible using their Document ID instead of by their location in the information architecture of your SharePoint 2016 environment.

# App Launcher

Even though this feature was announced at TechEd Europe back in October 2014 and made its appearance in Office 365 only a few weeks after the event, SharePoint 2016 is the very first time it makes an appearance in the on-premises world. The app launcher allows you to add shortcuts easily to your favorites Office 365 apps and SharePoint 2016 Add-Ins in the form of tile icons. The following two figures compare the app launcher in SharePoint 2016 on-premises and the one available in Office 365 (see Figure 2-5 and Figure 2-6).

***Figure 2-5.*** *The SharePoint 2016 App Launcher*

***Figure 2-6.*** *The Office 365 App Launcher*

On-premises, in order for the app launcher to be enabled, you need to provision an instance of the User Profile Service Application. The PowerShell cmdlet involved in creating an instance of that service application is New-SPProfileServiceApplication. At a minimum, it requires you to pass it an Internet Information Services (IIS) application pool. An IIS application pool is created in PowerShell using the New-SPIISWebServiceApplicationPool cmdlet:

```
$account = Get-SPManagedAccount "contoso\<App Pool User Account>"
$appPool = New-SPServiceApplicationPool -Name "UserProfile" -Account $account
```

The following line of PowerShell will then allow you to quickly provision such an instance by providing the minimum level of information required by the service application to function properly:

```
$userProfileSA = New-SPProfileServiceApplication -ApplicationPool $appPool -Name "UPS"
```

This PowerShell code creates the service application instance; however, before it can be fully operational, we still need to create a related service application proxy instance. To achieve this, we need to call the New-SPProfileServiceApplicationProxy PowerShell cmdlet and pass it a reference to the service application instance we just created (see Figure 2-7).

```
New-SPProfileServiceApplicationProxy -ServiceApplication $userProfileSA -Name "UPSProxy"
```

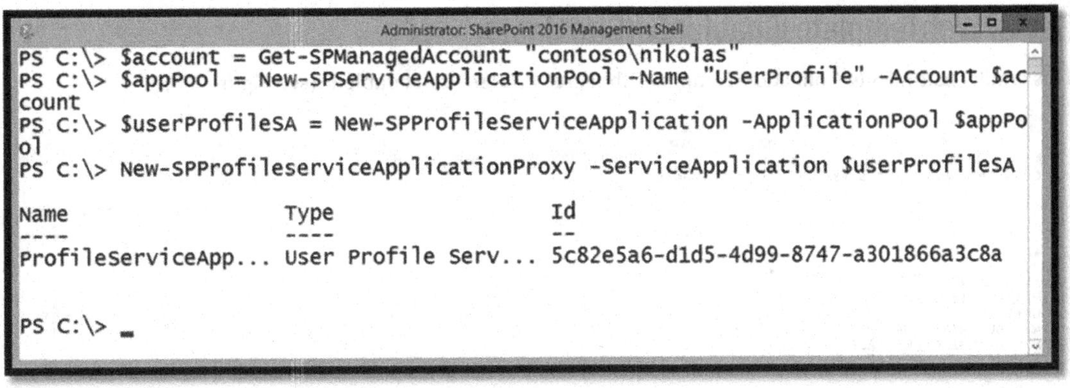

*Figure 2-7.* *Provisionning the User Profile Service Application in SharePoint 2016 using PowerShell*

After executing this code, you should be able to simply refresh any of your SharePoint 2016 pages and see the app launcher appear in the top-left section of the suite bar.

## Fast Site Creation

*Fast site creation* is a new feature introduced in SharePoint 2016 that allows a user to speed up the time taken to create a new site collection. Using this mechanism takes half the time the default New-SPSite PowerShell cmdlet would normally take to instantiate a new site collection in the SharePoint 2016 farm. This feature works by operating directly at the SQL Server level, not going through the Object Model to perform its tasks, and thereby saving several round trips to the database server and back to the actual SharePoint 2016 servers.

While you may wonder why Microsoft would spend time and effort improving such a basic operation, you need to put yourself in the shoes of an organization that is hosting and maintaining a large scaled multi-tenancy instance of SharePoint 2016. Some such companies must instantiate thousands of site collections a day, so each second saved is important to them; and let's face it, faster is always better when it comes to executing a PowerShell command.

The concept behind the fast site creation feature is that each site collection is associated with a blank template called a "site master." This site master is nothing more than a generic site based on a specific template (such as Team Site, Blank Site, and so on). Upon initiating the fast site creation process, SharePoint 2016 simply takes a copy of that site from SQL and copies it over to the destination site collection.

The Microsoft SharePoint 2016 PowerShell snap-in introduces six new cmdlets to allow us to interact with the site masters:

```
Disable-SPWebTemplateForSiteMaster
Enable-SPWebTemplateForSiteMaster
Get-SPSiteMaster
Get-SPWebTemplatesEnabledForSiteMaster
New-SPSiteMaster
Remove-SPSiteMaster
```

Let's take a quick look at what each of these cmdlets does.

## Get-SPWebTemplatesEnabledForSiteMaster

This cmdlet lists all Site Collection Templates that are "fast creation enabled" (see Figure 2-8).

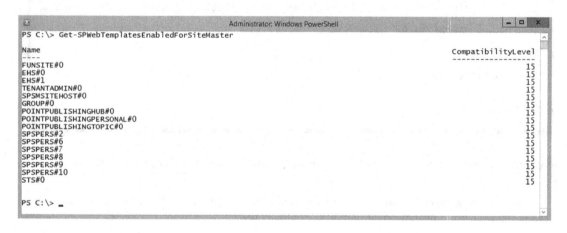

***Figure 2-8.*** *Calling the Get-SPWebTemplatesEnabledForSiteMaster PowerShell cmdlet*

## Disable-SPWebTemplateForSiteMaster

This cmdlet disables a site template that was enabled for fast site creation. Before SharePoint can allow a site template to be used for fast site creation, it needs to have been enabled. In the following example, we disable the STS#0 template (see Figure 2-9):

```
Disable-SPWebTemplateForSiteMaster -Template #STS#0
```

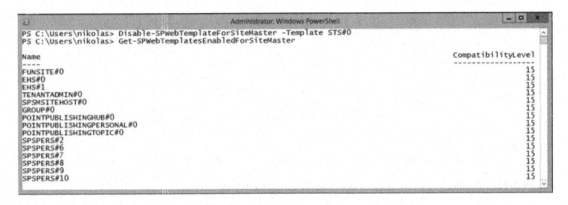

**Figure 2-9.** *Disabling the Team Site template for fast site creation*

## Enable-SPWebTemplateForSiteMaster

This cmdlet enables a site template to be used for fast site creation. For example, after disabling fast site creation on template STS#0 as we just did, if we wish to re-enable it, we need to run the following cmdlet (see Figure 2-10):

```
Enable-SPWebTemplateForSiteMaster -Template STS#0
```

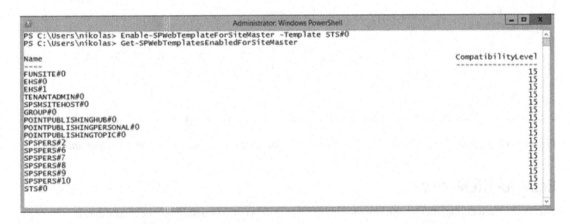

**Figure 2-10.** *Enabling the Team Site template for fast site collection using PowerShell*

## New-SPSiteMaster

Now that we have our site template ready for fast site creation, we need to create what we call a new site master. Think of a site master as being a cookie cutter. It is a mold from which all site collections created via fast site creation will be made (Figure 2-11).

```
New-SPSiteMaster -Template STS#0 -ContentDatabase "WSS_Content"
```

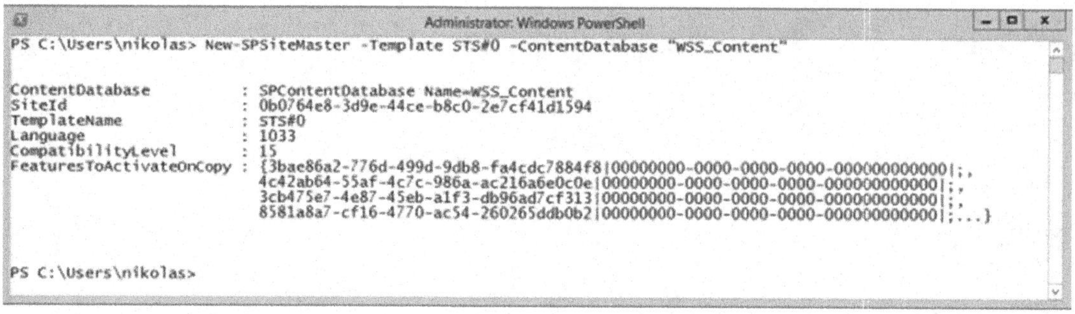

*Figure 2-11.* *Creating a new Site Master using the Team Site template*

## Get-SPSiteMaster

This PowerShell cmdlet returns a reference to the site master associated with a content database (see Figure 2-12):

```
Get-SPSiteMaster -ContentDatabase "WSS_Content"
```

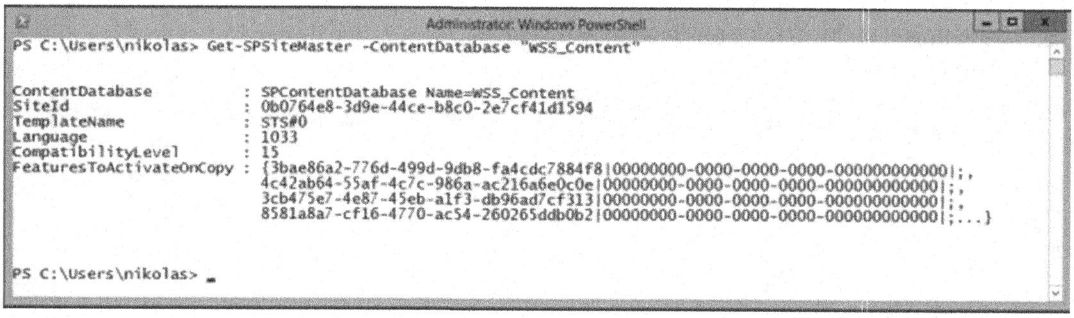

*Figure 2-12.* *Getting a reference to a site master object associated with a SharePoint 2016 content database*

## Remove-SiteMaster

This PowerShell cmdlet deletes the site master instance from a content database (see Figure 2-13):

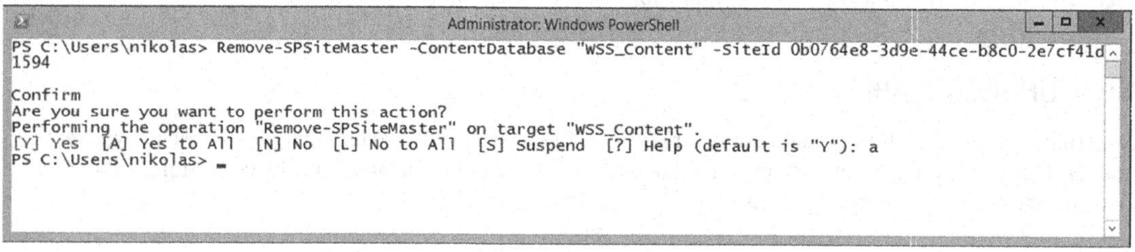

*Figure 2-13.* *Deleting a site master instance from a content database using PowerShell*

## How Fast Site Creation Works

After having properly created a site master for a specific site collection, we need to call the `New-SPSite` PowerShell cmdlet, but ensure that we pass it the switch parameter `-CreateFromSiteMaster` to tell it to use the fast site creation process instead of the classic way of creating a site collection. The following example uses the Site Master created for our root site collection (`http://localhost`) and will be creating a new site collection located at `http://localhost/sites/FC1` using the fast site creation process. The following lines of PowerShell code will allow us to achieve that (see Figure 2-14):

```
New-SPSite http://localhost/sites/FC1 -Template "STS#0" -ContentDatabase
"WSS_Content" -OwnerAlias "Contoso\<user account>" -CreateFromSiteMaster
```

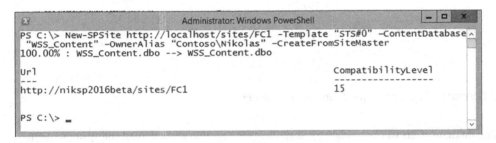

*Figure 2-14.* *Creating a new site collection in SharePoint using fast site creation*

# Filename Support

While there have not been any changes in the set of PowerShell cmdlets available in SharePoint 2016 for working with filenames, it is important to note that Microsoft has removed the restriction on filename length for documents. In previous versions of the product, it was not possible for someone to upload a document that had more than 128 characters in its name. In SharePoint 2016, this restriction has been removed and it is now possible for users to store documents having filenames up to any length. The restriction in the length of the file name will actually come from the operating system itself and not from SharePoint (see Figure 2-15).

*Figure 2-15.* *Long file name for documents in SharePoint 2016*

# Hybrid Search

Hybrid search, introduced in SharePoint 2016, is the feature that was by far the most awaited by the SharePoint community. This feature allows users to have the Office 365 search engine crawl and index on-premises content and have it exposed through its results page.

## Sharing of Documents with QR Code

SharePoint 2016 makes it easier than ever to share documents on mobile devices. By default, every document library has a feature enabled that allows all documents in it to expose a QR code for users to easily share access to them. When you access the document's properties overlay menu, a new QR code icon will be displayed, allowing you to easily generate a QR code for that specific document (see Figure 2-16).

*Figure 2-16. Generate a QR code icon for documents in SharePoint 2016*

By clicking this icon, users will be brought to an application page that will automatically generate a QR code for the document (see Figure 2-17).

Scan this QR code with your phone or tablet to open
http://niksp2016beta/Shared%20Documents/ProPlus_en-us_x86.xml

*Figure 2-17. Generated QR code for a document in SharePoint 2016*

## Office Online Server (OOS)

The next evolution of what used to be known as Office Web Apps has been rebranded in SharePoint 2016 and is now called Office Online Server (OOS). As was the case in the 2013 version, this component needs to be deployed to its own server and can be used as a standalone product. Some components, such as durable links and real-time co-authoring in Office clients, require this component to be part of the SharePoint 2016 farm in order to function as expected.

# Automatic Indexing for Large SharePoint Lists

It has always been a problem with SharePoint that handling lists of over 5,000 items is difficult. SharePoint 2016 makes our life a little better by introducing a feature that automatically creates indexes on various fields the moment the list contains more items that half of what is allowed by the list threshold. Let us clarify this a bit more. If the list threshold is set to 5,000 items, that means that the moment your list has more than 2,500 items in it, the automatic indexing process will kick in. this automatic process is actually handled by a timer job called `Job-List-Automatic-Index-Management`.

If you were to take a closer look at the options available in the list settings application page and compare it with what was available in SharePoint 2013, you will see that a new option made its appearance in the Advanced Settings section of the list's settings. Scrolling down to the very last setting on that page will reveal a new *Automatic Index Management* option that you can turn on or off (see Figure 2-18). This is the option that determines whether this list should automatically start indexing its fields when its item count reaches half of what the threshold allows (see Figure 2-18).

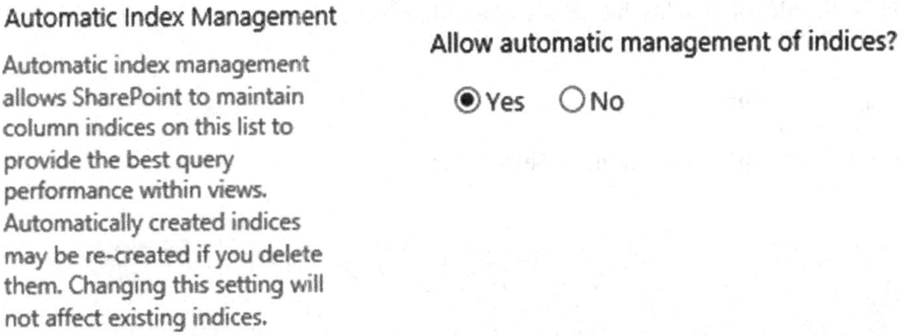

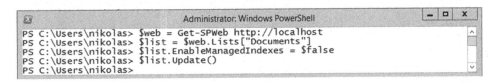

**Automatic Index Management**

Automatic index management allows SharePoint to maintain column indices on this list to provide the best query performance within views. Automatically created indices may be re-created if you delete them. Changing this setting will not affect existing indices.

**Allow automatic management of indices?**

◉ Yes   ○ No

***Figure 2-18.*** *Enabling automatic list index management in SharePoint 2016*

Using PowerShell, you can turn this setting on or off by changing the `EnableManagedIndexes` property on a list. This property is a Boolean value, meaning that you need to set it to true to enable it or to false to disable it. The following example shows you how to disable the automatic index setting on a document library named "Documents" (see Figure 2-19).

```
$web = Get-SPWeb http://localhost
$list = $web.Lists["Documents"]
$list.EnableManagedIndexes = $false
$list.Update()
```

```
Administrator: Windows PowerShell                                    _  □  x
PS C:\Users\nikolas> $web = Get-SPWeb http://localhost
PS C:\Users\nikolas> $list = $web.Lists["Documents"]
PS C:\Users\nikolas> $list.EnableManagedIndexes = $false
PS C:\Users\nikolas> $list.Update()
PS C:\Users\nikolas>
```

***Figure 2-19.*** *Disabling the automatic indexing of a SharePoint 2016 list using PowerShell*

After executing these PowerShell lines, you can go back through the SharePoint 2016 graphical interface and see for yourself that the setting was changed and that it is now turned off (see Figure 2-20).

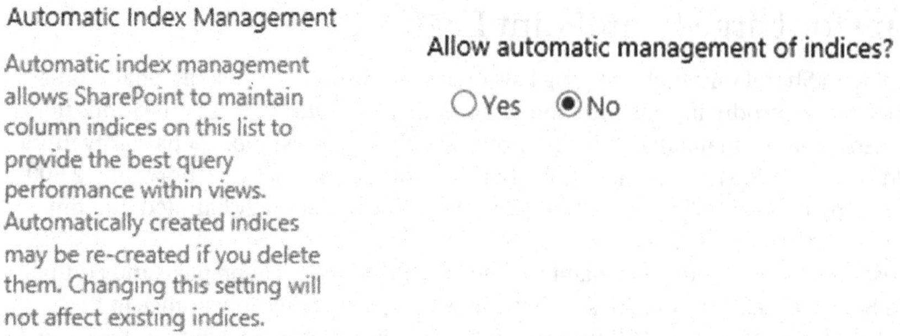

## Automatic Index Management

Automatic index management allows SharePoint to maintain column indices on this list to provide the best query performance within views. Automatically created indices may be re-created if you delete them. Changing this setting will not affect existing indices.

**Allow automatic management of indices?**

○ Yes   ◉ No

***Figure 2-20.*** *Automatic list indexing setting turned off*

Now, you may ask how to determine which fields are set to be included as part of the automatic feature (which fields will be indexed automatically). This information can be easily obtained using PowerShell. The following lines will return the titles of all fields that are set to be indexed by the automatic feature for the Documents list (see Figure 2-21).

```
$web = Get-SPWeb http://localhost
$list = $web.Lists["Documents"]
$list.Fields | Where{$_.Indexable -eq $true} | Select Title
```

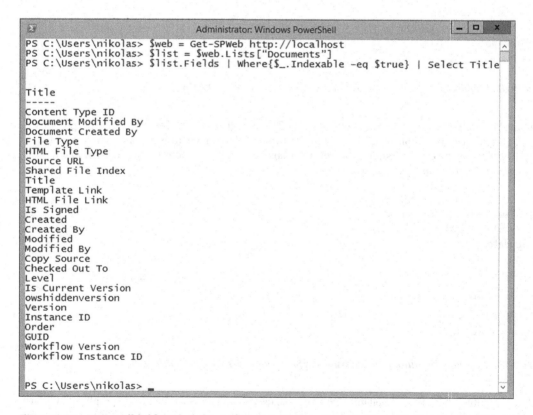

***Figure 2-21.*** *Listing all fields included in a SharePoint list's index using PowerShell*

## MinRoles

You can now specify just the role that you want on particular SharePoint 2016 servers, a feature known as *MinRoles*. Doing so will install only the components required for the specified role. You will also be able to convert servers to run new roles if needed (see Figure 2-22).

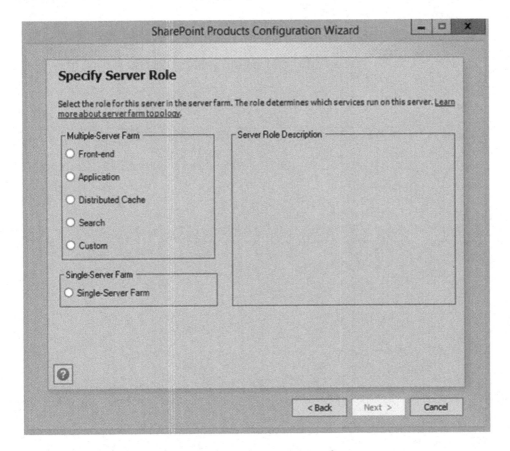

***Figure 2-22.*** *Selecting a server role in the configuration wizard*

There are more features available in SharePoint 2016, which is a very cool product and offers the best way to start getting your hands into Office 365. SharePoint 2016 is very suitable for hybrid models and integration with Office 365. To learn about more of the features available to you, go to: `https://technet.microsoft.com/en-us/library/mt346121(v=office.16).aspx`

# Summary

In this chapter we have given a brief look at the some of the new functionality available for you in SharePoint 2016. From what we are seeing, Microsoft is moving toward strong integration between Office 365 and the cloud to encourage using hybrid models (that is, using both on-premise and cloud storage), so we are going to speak in this book about PowerShell for Office 365.

# CHAPTER 3

■ ■ ■

# PowerShell Basics

Throughout this book, it is assumed that readers have had some level of exposure to SharePoint but no experience whatsoever with the PowerShell technology. The content of this chapter will help readers become familiar with the core elements of PowerShell.

Here is a summary of what you will learn in the current chapter:

- How PowerShell sessions work

- The common PowerShell operators

- Customizing your PowerShell sessions

- How to extend the list of default available methods (cmdlets)

- The difference between a PowerShell snap-in and a PowerShell module

## Terminology

Before diving any further into the core of what PowerShell really is, there are several terms and expressions define so that you will better understand all the elements this chapter will discuss.

### Session

Think of a PowerShell *session* as being the current PowerShell window in which you are working. PowerShell resembles the default command line in many aspects. However, it is important to remember that PowerShell is built on top of the .NET Framework. You can therefore use it to access and manipulate any .NET object loaded in memory. Normal command-line methods and operations will still work inside PowerShell (dir, copy, and so on). Objects and variables declared in a PowerShell session will continue to exist and to be accessible throughout the lifetime of the session. Closing the Windows PowerShell window will automatically terminate the session.

### Cmdlets

Pronounced "command-lets," these represent the set of methods that are available in the current session. They are normally written in the form of verb-object (for example, Get-SPSite, Set-ExecutionPolicy, Delete-SPListItem, and so on). As you will learn later in this chapter, it is possible to extend the default set of available cmdlets by adding your own to the PowerShell ecosystem.

N. Charlebois-Laprade and J. E. Naguib, *Beginning PowerShell for SharePoint 2016*,
DOI 10.1007/978-1-4842-2884-5_3

## Profile

A PowerShell *profile* is a script that is executed every time a PowerShell session is initialized. It allows users to modify their global settings for all PowerShell sessions and to instantiate global objects and variables by default. The PowerShell profile is where you'll need to start looking if you'd like to personalize and customize your PowerShell environment.

## Snap-In

*Snap-ins* in the PowerShell world are sets of methods and objects that can be imported into a session. Think of them as .NET namespaces that would be imported at the beginning of your classes by calling the using statement. When you launch the SharePoint Management Shell, all you are really doing in the background is starting a new PowerShell session and importing the SharePoint packages into the current session by calling Add-PSSnapin Microsoft.SharePoint.PowerShell. Snap-ins contain only PowerShell cmdlets and nothing else. All PowerShell snap-ins must be written in .NET and compiled as assemblies. Snap-ins are by default saved in the registry under \HKEY_LOCAL_MACHINE\SOFTWARE\Microsoft\PowerShell\1\PowerShellSnap-ins\. You can get a list of all registered PowerShell snap-ins for the current session by using the Get-PSSnapin -Registered cmdlet. Figure 3-1 provides an overview of how you can use this cmdlet to get the list of registered cmdlets in a PowerShell session in which we have registered the SharePoint snap-ins.

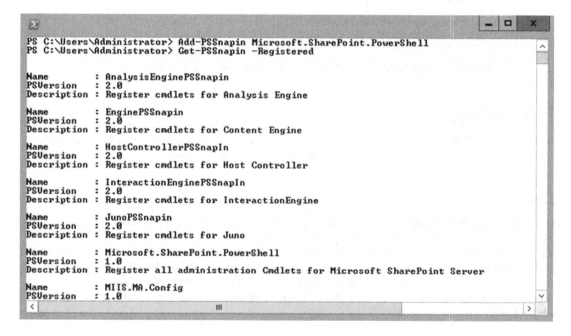

```
PS C:\Users\Administrator> Add-PSSnapin Microsoft.SharePoint.PowerShell
PS C:\Users\Administrator> Get-PSSnapin -Registered

Name         : AnalysisEnginePSSnapin
PSVersion    : 2.0
Description  : Register cmdlets for Analysis Engine

Name         : EnginePSSnapin
PSVersion    : 2.0
Description  : Register cmdlets for Content Engine

Name         : HostControllerPSSnapIn
PSVersion    : 2.0
Description  : Register cmdlets for Host Controller

Name         : InteractionEnginePSSnapIn
PSVersion    : 2.0
Description  : Register cmdlets for InteractionEngine

Name         : JunoPSSnapin
PSVersion    : 2.0
Description  : Register cmdlets for Juno

Name         : Microsoft.SharePoint.PowerShell
PSVersion    : 1.0
Description  : Register all administration Cmdlets for Microsoft SharePoint Server

Name         : MIIS.MA.Config
PSVersion    : 1.0
```

***Figure 3-1.** Listing all registered snap-ins with PowerShell*

## Module

The concept of modules was introduced in PowerShell version 2.0. A *module* represents a set of PowerShell functionalities that can be added to a PowerShell session. It can contain cmdlets, functions, variables, and so on. Unlike PowerShell snap-ins, modules don't have to be compiled assemblies; they can be, for example, external PowerShell scripts that are referenced by the current session. As an example, assume that you are writing a new script that simply contains a set of mathematical functions, say, Add, Subtract, Multiply, and Divide. This script is just a text file saved on disk as a custom PowerShell extension (.psd1 or .psm1). By importing it as a module into your current session, you will be able to access all of its declared mathematical functions as if they were part of the script that you were currently writing. To achieve this with snap-ins, your functions would need to have been compiled as a .NET assembly (.dll file), which would have made it harder to make any modifications to your functions.

By default, when trying to import a module, PowerShell looks in the %windir%\System32\ WindowsPowerShell\v1.0\Modules directory. You can list all available PowerShell modules in your environment by using the Get-Module -ListAvailable cmdlet (see Figure 3-2).

```
PS C:\> Get-Module -ListAvailable


    Directory: C:\Program Files\WindowsPowerShell\Modules


ModuleType Version    Name                    ExportedCommands
---------- -------    ----                    ----------------
Binary     1.0.0.0    PackageManagement       {Find-Package, Get-Package, Get-PackageProvider, Ge...
Script     3.3.5      Pester                  {Describe, Context, It, Should...}
Script     1.0.0.1    PowerShellGet           {Install-Module, Find-Module, Save-Module, Update-M...
Script     1.1        PSReadline              {Get-PSReadlineKeyHandler, Set-PSReadlineKeyHandler...


    Directory: C:\WINDOWS\system32\WindowsPowerShell\v1.0\Modules


ModuleType Version    Name                    ExportedCommands
---------- -------    ----                    ----------------
Manifest   1.0.0.0    AppBackgroundTask       {Disable-AppBackgroundTaskDiagnosticLog, Enable-App...
Manifest   2.0.0.0    AppLocker               {Get-AppLockerFileInformation, Get-AppLockerPolicy,...
Manifest   2.0.0.0    Appx                    {Add-AppxPackage, Get-AppxPackage, Get-AppxPackageM...
Script     1.0.0.0    AssignedAccess          {Clear-AssignedAccess, Get-AssignedAccess, Set-Assi...
Manifest   1.0.0.0    BitLocker               {Unlock-BitLocker, Suspend-BitLocker, Resume-BitLoc...
Manifest   2.0.0.0    BitsTransfer            {Add-BitsFile, Complete-BitsTransfer, Get-BitsTrans...
Manifest   1.0.0.0    BranchCache             {Add-BCDataCacheExtension, Clear-BCCache, Disable-B...
```

***Figure 3-2.*** *Listing all available modules in PowerShell*

As you can see in Figure 3-2, several types of modules can exist. There are currently five types of supported modules in PowerShell v3.0:

Binary (.dll): A module that is defined in an assembly. This type includes snap-ins and class libraries that contain cmdlet classes.

Cim (.cdxml): Called *cmdlets-over-objects*. These are saved in a file format referred to as cmdlet definition XML (CDXML). They define a mapping between Windows PowerShell cmdlets and CIM class operations or methods. Think of using them as a way to make calls into external APIs as if their methods were accessible as PowerShell cmdlets.

Manifest (.psd1): A Windows PowerShell data file that is used to describe and define how a module is being processed. Module manifest files contain a hash table with keys and values. These are not required, but they can help describing existing modules by providing information about the author and giving more details about what the specified module actually does. Thus they are important for versioning.

Script (.psm1): A module whose members are declared in an external script. Script modules normally contain cmdlet definitions. For example, if we look at the Script module for the Integrated Scripting Environment (ISE), we see that it contains several cmdlet definitions, such as New-IseSnippet, Import-IseSnipper, and Get-IseSnippet.

Workflow (.xaml): Some of you probably recognize the extension associated with this type of PowerShell modules. Pronounced "zammel," XAML stands for Extensible Application Markup Language, and it is Microsoft's XML-based markup language behind the Windows Presentation Framework (WPF). It is used to abstract the visual presentation layer of applications from their actual logic. However, in this case, the Windows Workflow Foundation (WWF) is responsible for executing our workflow's logic. A workflow module is basically a special script structure that PowerShell is able to interpret and convert into Windows Workflow Foundation code. The WWF engine is then called to execute the workflow's activities. PowerShell workflow methods are identified by using the keyword workflow instead of function. Code in a workflow method is able to fork its logic, meaning that several activities can execute in parallel.

# PowerShell Operators and Common Operations

For every new language you learn, there is a new syntax to become familiar with, and PowerShell is no different. The beauty of it, however, is that if you are familiar with the C# syntax, you'll find lots of commonalities with the scripting language. The following section gives you an overview of the various PowerShell operators that you will need to master in order to become a skilled SharePoint administrator.

## Printing Values on Screen

During a script execution, you'll want to interact with the user. The two main methods you'll need to remember are the write-host cmdlet to print a string on screen, and the read-host cmdlet to capture a user's input from the console. Both cmdlets are shown in use in Figure 3-3.

```
PS C:\> $favoriteColor = Read-Host "What is your favorite color?"
What is your favorite color?: Green

PS C:\> Write-Host "Your favorite color is $favoriteColor"
Your favorite color is Green

PS C:\> |
```

*Figure 3-3.* *Usage of the* write-host *and* read-host *cmdlets*

## Console Colors

One of the great advantages of PowerShell over its command-prompt predecessor is its ability to interact with the graphical interface. This allows users to use visual cues in their scripts to help identify different information elements that you would otherwise have to spend time figuring out manually. Within your PowerShell session, you have the option of specifying the colors to use for both the text's background and foreground. The following line will print a line of red text on a yellow background:

```
Write-Host "See how cool this is?" -Backgroundcolor yellow -Foregroundcolor red
```

This can prove to be very useful when displaying lots of information on screen. Imagine, for example, a PowerShell script that will loop through all subsites on a SharePoint site collection that has over 1,000 sites. Let's suppose that the purpose of this script is to identify subsites that have unique permissions but that you also want to obtain a full list of all sites. Your script could introduce some conditional logic that would display the URLs of all sites that inherit permissions from the parent with a green background, and the URLs of all subsites that have unique permissions with a red background. This would achieve both goals, providing you with a full list of the URLs for all subsites as well as giving you an easy visual cue to identify subsites that don't inherit permissions from their parents.

## Variables

Variables in PowerShell are declared and referenced using the $ operator. In the earlier example, when capturing the user's input for their favorite color, you assigned the value to a variable. This value is later reused to print out a confirmation message to the users, as seen in this example:

```
$myVariableText = "My favorite number is:"
$myVariableNumber = 7
Write-Host $myVariable $myVariableNumber
```

Executing this code will print the following message on the PowerShell console: "My favorite number is: 7".

## Comments

What good would a piece of code be without proper comments to describe what it is actually doing? Commenting the logic of code or script is something every good IT professional should learn the discipline to do. Comments in PowerShell are preceded with the # symbol. It is possible to create comments blocks by enclosing them in <# #> tags. The following example demonstrates how comments can be used to describe a script to help future users understand its logic:

```
# The following variable contains the number of Days in the week
$numDaysInWeek = 7
<# The following lines of code does two things:
1 - Reads the answer  to the question from the user;
2 - Validate the answer #>
$answer = Read-Host "How many days in a week?"
if($answer -eq 7)
{
    Write-Host "You are correct"
}
else
{
Write-Host "Wrong answer!"
}
```

## Casting

This is the process of converting an object from one type to another. Casting operations are represented by a type name placed between square brackets ([]), followed by the object to convert. For example, converting a string to an integer could be done as shown in Figure 3-4.

```
$stringValue = "12"
Write-Host ([int] $stringValue +13)
Write-Host $stringValue + 13
```

```
PS C:\> $stringValue = "12"

PS C:\> Write-Host ([int]$stringValue + 13)
25

PS C:\> Write-Host $stringValue + 13
12 + 13

PS C:\> |
```

*Figure 3-4.  Converting a string into an integer*

In this demo, you can see that the first statement casts the string value of variable $stringValue into a number and then adds 13 units to it. The resulting value, 25 in this case, is of type integer. The second statement doesn't cast the variable's value as a number but considers it to be a string. The write-host then treats the entire statement as a string and prints out the operation in a textual fashion.

## Conditional Logic

In many cases, you'll need to gate and branch your code's logic in one direction or another based on a decision. PowerShell includes its own set of operators, just like any other good programming language.

## Decisions

Decisions in the context of PowerShell are expressed by using if and else statements. These allow your script to make a decision based on values you wish to evaluate against a specific condition. The code following an if statement will be executed only if specific conditions are met. Otherwise, the script proceeds with the code contained in the else statement. For example, assume you are writing a very simple script to teach math to young kids in school. The script will ask the students to input any positive number, and will print out a message stating whether the number is even or odd. The following lines represent how you could create such a script using PowerShell:

```
$number = Read-Host "Please enter a positive number:"
<# Use the modulo operation to divide the number by 2. Module returns the remainder of a
division operation. If the result is 0 then the number is even, otherwise it is odd. #>
$result = $number % 2
if($result -eq 0)
{
Write-Host "The number is even!"
}
else
{
Write-Host "The number is odd!"
}
```

# Comparison

Table 3-1 lists the comparison operators that can be used to validate conditional statements.

**Table 3-1.** *Comparison Operators*

| Operator | Meaning |
|----------|---------|
| -ge | Greater-than or equal to<br>≥ |
| -gt | Greater than<br>> |
| -le | Less-than or equal to<br>≤ |
| -lt | Less than<br>< |
| -eq | Equal to<br>= |
| -ne | Not equal<br>≠ |
| -like | Wildcard<br>%word% |
| -notlike | Not matching wildcard |

In addition to the operators mentioned in Table 3-1, there are additional operators that enforce case-sensitivity. Simply prefix any of the operators in Table 3-1 with a c (for example -ceq, -clike, and so on). Figures 3-5 and 3-6 show examples of using some of the comparison operators.

```
Script5.ps1 X
1    $value = Read-Host "Choose a number between 1 and 5"
2
3    if($value -eq 2)
4    {
5        Write-Host "Congrats, you've found the secret number!"
6    }
7    else
8    {
9        Write-Host "The number you chose was incorrect"
10   }
```

```
PS C:\> C:\Users\NikCharlebois\OneDrive\Books\PowerShell for SharePoint 2016\Chapters\Chapter 4 - PowerShell Basics\
Choose a number between 1 and 5: 3
The number you chose was incorrect

PS C:\> C:\Users\NikCharlebois\OneDrive\Books\PowerShell for SharePoint 2016\Chapters\Chapter 4 - PowerShell Basics\
Choose a number between 1 and 5: 2
Congrats, you've found the secret number!

PS C:\>
```

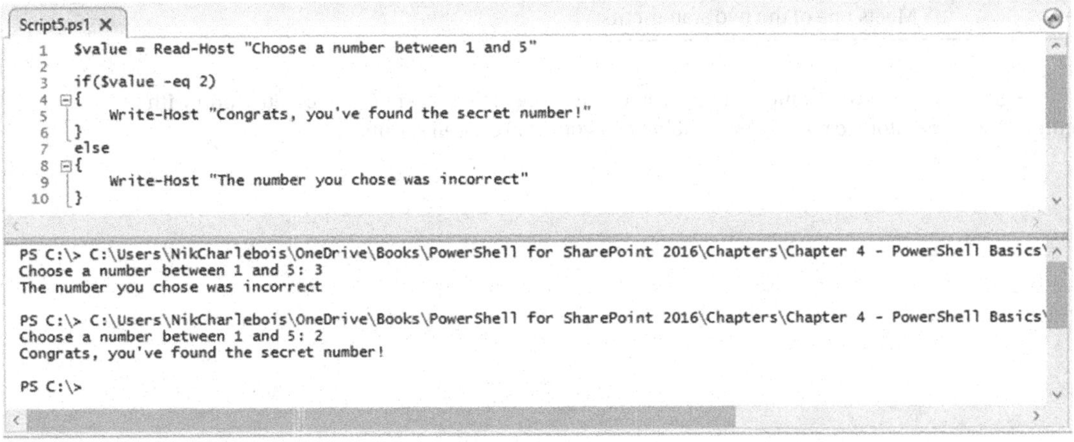

**Figure 3-5.** *Comparing numbers*

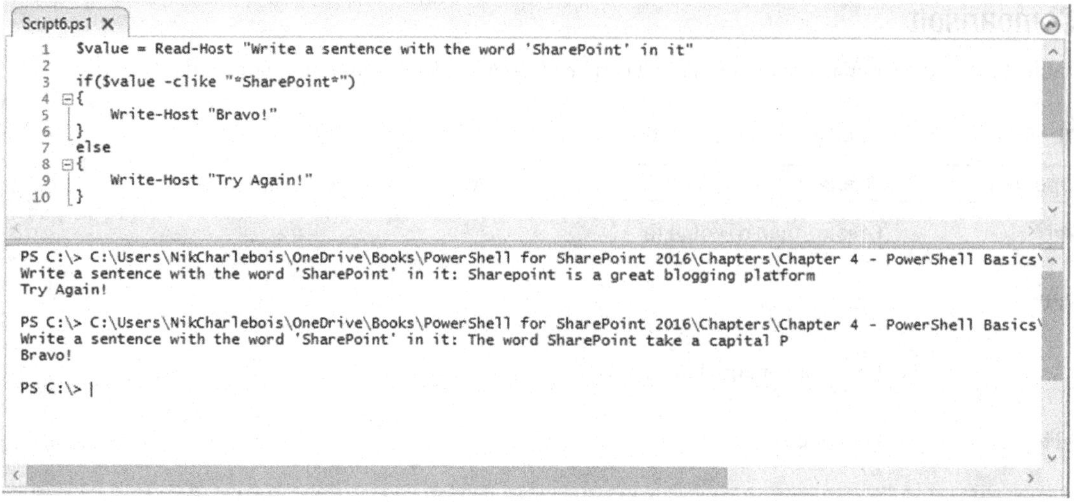

```
Script6.ps1 ✕
 1    $value = Read-Host "Write a sentence with the word 'SharePoint' in it"
 2
 3    if($value -clike "*SharePoint*")
 4  ⊟{
 5  |      Write-Host "Bravo!"
 6  |}
 7    else
 8  ⊟{
 9  |      Write-Host "Try Again!"
10  |}
```

```
PS C:\> C:\Users\NikCharlebois\OneDrive\Books\PowerShell for SharePoint 2016\Chapters\Chapter 4 - PowerShell Basics\
Write a sentence with the word 'SharePoint' in it: Sharepoint is a great blogging platform
Try Again!

PS C:\> C:\Users\NikCharlebois\OneDrive\Books\PowerShell for SharePoint 2016\Chapters\Chapter 4 - PowerShell Basics\
Write a sentence with the word 'SharePoint' in it: The word SharePoint take a capital P
Bravo!

PS C:\> |
```

***Figure 3-6.*** *Comparing strings*

## Logical Operators

Table 3-2 lists the different logical operators that can be used to make up conditional statements.

***Table 3-2.*** *Logical Operators*

| Operator | Meaning |
|----------|---------|
| -not | Does not meet the following condition |
| ! | Same as -not |
| -and | Meets both statements |
| -or | Meets one of the two statements |

Figure 3-7 shows an example of how you can use the logical operators in conjunction with the comparison operators to create powerful logic in your PowerShell scripts.

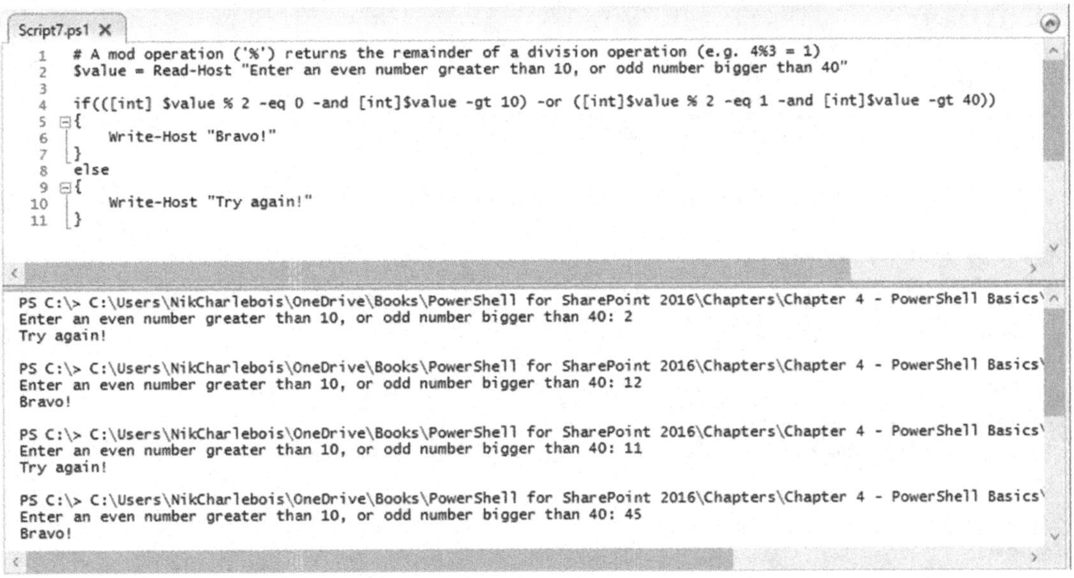

```
Script7.ps1 ✕
1    # A mod operation ('%') returns the remainder of a division operation (e.g. 4%3 = 1)
2    $value = Read-Host "Enter an even number greater than 10, or odd number bigger than 40"
3
4    if(([int] $value % 2 -eq 0 -and [int]$value -gt 10) -or ([int]$value % 2 -eq 1 -and [int]$value -gt 40))
5    {
6        Write-Host "Bravo!"
7    }
8    else
9    {
10       Write-Host "Try again!"
11   }
```

```
PS C:\> C:\Users\NikCharlebois\OneDrive\Books\PowerShell for SharePoint 2016\Chapters\Chapter 4 - PowerShell Basics\
Enter an even number greater than 10, or odd number bigger than 40: 2
Try again!

PS C:\> C:\Users\NikCharlebois\OneDrive\Books\PowerShell for SharePoint 2016\Chapters\Chapter 4 - PowerShell Basics\
Enter an even number greater than 10, or odd number bigger than 40: 12
Bravo!

PS C:\> C:\Users\NikCharlebois\OneDrive\Books\PowerShell for SharePoint 2016\Chapters\Chapter 4 - PowerShell Basics\
Enter an even number greater than 10, or odd number bigger than 40: 11
Try again!

PS C:\> C:\Users\NikCharlebois\OneDrive\Books\PowerShell for SharePoint 2016\Chapters\Chapter 4 - PowerShell Basics\
Enter an even number greater than 10, or odd number bigger than 40: 45
Bravo!
```

*Figure 3-7.* *Multiple logical operators*

# Functions

A *function* is a reusable block of code that can receive parameters and return a specific output. Think of it as being a black box in which you input something, and something else comes out of it. A function normally takes in a set of parameters, and often returns a specific value. Some functions don't return any value; these are called *void methods*. These functions will normally perform an operation or a modification on an existing object but do not need to return the value back to the main portion of the script. PowerShell functions are declared using the function keyword and don't require you to specify a return type. In that sense, they are closer to JavaScript functions than to C# methods. Variables declared inside a method are said to be *local*, meaning they exist only within its context. To illustrate what we mean by a local variable, let's take a look at the demo in Figure 3-8.

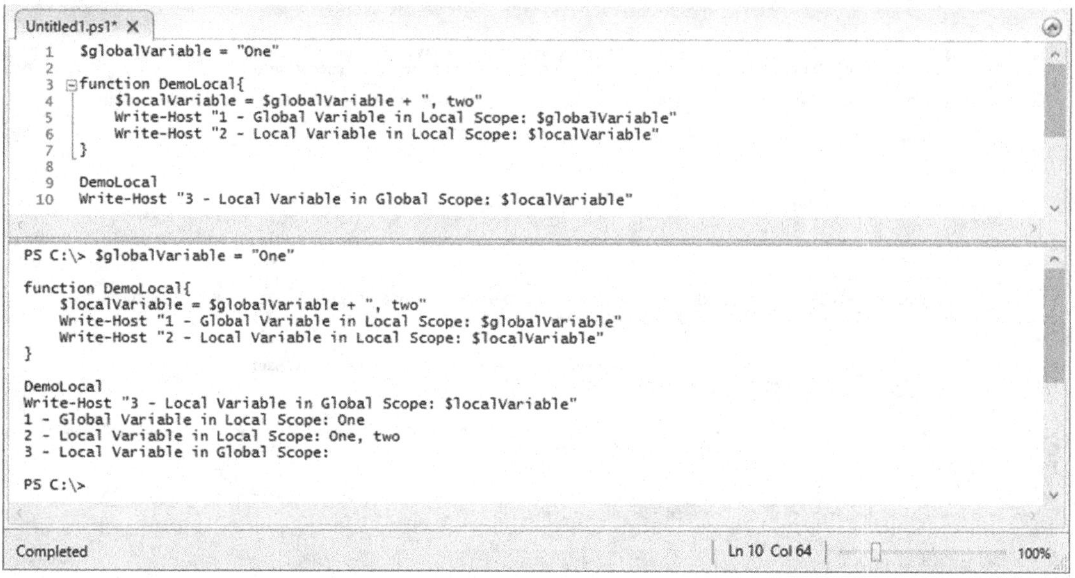

```
Untitled1.ps1* X
  1   $globalVariable = "One"
  2
  3  ⊟function DemoLocal{
  4        $localVariable = $globalVariable + ", two"
  5        Write-Host "1 - Global Variable in Local Scope: $globalVariable"
  6        Write-Host "2 - Local Variable in Local Scope: $localVariable"
  7   }
  8
  9   DemoLocal
 10   Write-Host "3 - Local Variable in Global Scope: $localVariable"
```

```
PS C:\> $globalVariable = "One"

function DemoLocal{
    $localVariable = $globalVariable + ", two"
    Write-Host "1 - Global Variable in Local Scope: $globalVariable"
    Write-Host "2 - Local Variable in Local Scope: $localVariable"
}

DemoLocal
Write-Host "3 - Local Variable in Global Scope: $localVariable"
1 - Global Variable in Local Scope: One
2 - Local Variable in Local Scope: One, two
3 - Local Variable in Global Scope:

PS C:\>
```

Completed                                          Ln 10 Col 64                    100%

***Figure 3-8.*** *Usage of local variables*

We see from the script's output that the host's output from line 10 is not printing anything. This is because the variable $localVariable does not exist outside the function in which it was declared. Globally declared variables, by contrast, are accessible through the script because they have been declared outside of functions, in what we call *global* scope.

# Loops

There are two types of loops in PowerShell, for loops and while loops. The first type normally has a specific number of iterations specified, whereas the second one tends to run indefinitely until a certain condition is met. The condition for a while loop is evaluated before beginning the execution of each loop. There is also another type of loop called the do-while loop, but it is basically a while loop for which you evaluate the condition to continue execution after each loop has completed. In the example in Figure 3-9, the two loops are equivalent.

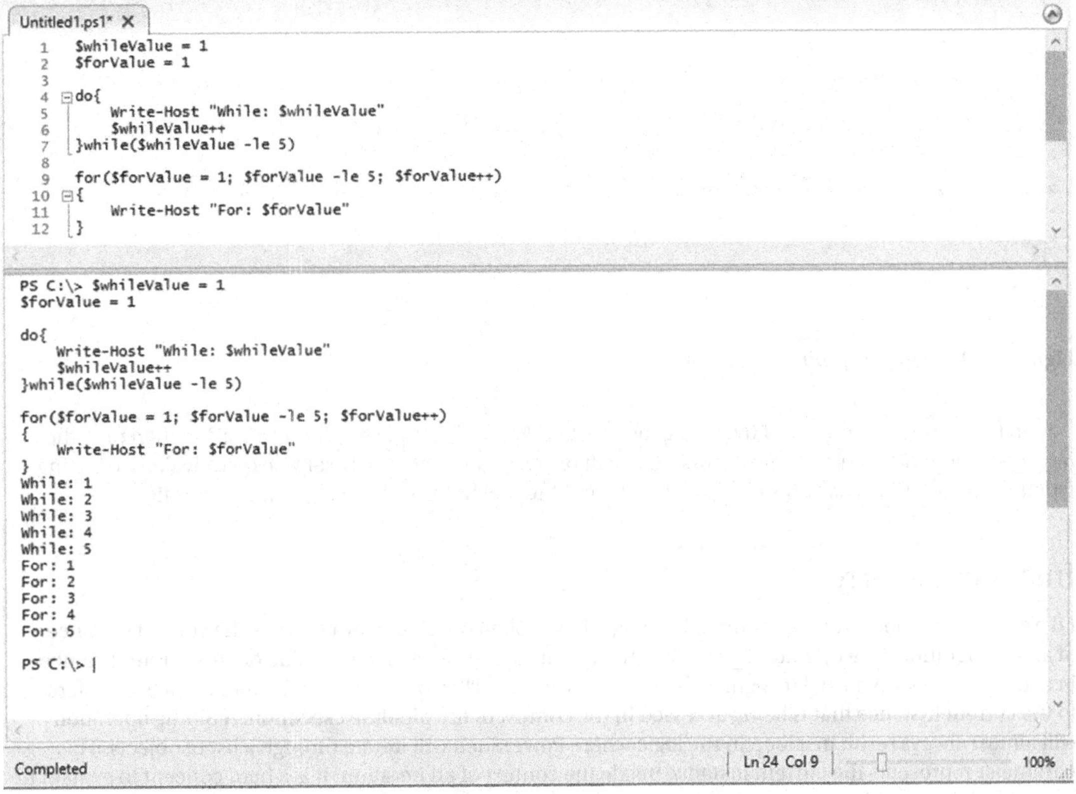

```
Untitled1.ps1* X
 1    $whileValue = 1
 2    $forValue = 1
 3
 4  ⊟do{
 5        Write-Host "While: $whileValue"
 6        $whileValue++
 7    }while($whileValue -le 5)
 8
 9    for($forValue = 1; $forValue -le 5; $forValue++)
10  ⊟{
11        Write-Host "For: $forValue"
12   }
```

```
PS C:\> $whileValue = 1
$forValue = 1

do{
    Write-Host "While: $whileValue"
    $whileValue++
}while($whileValue -le 5)

for($forValue = 1; $forValue -le 5; $forValue++)
{
    Write-Host "For: $forValue"
}
While: 1
While: 2
While: 3
While: 4
While: 5
For: 1
For: 2
For: 3
For: 4
For: 5

PS C:\> |
```

*Figure 3-9.* *A for loop and a while loop*

# Piping

The concept of *piping* is not something new, and it's been around since the old days of MS-DOS. Piping is the idea of taking an object or a result of a function, and sending it to another function. A piping operation is represented by the | (pipe) symbol, and the flow of action is from left to right. A very important tip that you should always remember is that piping an object to the get-member cmdlet allows you to display all properties and methods of an object and exposes them for you to use. For example, piping an SPSite object (SharePoint Site Collection) with the Get-Member cmdlet will return all properties of the SPSite object (for example, Title, URL, UIVersion, and so on), as well as all methods that can be called on that object (Update(), Delete(), and so on). Think of this as being a reflection mechanism to get some insights into external objects. The example in Figure 3-10 illustrates how parameters and values are passed through the piping operation.

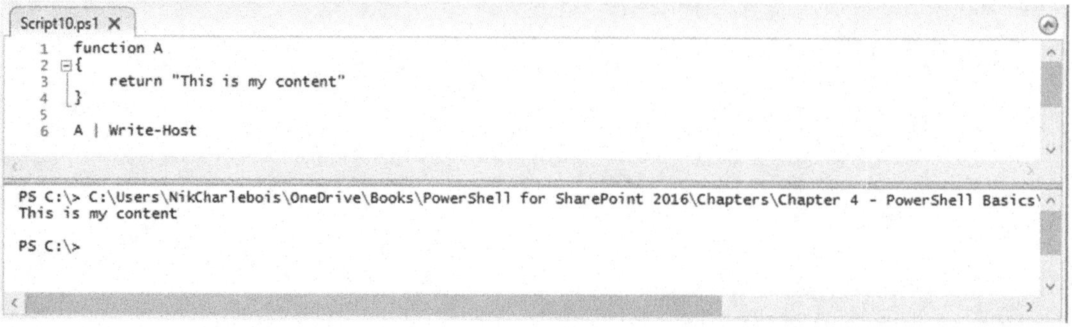

```
Script10.ps1 ✕
 1    function A
 2  ⊟{
 3         return "This is my content"
 4  └}
 5
 6    A | Write-Host
```

```
PS C:\> C:\Users\NikCharlebois\OneDrive\Books\PowerShell for SharePoint 2016\Chapters\Chapter 4 - PowerShell Basics\
This is my content

PS C:\>
```

***Figure 3-10.*** *Using the piping operation*

In this example, we start off by calling the function A, which simply returns a string. We then pipe the returned string into the write-host cmdlet, which prints it to screen. This example is equivalent to having typed write-host A. It simply helps you understand the mechanisms behind the pipe operation.

# Instance Referrer

Like every other modern programming language, PowerShell provides way to access the current instance of an enumeration. The operator $_ ensures that you always get access to the value of the current instance in a loop. C# developers will recognize this concept from the this operator. The $_ operator always refers to the current instance that is being accessed in the context of the pipeline execution. A piping operation will almost always result in a loop in the logic where PowerShell will iterate through a list of objects. This parameter represents the current instance inside the context of an iteration. It is a hard concept to explain in words, so let's look at some examples. For instance, assume the following line of PowerShell:

```
"a","b","c","d" | %{write-host $_}
```

In this example, the % operator is used as a shortcut to the ForEach-Object operator, which loops through objects in a collection. This line will loop through each value of the string array and pass it on to the write-host cmdlet. Notice that the value we're trying to print is the instance referrer operator, meaning that for each value in the array, we will print the currently accessed value on the screen. The result of this line of code will be the following:

```
a
b
c
d
```

Another useful way to use this operator is to query large lists of objects. Assume that we are trying to list every single command that is available to us in the current PowerShell session using the Get-Command cmdlet. Just running this command will return over 2,000 various cmdlets available in PowerShell 3.0. What if we only wanted to list, for example, the cmdlets that allow us to interact with group policies? Using the pipe operator in conjunction with the instance referrer, we could build a select statement that would filter the list of all available cmdlets, and return only those that apply to a group policy object. Consider the following line of PowerShell:

```
$gpCmdlets = Get-Command | Where{$_.ModuleName -eq "GroupPolicy"}
```

This line of code will return only the list of cmdlets that belong to the GroupPolicy module and assign them to the gpCmdlets variable. PowerShell will start by looping through each cmdlet returned by the Get-Command call and will pass it to our query selector through the pipe operator. The Where statement will then examine each cmdlet received, by getting its instance using the instance referrer. It will then decide to add the current cmdlet to the results or not based on whether it meets the condition that its module name must be equal to GroupPolicy.

# Error Handling

There is nothing scarier for an administrator running a script on a production server than to see a bunch of red error messages being printed on screen. There are times when even the best of scripts will generate exceptions. Some exceptions might even be part of the normal flow of your script. For example, when developing a PowerShell script that automatically uninstalls a SharePoint solution from a server and redeploys it, you'll get an exception the first time you run your script, because the solution you're trying to uninstall doesn't already exist on the destination server. If you leave your script as is, administrators will see several lines in red, and will probably freak out. To solve this issue, there are two possible solutions. One would be to override the default PowerShell color scheme to display error messages in another color, but that won't do any good. The other option would be to trap the exception within a try/catch block.

Error handling in PowerShell works just as it does in C#. Code inside the try statement will execute, and if any error is encountered, the execution flow of your script will be passed down to the catch statement along with the exception's related information. You will then be able to handle the exception thrown and decide what to do with it. You also have the option of adding an optional finally block to your try/catch statement. Code in the finally statement will always be executed; it doesn't matter if an exception is thrown or not. It is normally best practice to include in your finally statement the code that ensures you dispose of any objects instantiated within the try statement to ensure that memory taken by these objects is freed even in case of errors.

You can specify what type of exception to look for in your statement by specifying the exception's type as a declaration in your code's block. Remember that every exception thrown inherits the System.Exception class, which means that specifying [System.Exception] as a type of exception to catch comes back to not specifying any type of exception whatsoever. In this case, every exception thrown will be handled by this error-handling declaration. The example shown in Figure 3-11 shows how to catch different exceptions thrown by your PowerShell code.

```
Script11.ps1 ×
  1    function MakeMeCrash($value)
  2  ⊟{
  3  |      switch($value)
  4  ⊟      {
  5  |          1{throw New-Object InvalidOperationException}
  6  |          2{throw New-Object AccessViolationException}
  7  |          default{throw New-Object Exception}
  8  |      }
  9  └}
 10
 11    try
 12  ⊟{
 13  |      $value = Read-Host "Enter a number to throw an exception"
 14  |      MakeMeCrash([int]$value)
 15  └}
 16    catch [System.InvalidOperationException]
 17  ⊟{
 18  |      Write-Host "1 - Catched InvalidOperationException"
 19  └}
 20    catch [System.AccessViolationException]
 21  ⊟{
 22  |      Write-Host "2 - Catched AccessViolationException"
 23  └}
 24    catch [System.Exception]
 25  ⊟{
 26  |      Write-Host "Default - Catched Generic Exception"
 27  └}
```

```
PS C:\> C:\Users\NikCharlebois\OneDrive\Books\PowerShell for SharePoint 2016\Chapters\Chapter 4 - PowerShell Basics\
Enter a number to throw an exception: 1
1 - Catched InvalidOperationException

PS C:\> C:\Users\NikCharlebois\OneDrive\Books\PowerShell for SharePoint 2016\Chapters\Chapter 4 - PowerShell Basics\
Enter a number to throw an exception: 2
2 - Catched AccessViolationException

PS C:\> C:\Users\NikCharlebois\OneDrive\Books\PowerShell for SharePoint 2016\Chapters\Chapter 4 - PowerShell Basics\
Enter a number to throw an exception: 5
Default - Catched Generic Exception

PS C:\>
```

*Figure 3-11.* Error handling with multiple types of exceptions

# Enumerations

Just like any other good programming language, PowerShell allows you to declare enumeration objects. You can think of an enumeration as being a list of keys with predefined constant values that your script can reference. Enumerations in PowerShell are accessed by making calls to the object in the following fashion;

```
[Enumeration Object's Name]::[Key Name]
```

A good example of this is the DayOfWeek property of the .NET DateTime object. You can get a reference to the week's day enumeration by calling the following:

```
[Enum]::GetNames([System.DayOfWeek])
```

Figure 3-12 shows the onscreen result.

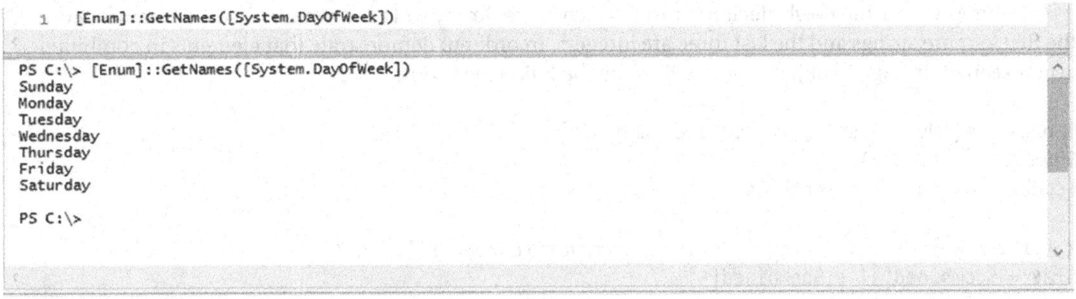

```
  1    [Enum]::GetNames([System.DayOfWeek])
```

```
PS C:\> [Enum]::GetNames([System.DayOfWeek])
Sunday
Monday
Tuesday
Wednesday
Thursday
Friday
Saturday

PS C:\>
```

**Figure 3-12.** *Enumeration of the days of the week*

You can also get a reference to a specific day by calling an element directly:

```
[System.DayOfWeek]::Thursday
```

# Arrays

In many scenarios, arrays will play an important part in your scripts. They represent lists of values that can be accessed using an integer index. In PowerShell, an array is declared by using the @ symbol followed by the list of values you wish to declare between parentheses:

```
$myArray = @('Red', 'Green', 'Blue')
```

In order to access a specific element of the array, you need to specify its index position between square brackets. Remember, the first element of an array is always located at position 0. For example, calling:

```
$myArray[1]
```

will return element 'Green' from the declared array. Arrays in PowerShell behave like dynamic vectors, meaning that you can add additional elements and remove others as you wish. The following line of code will insert a new value 'Yellow' at the end of your array:

```
$myArray += 'Yellow'
```

To verify that the command worked, and that it did in fact append the new value to the existing array, you can print out the length of your array variable to ensure that it now contains four values:

```
$myArray.Length
```

The line of script should write the value 4 on screen. It is also possible to combine two arrays of different types in PowerShell. Assume that you declare a new array that contains only numbers:

```
$myArray2 = @(1, 2, 3)
```

You can combine the two arrays, even if the first one contains a list of string values and the second one contains a list of integers. To combine arrays, you simply use the + operand:

```
$combinedArray = $myArray + $myArray2
```

In our example, the newly declared variable $combinedArray will now contain seven elements, of which the first four are strings and the last three are integers. In order to demonstrate that elements in combined arrays keep their original object type, we'll create the following script:

```
$words = @('My', 'is ' , ' favorite number ')
$numbers = @(2,3,2)
$combined = $words + $numbers

# Array now looks like ('My ', ' is ', ' favorite number ', 2, 3, 2)
$fav = $combined[3] + $combined[5]
$sentence = $combined[0] + $combined[2] + $combined[1]

$sentence + $fav
```

Running this script will display the message "My favorite number is 4," as shown in Figure 3-13.

```
1   $words = @('My', 'is ' , ' favorite number ')
2   $numbers = @(2,3,2)
3   $combined = $words + $numbers
4
5   # Array now looks like ('My ', ' is ', ' favorite number ', 2, 3, 2)
6   $fav = $combined[3] + $combined[5]
7   $sentence = $combined[0] + $combined[2] + $combined[1]
8
9   $sentence + $fav
```

```
PS C:\> C:\Users\NikCharlebois\OneDrive\Books\PowerShell for SharePoint 2016\Chapters\Chapter 4 - PowerShell Basics\
My favorite number is 4

PS C:\>
```

***Figure 3-13.*** *Result of combining arrays with different types*

## Environment Variables

It is possible to get direct access to all global environment variables declared on a machine. By default, PowerShell declares the following global variable: $env. You can access different information regarding your current environment by calling $env:[Variable Name]. For example, if you want to get the current computer name, you can simply call:

```
$env:computername
```

## WhatIf Rollback

Those familiar with the Transact SQL syntax will recognize this neat little feature that allows you to run a command that tries to modify or delete existing content, and that displays the end result, but that never actually commits the transaction. This comes in very handy when you want to test a script or procedure against production data that continuously changes and that can't be accurately replicated in a dev environment. In order to use the PowerShell rollback features, simply include the -WhatIf switch after your actual command. You will be presented with the results of your query on screen, if you are satisfied with the results, all you'll need to do is remove the switch and run the command again to have it committed.

## Graphical User Interface

Guess what? You can build interactive user experiences with a PowerShell script. Remember, PowerShell is .NET in the back-end, so we can reuse the control libraries exposed by the framework to create a visual interface for our scripts. For example, assume you are writing a script that simply asks for a user's name and displays a greeting message on screen. Instead of using the default write-host cmdlet to display the greeting message, you could build a graphic form that displays the welcome text in a visual fashion. The following lines of code take you through the process of creating such a script:

```
Add-Type -AssemblyName System.Windows.Forms
$form = New-Object Windows.Forms.Form
$form.Height = 100

$name = read-host "What is your name?"

$lblWelcome = New-Object System.Windows.Forms.Label
$lblWelcome.Text = "Welcome $name !"

$form.Controls.Add($lblWelcome)
$form.ShowDialog()
```

The resulting script will prompt the user for their name in the PowerShell console, and once the user has entered the information, a Windows form will be displayed with the greeting message appearing in a text label (see Figure 3-14).

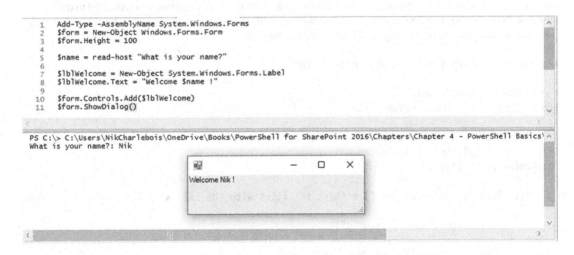

***Figure 3-14.*** *Result of the graphical interface script*

## Demo Project—Selective Deletion of Files in a Folder

In the following demo, you will learn how you can use PowerShell to interact with files stored on your machine, and how you can use the -WhatIf switch to test the execution of your script before committing any changes. Assume the following scenario, in which you are asked to develop a PowerShell script that will loop through all the files in a specified folder delete only files that have the extension .txt. The script will need to prompt the user to enter the path for the folder containing the files. Your script should also prompt the user to choose to run the script in "test" mode, which will implement the -WhatIf switch, and not commit the changes directly. Figure 3-15 shows the files that exist in the folder against which you will execute your script.

| Name | Date modified | Type | Size |
|---|---|---|---|
| A001.txt | 2015-10-06 23:29 | Text Document | 1 KB |
| A002Table.xls | 2015-10-06 23:29 | Microsoft Excel 97... | 1 KB |
| A003.docx | 2015-10-06 23:29 | Microsoft Word D... | 1 KB |
| A004.txt | 2015-10-06 23:29 | Text Document | 1 KB |
| A005.pptx | 2015-10-06 23:29 | Microsoft PowerP... | 1 KB |
| A006.txt | 2015-10-06 23:29 | Text Document | 1 KB |
| A007.txt | 2015-10-06 23:29 | Text Document | 1 KB |
| A008.pdf | 2015-10-06 23:29 | PDF File | 1 KB |
| A009.txt | 2015-10-06 23:29 | Text Document | 1 KB |
| A010.mdb | 2015-10-06 23:29 | Microsoft Access ... | 1 KB |

*Figure 3-15.* *Files listing of folder*

The script that you will be developing will need to capture two inputs from the user: a value, y or n, that will identify if the user wants to run the script in "test" mode or not, and the location of the folder containing the files, in this case C:\Demo 1\Files. The script will then need to loop through all files in that folder and check each one's extension. Whenever you encounter a file with the .txt extension, you will need to decide, based on the user's input, whether to call the method that will delete the current file with the rollback switch (-WhatIf) or not. The resulting script will look like the following:

```
$rollback = Read-Host "Run in Test mode? (Y/N)"

# Get path the the folder
$folderPath = read-host "Folder Path"

# Get all files in specified folder and loop through each;
$files = Get-ChildItem $folderPath
foreach($file in $files)
{
    if($file.Extension -eq ".txt") # Check for files with the TXT extension
    {
        if($rollback.ToLower() -eq "y")
        {
            Remove-Item $file.FullName -WhatIf
        }
        elseif($rollback.ToLower() -eq "n") #Notice how elseif is spelled in one word in PowerShell
        {
            Remove-Item $file.FullName
        }
    }
}
```

Figure 3-16 shows the execution of this script against your folder.

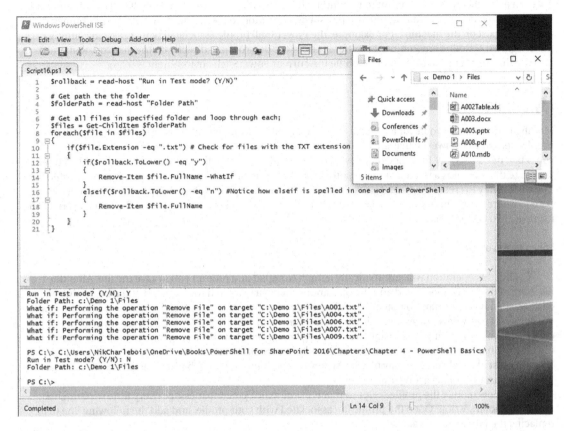

***Figure 3-16.*** *Result of script deleting text files only*

## Customization

Another nice feature of PowerShell is its ability to create predefined customized sessions for different users. For example, we're SharePoint developers, so almost any PowerShell script that we write and execute will be committed against a SharePoint environment. Therefore, it would be nice if, by default, every time we open a new PowerShell session window, the Microsoft.SharePoint.PowerShell snap-in was registered, instead of having to manually register it every time. Also, some people may have preferences for how the text and background of the PowerShell window should look by default. These are only a few of the scenarios that led the PowerShell team to come up with something called PowerShell profiles. These allow you to save various configurations and artifacts such as custom modules in a separate file that will automatically be preloaded every time you launch a new PowerShell session.

Profiles are simply .ps1 files that are stored on disk. These profile files are stored in each user's personal documents folder. You can view where your current profile is stored by calling the following variable:

```
$profile
```

In this case, the profile on your server is located at:

```
c:\Users\Administrator\Documents\WindowsPowerShell\Microsoft.PowerShell_profile.ps1
```

Every time a new session is launched, this .ps1 PowerShell script will try to execute. By default, the file does not exist; this is very important to remember. If the file does not exist, PowerShell will simply continue its normal execution flow. You should also pay special attention to the various PowerShell environments that can coexist on the machine. For example, the PowerShell profile associated with a session running in the integrated scripting environment is different from the one running directly on the desktop. Remember to also use the $profile call to see which profile the current PowerShell environment is using.

## My Profile

Modifying the default profile for a specific user is as simple as modifying the .ps1 file associated with its profile. Remember, however, that the file does not exist by default, so to begin modifying your profile, you'll first need to create the associated .ps1 file. By default, PowerShell declares a default variable named $profile that contains a reference to the path where PowerShell is looking for the current user's profile file. The easiest way to create the file if it doesn't already exist is to call the Notepad application, passing it the path to where your profile should be located. This will automatically create the profile file and let you edit it using the text editor tool:

```
Notepad $profile
```

Calling this operation will automatically launch Notepad and prompt you to save the file. After the file is created, simply open it and add the operations that you want to have executed at the beginning of each session. It is important to note that adding too many operations by default could very well slow down the launch of every new PowerShell window in your environment. Thus you should keep the preloaded commands to a minimum, and abstain from calling operations that take a long time to load. For example, the default SharePoint PowerShell console tries to load all SharePoint modules every time you launch it. You will most likely observe a delay of a few seconds every time you launch a new instance of it, because PowerShell snap-ins take a long time to load.

Let us now modify the profile script so that it prints a nice greeting message every time we launch a new PowerShell session. Open the profile file associated with your profile, and add the following line to it, replacing the {Your Name} value:

```
Write-host "Welcome {Your Name}!"
```

Save your changes, and launch a new PowerShell session. If everything worked, you should now see your greeting message displayed as the first line after the PowerShell copyright information.

Other types of customization that you may want to apply could be related to the visual aspect of your default PowerShell windows. For example, because the illustrations in the current book are in black and white, we'll want to change the default background color of the sessions to white and the default foreground to black. In order to achieve this, we'll add the following lines of code in our default PowerShell profile's script:

```
$console = Get-Host
$console.UI.RawUI.BackgroundColor = "White"
$console.UI.RawUI.ForegroundColor = "Black"

# Need to call Clear-Host to wipe out the navy blue color that has already been put on screen.
Clear-Host
```

Save your modified profile file, and launch a new PowerShell session window. You should see it flash on hitting the Clear-Host command, and then the entire PowerShell window should be in black and white.

# Custom Modules

In some cases, you may have developed useful methods that are generic enough that you would like to have them included in every PowerShell session so that you can call them as you want, just as if they were part of the baseline product. In such a case, you'll want to expose your method as a PowerShell module, to ensure that it is made available to all users using PowerShell on the current machine. The most common scenario for creating custom modules is to take a PowerShell script (.ps1) containing the logic of the method you want to expose, and convert it to a module. Consider the following script:

```
$script:Owner = "Nik"
function Get-Owner
{
    return $script:Owner
}

function Set-Owner($owner)
{
$script:Owner = $owner
}
```

This represents a very simple way of specifying who the current owner of a script is. It contains two methods, a "getter" and a "setter," and a generic script variable that stores the information pertaining to the owner's name. In order for this script to be converted into a PowerShell module, we'll need to save it with a .psm1 extension. Create a new folder at the root of your c:\ drive on your environment, and name it PSModules. Save this script in the newly created folder and name it MyOwnerModule.psm1. Now, open a new PowerShell session, and execute the following line of code to convert your script into a reusable module:

```
Import-module c:\PSModules\MyOwnerModule.psm1
```

That's it; your new custom module is now loaded into your PowerShell session. To confirm that it is loaded in memory, type the following command in your current PowerShell session:

```
Get-Module
```

You should see it listed among the available modules. Please note that, at this point, your module exists only while your PowerShell session remains open. If you close your PowerShell window and open a new one, you'll need to reimport it in order for it to be usable. If you want to make sure it stays available for all of your sessions, it would be a good idea to add the Import command in your personal PowerShell profile. Now that your module is loaded, you can make direct calls to your method in the following fashion:

```
Get-Owner # Will print Nik
Set-Owner "Bob"
Get-Owner # Will print Bob
```

You should always consider creating a module when you want to reuse a set of methods and objects.

# Leaping Ahead

As this book is being written, the Windows Server 2016 Technical Preview 3 has just been made available. This new version of Microsoft's popular server operating system comes preloaded with PowerShell version 5.0. This section will give you a quick overview of what new features and tools have been introduced with the latest version of the scripting engine.

## Desired State Configuration

This new feature is something administrators have been asking for since the early days of PowerShell. It allows a user to specify what the minimum conditions should be for the script to be able to execute properly. You can use Desired State Configuration code block, or DSC for short, in your scripts to specify what software, features, resources, or components should be present on specific machines, and what their status should be. PowerShell will then go and perform the required installation of the specified items before running your script. PowerShell Desired State Configuration will be covered in detail in later chapters of this book.

## Dynamic Method and Property Names

Imagine that you have a script in which you need to store information about what method or property of an object to call. In some previous versions of PowerShell (version 3.0 and earlier), calling such an element using a value stored in a variable would require you to call in to some reflection assemblies. Starting with PowerShell version 4, you can now make calls on objects using variables values. The following example illustrates what we mean by dynamic naming:

```
$now = Get-Date
$dynamicProperty = "Month"

$now.$dynamicProperty
```

This example declares a new string variable that contains the name of the property you will want to call on the DateTime object, in this case Month, which will return the name of the current month. Instead of calling the Month property directly on the DateTime object, you now call the variable name that contains a string reference to the property name. This example is perfectly valid in PowerShell v5, and will return the name of the current month on screen.

# Summary

In this chapter, you have learned the fundamentals of PowerShell. You should now be able to create and run your own PowerShell scripts and modules, and be able to customize your PowerShell experience using profiles. This chapter gave you an overview of the possibilities that PowerShell offers the system administrator. Without getting into the low-level specifics of PowerShell, this chapter taught you the general concepts behind the use of PowerShell in real-life scenarios. You have now learned the fundamentals you require in order to start configuring and managing your SharePoint environment. The next chapter will focus on configuring a SharePoint 2016 environment from the ground up. From this point on, we will assume that you have a good understanding of all elements of PowerShell scripts. Refer to this chapter as needed throughout the rest of this book, as you may need to revisit certain concepts explained in it for future examples.

# CHAPTER 4

■ ■ ■

# Installing and Deploying SharePoint with PowerShell

We are now ready to start digging into what PowerShell has to offer to us, SharePoint people. This chapter will go over the basic commands you can use in PowerShell to help automate the build of your SharePoint environment. Through a set of demos, you'll learn how you can write your own custom scripts and reuse them to create new SharePoint machines on demand. We will cover how to automate the installation of the following aspects of a new SharePoint farm:

- Installation and configuration of the Server Operating System's roles and features

- Installation and configuration of SQL Server

- Installation of the SharePoint prerequisites

- Installation of the SharePoint core components

- Configuration of your new SharePoint Farm

The SharePoint Farm environment that we will have created and configured by the end of this chapter will act as the foundation for all other chapters to come. The environment will be "self-contained," meaning that all required components will be installed on a single box. In real-life scenarios, you'll always want to offload the domain controller role to a separate server as well as have your SQL Server installation hosted elsewhere. SharePoint 2016 also gives us more flexibility than its predecessors, by allowing us to assign predefined roles to our servers to ensure that the proper services are run on the appropriate server.

Components like the workflow engine, machine translation, and search services would normally be installed on external application servers in order to keep the SharePoint Web front-end servers as lightweight as possible. It is important to note that the end-goal architecture we will create in this chapter is for learning purposes only, and should not be something you aim to replicate in a production environment. The rest of this chapter assumes that your test environment has a fresh baseline copy of Windows Server 2012 R2 Standard with Update (x64) edition installed.

## Requirements

The following section will cover both the hardware and the software requirements you will need in order to re-create the same development environment created in this chapter. Pay specific attention to the various drives that are required along with their respective installation media, as the script produced at the end of the chapter will not work otherwise.

© Nikolas Charlebois-Laprade and John Edward Naguib 2017

N. Charlebois-Laprade and J. E. Naguib, *Beginning PowerShell for SharePoint 2016*,

DOI 10.1007/978-1-4842-2884-5_4

# Hardware Requirements

For you to be able to get through the rest of this book trying out all of the examples that follow in a reasonable fashion, you will need to create your new SharePoint 2016 farm on a machine that meets the following list of minimum requirements. These requirements are in line with Microsoft's recommendations:

- 16 GB of RAM available

- 80 GB of disk space

- 64-bit, 4 cores

- Windows Server 2012 R2 Standard with Update (x64) as the operating system

- Three DVD drives assigned to your machine (D:\, E:\, and F:\)

# Software Requirements

The scripts and examples given in this chapter will require you to have a copy of the installation files for the following software:

- SQL Server 2014 Standard Edition with Service Pack 1 (x64)

- SharePoint Server 2016 (x64)

In addition, all of these scripts assume that you have the media shown in Table 4-1 available to automate the installation.

***Table 4-1.*** *Required Media and Associated Drives*

| Drive | Media |
| --- | --- |
| D:\ | SQL Server 2014 with SP1 |
| E:\ | Windows Server 2012 R2 Standard with Update |
| F:\ | SharePoint Server 2016 |

Figure 4-1 shows the various drives that are required and their associated installation media in Windows Explorer.

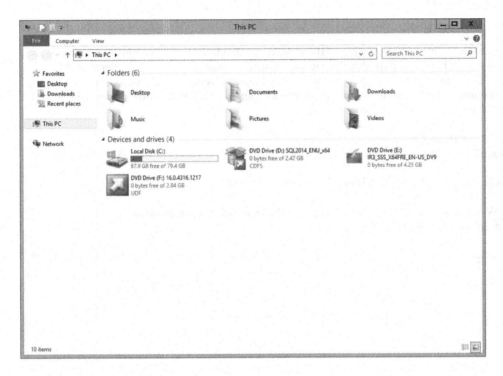

***Figure 4-1.*** *Overview of the required installation media*

Another requirement is that you must have the PowerShell execution policy set to be unrestricted. Please refer to Chapter 3 to learn how this can be achieved. Without this set properly, the scripts produced in this chapter will not execute as expected, because PowerShell will block their execution.

# Roles and Features

This section will help you automate the configuration of all Windows Server 2012 R2 roles and features required by SQL Server 2014 and SharePoint 2016. We will go into the details of the various roles and which PowerShell commands are required to have them enabled on your server.

---

■ **Caution**    Please note that the intent of this book is to help you understand the internals of how PowerShell works and how it can be used. Some of the scripts that you'll encounter in the following chapters may contain passwords that are exposed in plain text. This is not considered to be best practice, and you should always be careful how you expose sensitive information in your scripts.

---

# Domain Controller

This role is probably the most important one of them all. Remember that your SharePoint 2016 machine will be self-contained; therefore, it needs to host its own domain. PowerShell in Windows Server 2012 R2 provides us with a set of various cmdlets that allow us to interact directly with the various Active Directory components. The following script excerpt will configure the domain controller role on the server environment (Figure 4-2 shows the script running):

```
$domainName = "contoso.com"
$safeModeAdminPassword = ConvertTo-SecureString "pass@word1" -AsPlainText -Force

Add-WindowsFeature AD-Domain-Services -IncludeManagementTools

Install-ADDSForest -DomainName $domainName -SafeModeAdministratorPassword
$safeModeAdminPassword -Confirm:$false
```

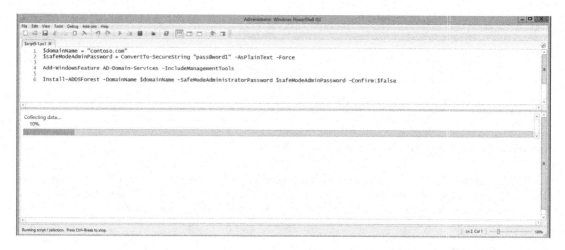

***Figure 4-2.** Installing the Domain Controller role with PowerShell*

Running this script will declare a new domain, called contoso.com, and will automatically promote it. After running this script, the machine will automatically reboot after a few seconds to ensure that the new configuration takes effect. After the machine reboots, you should see your new domain name appended in front of your user name on the login screen (see Figure 4-3).

***Figure 4-3.** Login screen with domain information*

## Users and Groups

The next step will be to create a few test users and groups in your new Active Directory structure. We will try to mimic a real-world scenario with an environment in which we will have fictive users spread out across different business units in the Contoso organization. we will use PowerShell to create the following Active Directory groups to represent the following functional business units:

- Administration

- Finance

- Human Resources

- Directors

- Tech Support

The following lines of script will take care of automatically creating these groups.

```
New-ADGroup -DisplayName "Administration" -GroupScope DomainLocal -Name "Administration"
New-ADGroup -DisplayName "Finance" -GroupScope DomainLocal -Name "Finance"
New-ADGroup -DisplayName "Human Resources" -GroupScope DomainLocal -Name "Human Resources"
New-ADGroup -DisplayName "Directors" -GroupScope DomainLocal -Name "Directors"
New-ADGroup -DisplayName "Tech Support" -GroupScope DomainLocal -Name "Tech Support"
```

We will now create a user for each security group that we have just created, using the following script. The default password for each of these users will be *pass@word1*. This will prove useful in future examples, when you will need to log into SharePoint as various users to test permissions. Figure 4-4 shows the created users.

```
$usersPassword = ConvertTo-SecureString "pass@word1" -AsPlainText -Force

New-ADUser -Name "JSmith" -GivenName "John" -Surname "Smith" -AccountPassword
$usersPassword  -UserPrincipalName "jsmith@contoso.com" -DisplayName "John Smith"
Enable-ADAccount -Identity "JSmith"
Add-ADGroupMember -Identity "Administration" -Member "JSmith"

New-ADUser -Name "BMoores" -GivenName "Bob" -Surname "Moores" -AccountPassword
$usersPassword  -UserPrincipalName "bmoores@contoso.com" -DisplayName "Bob Moores"
Enable-ADAccount -Identity "BMoores"
Add-ADGroupMember -Identity "Finance" -Member "BMoores"

New-ADUser -Name "PHarris" -GivenName "Peter" -Surname "Harris" -AccountPassword
$usersPassword -UserPrincipalName "pharris@contoso.com" -DisplayName "Peter Harris"
Enable-ADAccount -Identity "PHarris"
Add-ADGroupMember -Identity "Human Resources" -Member "PHarris"

New-ADUser -Name "KButtler" -GivenName "Kyle" -Surname "Buttler" -AccountPassword
$usersPassword -UserPrincipalName "kbuttler@contoso.com" -DisplayName "Kyle Buttler"
Enable-ADAccount -Identity "KButtler"
Add-ADGroupMember -Identity "Directors" -Member "KButtler"
```

```
New-ADUser -Name "MRanger" -GivenName "Mike" -Surname "Ranger" -AccountPassword
$usersPassword  -UserPrincipalName "mranger@contoso.com" -DisplayName "Mike Ranger"
Enable-ADAccount -Identity "MRanger"
Add-ADGroupMember -Identity "Tech Support" -Member "MRanger"
```

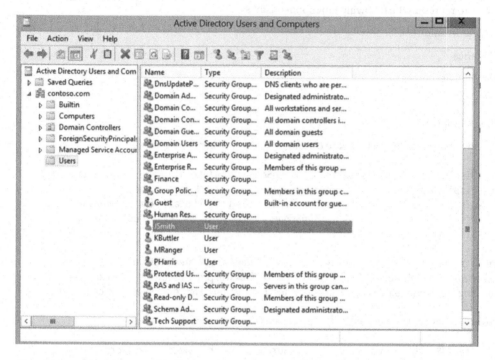

***Figure 4-4.*** *List of users and groups*

## Application Server Role

SharePoint 2016 requires your server to have the Application Server role enabled to leverage many .NET features, such as the Windows Communication Foundation for web service calls. Besides activating this role, there are several specific features that also need to be turned on in order for SharePoint to install properly. The list in Table 4-2 identifies all features required.

***Table 4-2.*** *All of the Features Required for Your Application Server Role*

| | | |
|---|---|---|
| Application-Server | AS-HTTP-Activation | AS-Named-Pipes |
| AS-Net-Framework | AS-TCP-Activation | AS-TCP-Port-Sharing |
| AS-WAS-Support | AS-Web-Support | Net-Framework-Features |
| Server-Media-Foundation | WAS | WAS-Config-APIs |
| WAS-NET-Environment | WAS-Process-Model | Web-App-Dev |
| Web-Asp-Net | Web-Basic-Auth | Web-Common-Http |
| Web-Default-Doc | Web-Digest-Auth | Web-Dir-Browsing |
| Web-Dyn-Compression | Web-Filtering | Web-Health |
| Web-Http-Errors | Web-Http-Logging | Web-Http-Tracing |
| Web-ISAPI-Ext | Web-ISAPI-Filter | Web-Lgcy-Scripting |
| Web-Log-Libraries | Web-Metabase | Web-Mgmt-Compat |
| Web-Mgmt-Console | Web-Mgmt-Tools | Web-Net-Ext |
| Web-Performance | Web-Request-Monitor | Web-Security |
| Web-Server | Web-Stat-Compression | Web-Static-Content |
| Web-WebServer | Web-Windows-Auth | Windows-Identity-Foundation |
| Xps-Viewer | | |

If you count, that's over 45 different features required. We could go and manually add each of them using the Server Manager console, but because this is a PowerShell book, after all, we'll just run a one-line command to have it all done automatically for us. The following line of script will take care of it all, as illustrated in Figure 4-5. Please give it a few minutes to complete.

```
Add-WindowsFeature Application-Server, AS-HTTP-Activation, AS-Named-Pipes, AS-Net-Framework,
AS-TCP-Activation, AS-TCP-Port-Sharing, AS-WAS-Support, AS-Web-Support, Net-Framework-Features,
Server-Media-Foundation, WAS, WAS-Config-APIs, WAS-NET-Environment, WAS-Process-Model,
Web-App-Dev, Web-Asp-Net, Web-Basic-Auth, Web-Common-Http, Web-Default-Doc, Web-Digest-Auth,
Web-Dir-Browsing, Web-Dyn-Compression, Web-Filtering, Web-Health, Web-Http-Errors,
Web-Http-Logging, Web-Http-Tracing, Web-ISAPI-Ext, Web-ISAPI-Filter, Web-Lgcy-Scripting,
Web-Log-Libraries, Web-Metabase, Web-Mgmt-Compat, Web-Mgmt-Console, Web-Mgmt-Tools,
Web-Net-Ext, Web-Performance, Web-Request-Monitor, Web-Security, Web-Server, Web-Stat-Compression,
Web-Static-Content, Web-WebServer, Web-Windows-Auth, Windows-Identity-Foundation,
Xps-Viewer -Source:E:\source\sxs\
```

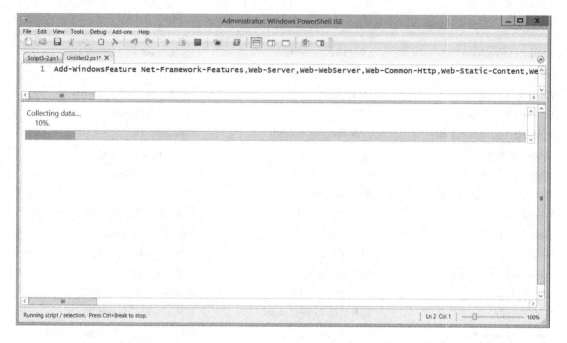

***Figure 4-5.*** *Features being installed*

After you are done running this command, you will need to restart the server. Figure 4-6 shows the features being configured on restarting the server. You can simply run:

```
Restart-Computer
```

***Figure 4-6.*** *Applying the prerequisite features on restarting*

# Installing the Software Components

You are now ready to start installing the various components that make up a SharePoint farm. As mentioned earlier in this chapter, the environment that you are building in this chapter is self-contained. We will therefore cover how you can automate the installation of the SQL Server components, the SharePoint 2016 prerequisites, and the SharePoint 2016 core components using PowerShell. In the next section, you will learn how to configure these components to make the most of your environment.

## Installing SQL Server 2014

Before you can properly install the required components of SQL Server 2014, you will need to enable the following roles on the server. The scripts that are detailed in the current section all assume that you have the SQL installation components loaded on a drive mapped to D:\. You will be doing a minimal installation of a default SQL standalone instance, installing only the Database Engine Services core bits. The following script will perform an unattended installation of SQL Server:

```
$sqlSAPassword = "pass@word1"

$sqlProcess = new-object System.Diagnostics.Process
$sqlProcess.StartInfo.Filename = "D:\setup.exe"
$sqlProcess.StartInfo.Arguments = "/QS /ACTION=install /IACCEPTSQLSERVERLICENSETERMS=1
/FEATURES=SQL /INSTANCENAME=MSSQLSERVER /INSTANCEID=MSSQLSERVER
```

```
/SQLSYSADMINACCOUNTS=contoso\Administrator /SECURITYMODE=SQL /SAPWD=$sqlSAPassword
/INDICATEPROGRESS /AGTSVCSTARTUPTYPE=Automatic /TCPENABLED=1"
$sqlProcess.Start()
$sqlProcess.WaitForExit()
```

During the installation process, you will see several installation windows appear (see Figure 4-7). You do not have to interact with any of them. The parameters passed to the setup executable will automatically fill in the appropriate information required for your installation. The installation process will take about 10 minutes to complete, so now may be a good time to grab a cup of coffee.

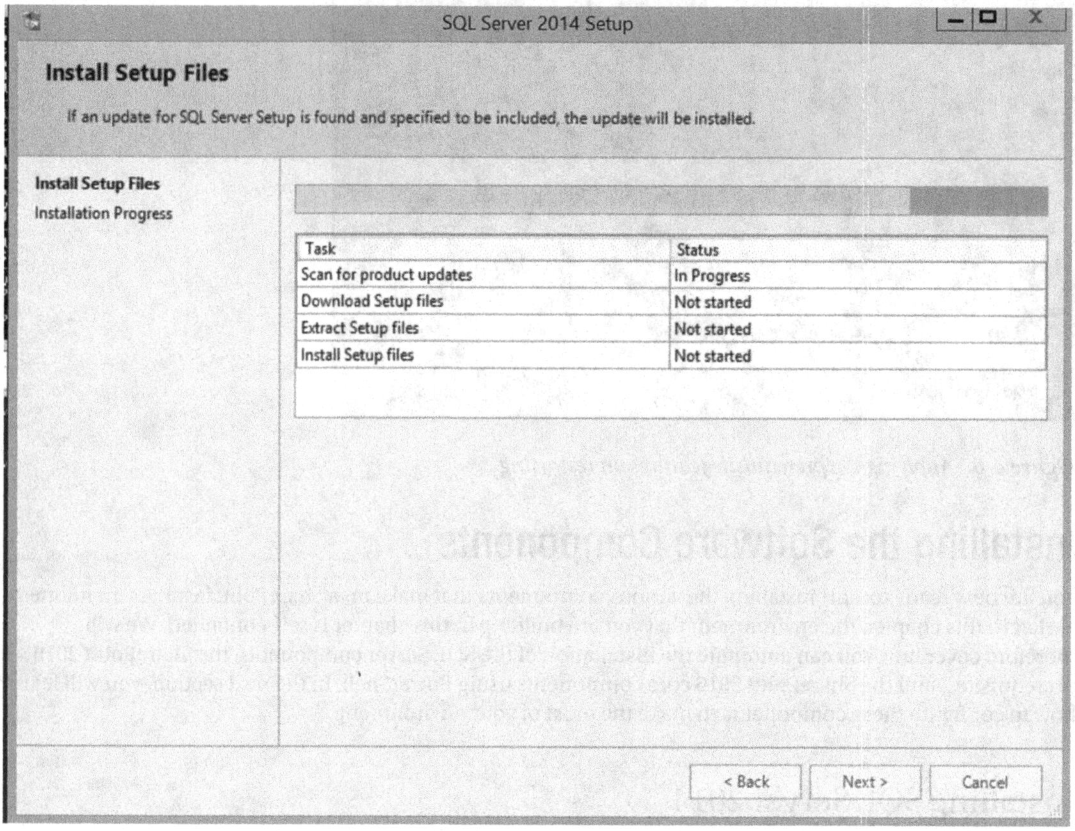

*Figure 4-7. Unattended SQL Server 2014 installation*

# Installing SharePoint Prerequisites

Finally! You are now ready to install the SharePoint components onto your server. The first step to installing SharePoint will be to download and install all of its prerequisites. You will be creating an automated PowerShell script that will automatically download each of them locally, and install them one at a time. The following list contains all the prerequisites that are required for the SharePoint Core installer to work:

- Microsoft SQL Server 2008 R2 SP1 Native Client

- Microsoft Sync Framework Runtime v1.0 SP1 (x64)

- Windows Server AppFabric

- Cumulative Update Package 1 for Microsoft AppFabric 1.1 for Windows Server (KB2671763)

- Windows Identity Foundation (KB974405)

- Microsoft Identity Extensions

- Microsoft Information Protection and Control Client

- Microsoft WCF Data Services 5.0

To download each of the required files, simply use the Invoke-WebRequest PowerShell cmdlet. The method takes two input parameters: the URL of the source file to download, and the local path in which to save the file. This method can be called in the following fashion:

```
$webClient = New-Object "System.Net.WebClient" $webClient.DownloadFile("http://<source file
URL>","c:\<local path>\<filename>" )
```

The automated script that you will create will have a list of all the prerequisite file URLs stored in an array. It will loop through each of them and download them locally. Once all of the files have been downloaded locally, the script will call the SharePoint 2016 Products Preparation Tool, passing it the list of prerequisite files as an argument. The installer tool will then take care of installing and properly configuring each of them (see Figure 4-8).

```
$LocalPath = "C:\SP2016Prereqs"

New-Item -ItemType Directory -Force -Path $localPath

# Array with all urls...a bit messy
$files = @("https://download.microsoft.com/download/9/1/3/9138773A-505D-43E2-AC08-
9A77E1E0490B/1033/x64/sqlncli.msi","https://download.microsoft.com/download/D/7/2/D72FD747-
69B6-40B7-875B-C2B40A6B2BDD/Windows6.1-KB974405-x64.msu", " http://download.microsoft.com/
download/0/1/D/01D06854-CA0C-46F1-ADBA-EBF86010DCC6/rtm/MicrosoftIdentityExtensions-64.
msi", " http://download.microsoft.com/download/E/0/0/E0060D8F-2354-4871-9596-DC78538799CC/
Synchronization.msi", "http://download.microsoft.com/download/A/6/7/A678AB47-496B-4907-
B3D4-0A2D280A13C0/WindowsServerAppFabricSetup_x64.exe", "http://download.microsoft.com/
download/7/B/5/7B51D8D1-20FD-4BF0-87C7-4714F5A1C313/AppFabric1.1-RTM-KB2671763-x64-ENU.
exe", "https://download.microsoft.com/download/3/C/F/3CF781F5-7D29-4035-9265-C34FF2369FA2/
setup_msipc_x64.exe", "https://download.microsoft.com/download/1/C/A/1CAA41C7-88B9-42D6-
9E11-3C655656DAB1/WcfDataServices.exe","https://download.microsoft.com/download/E/2/1/
E21644B5-2DF2-47C2-91BD-63C560427900/NDP452-KB2901907-x86-x64-AllOS-ENU.exe", "http://
download.microsoft.com/download/2/E/6/2E61CFA4-993B-4DD4-91DA-3737CD5CD6E3/vcredist_x64.
exe", "http://download.microsoft.com/download/C/6/9/C690CC33-18F7-405D-B18A-0A8E199E531C/
Windows8.1-KB2898850-x64.msu")

$fileName = ""
$pathParts

foreach($file in $files)
{
    $pathParts = $file.Split("/")
    $fileName = $pathParts[$pathParts.Length -1]
    $fullName = "$localPath\$fileName"
    Invoke-WebRequest $file -OutFile $fullName
}
```

```
$prereqProcess = new-object System.Diagnostics.Process
$prereqProcess.StartInfo.Filename = "F:\prerequisiteinstaller.exe"
$prereqProcess.StartInfo.Arguments = "/SQLNCli:$LocalPath\sqlncli.msi /IDFX:$LocalPath\
Windows6.1-KB974405-x64.msu /IDFX11:$LocalPath\MicrosoftIdentityExtensions-64.msi
/Sync:$LocalPath\Synchronization.msi /AppFabric:$LocalPath\WindowsServerAppFabricSetup_x64.exe
/KB2671763:$LocalPath\AppFabric1.1-RTM-KB2671763-x64-ENU.exe
/MSIPCClient:$LocalPath\setup_msipc_x64.exe /WCFDataServices56:$LocalPath\WcfDataServices.exe
/DotNet452:$LocalPath\NDP452-KB2901907-x86-x64-AllOS-ENU.exe /MSVCRT12:$LocalPath\vcredist_x64.exe
/KB2898850:$LocalPath\Windows8.1-KB2898850-x64.msu /unattended"
$prereqProcess.Start()
$prereqProcess.WaitForExit()
```

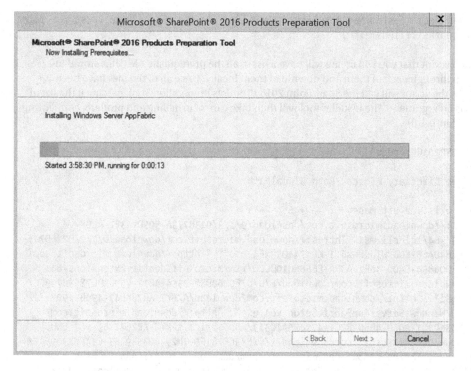

*Figure 4-8.* *Unattended Sharepoint 2016 prerequisites installation*

Allow this script about 5 to 10 minutes to finish its execution. Once it is completed, you will need to reboot the machine. After your machine has finished restarting, it will be properly configured and ready to receive the SharePoint installation elements.

## Installing SharePoint

Last but not least are the SharePoint core elements. The SharePoint 2016 installation media already contain a few predefined configuration files to help us do an unattended installation of the product. Unfortunately, each of them requires you to manually specify your product key before it can complete. The configuration files are nothing more than short XML files located under the /files/ folder at the root of the media.

In order to get your unattended installation working, you will need to copy the setupfarmsilent configuration file locally on drive C:\, modify it to include your product key, and then execute the installation process by referencing the newly modified configuration file:

```
$productKey = "XXXXX-XXXXX-XXXXX-XXXXX-XXXXX" # Replace with your own

$spLocalPath = "C:\SP2016\"
$spConfigFile = $spLocalPath + "config.xml"

New-Item -ItemType Directory -Force -Path $spLocalPath
Copy-Item F:\files\setupfarmsilent\config.xml $spLocalPath
$configContent =[io.file]::ReadAllText($spConfigFile)

Get-ChildItem $spConfigFile -Recurse |
    Where-Object {$_.GetType().ToString() -eq "System.IO.FileInfo"} |
    Set-ItemProperty -Name IsReadOnly -Value $false

$configContent = $configContent -Replace "<!--", ""
$configContent = $configContent -Replace "-->", ""
$configContent = $configContent -Replace "Enter Product Key Here", $productKey
$configContent = $configContent -Replace """none""", """basic"""

$configContent | Out-File $spConfigFile
```

This script takes care of copying the configuration file locally by creating a folder on your C:\ drive, and creating a copy of the XML configuration file used by SharePoint to install all of its components. Open the newly copied file, and modify its content to include your own product key for SharePoint 2016. As the script indicates, please replace the generic product key provided with the one provided on your installation media or MSDN subscription. Next, initiate a new process that will execute the SharePoint 2016 installation wizard in silent mode (no graphical interfaces) by referencing the XML configuration file that you have just created locally with the previous script. Figure 4-9 shows the installation in process.

```
$spProcess = new-object System.Diagnostics.Process
$spProcess.StartInfo.Filename = "F:\setup.exe"
$spProcess.StartInfo.Arguments = "/config C:\SP2016\config.xml"
$spProcess.Start()
$spProcess.WaitForExit()
```

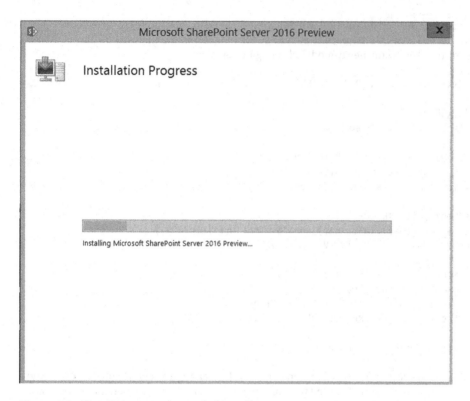

*Figure 4-9. SharePoint 2016 unattended installation*

# Configuring Your SharePoint Farm

Now that all parts of our SharePoint 2016 environment have been installed, you need to configure the farm. Once again for this task we will be using PowerShell to create the various databases and service instances required by SharePoint to run properly. At the end of this section, your environment will be fully usable and will be ready for you to start playing with it.

## Creating the Databases

Unless you've been living under a rock for the past few years, you've come to learn that since SharePoint 2010, the SharePoint Products Configuration Wizard, which is the default graphical tool to configure your SharePoint farm, adds a bunch of random numbers at the end of each database it creates. These numbers are referred to as a GUID, and are used by SharePoint to ensure that your databases are uniquely named because the tool doesn't trust you to pick one yourself. If you are like us, we just hate it when software assumes that we don't know what we're doing and makes decision on our behalf. Fear not my friends; with the help of some PowerShell goodness, there is a way to specify how you want these databases to be named.

In the SharePoint world, there are three main types of database that every farm should have: the Central Administration content database (referred to as the admin database), the configuration database (referred to as the config database), and the content database. The admin database is where the information about the central administration site collection is stored. There will always only be a single instance of this database per SharePoint farm. The config database stores information about all other SharePoint databases in the farm. It also keeps track of all custom solutions, webparts, web applications, site templates, and all other farm settings. The content database, by contrast, can have multiple instances. It stores all information about a site collection in it. There could be more than one site collection stored in each content database.

Throughout the next few sections, we will describe how to create each of these databases automatically using PowerShell. With the core parts of SharePoint now installed on your machine, you now have access to use the `Microsoft.SharePoint.PowerShell` cmdlets, which will make your job easier.

The first database that you'll need to create is the config database. Because it is the main database keeping track of everything going on in our SharePoint farm, it makes sense to create this first. With the SharePoint cmdlets now available, you can call the `New-SPConfigurationDatabase` cmdlet to do the work. Calling this cmdlet will also automatically create an empty admin database that will act as a placeholder for the eventual Central Administration site collection that will be created in the next section.

Starting with SharePoint 2016, the `New-SPConfigurationDatabase` Powershell cmdlet requires that we specify what MinRole to assign to our server. Because we are setting up a Single Server farm for the purpose of this book, we will need to specify to our PowerShell cmdlet that we wish to assign our server with the SingleServerFarm role. This is done by adding the `-LocalServerRole SingleServerFarm` parameters to the end of our command.

```
$spConfigDBName = "SPConfig" # Config DB name, replace by your own;
$spAdminDBName = "SPAdmin" # Admin DB name, replace by your own;
$spPassphrase = "pass@word1" # Recommendation is to change this to something else;
$spFarmAdminPassword = "pass@word1" # replace by your admin account password;

# Convert the provided Passphrase to a secure string
$securePassphrase = ConvertTo-SecureString $spPassphrase -asPlainText -force

# Convert the provided Admin account's password to secure string and create a new PowerShell
Credentials object to represent the Administrator's account;
$secureAdminPassword = ConvertTo-SecureString $spFarmAdminPassword -asPlainText -force
$spFarmAdmin = New-Object -TypeName System.Management.Automation.PSCredential -ArgumentList
"contoso\administrator", $secureAdminPassword

# Load the SharePoint PowerShell cmdlets
Add-PSSnapin Microsoft.SharePoint.PowerShell

New-SPConfigurationDatabase -DatabaseServer $env:COMPUTERNAME -DatabaseName $spConfigDBName
-AdministrationContentDatabaseName $spAdminDBName -Passphrase $securePassphrase
-FarmCredentials $spFarmAdmin -LocalServerRole SingleServerFarm
```

The operation should take about four to five minutes to complete. Once it is completed, you should be able to see that your two databases have been properly created on your server by using the SQL Server Management Studio tool (see Figure 4-10).

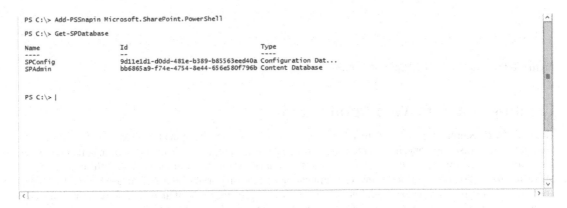

***Figure 4-10.*** *SharePoint 2016 databases*

## Configuring Central Administration

Now that your empty placeholder for Central Administration has been created (`config database`), go ahead and populate it with information about its site collection. It is normally a good practice to have your Central Administration site deploy on a nonstandard port that is higher than 999. The following script lets you specify what port number you'd like to use. Our personal preference is to always use port 7777 for development farms. Examples that will follow in the next few chapters will all assume that you have it deployed to this port, so unless you have a good reason to wanting to change it, we suggest that you leave it untouched. The execution of the PowerShell command should take about two minutes to execute.

```
$centralAdminPort = 7777
New-SPCentralAdministration -Port $centralAdminPort -WindowsAuthProvider "NTLM"
```

Once the process has completed, your Central Administration site will be all ready for you to use. Open a new browser window on your machine, and navigate to `http://localhost:7777/`. You should be able to view and navigate throughout the various administrative sections of the site (see Figure 4-11).

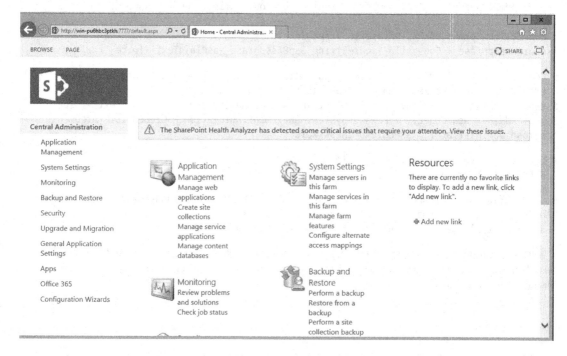

*Figure 4-11.* *Sharepoint 2016 Central Administration*

## Creating Your First Web Application

The title of this section is not 100 percent accurate; you already have a web application created in your farm, the Central Administration one. In order to start leveraging the collaborative side of SharePoint, you need to create another web application that will contain the site collections that you want to expose to the end users. My recommendation is to have your new web application created on port 80. That just makes it easier to access and prevents you from having to remember what port it's on. Again, examples that are to follow in this book all assume that you have it configured on port 80. Feel free, however, to change it to whatever port you would like.

New web applications in PowerShell are created by calling the New-SPWebApplication cmdlet. This requires you to specify the application's name as well as the name of the Internet Information Services (IIS) application pool that will be associated with it. Each web application in SharePoint gets its own IIS application pool to manage its resources.

In this example, even if it is not required, you will also provide the cmdlet with the port number on which to create your web application. You will also provide the account to use to run the application pool, in this case the administrator account. In SharePoint 2016, the classic mode authentication has been deprecated, so you will need to define a new authentication provider so that your web application can use claims-based authentication. The script to have it created is the following:

```
$webAppPort = 80

$authProvider = New-SPAuthenticationProvider
$adminManagedAccount = Get-SPManagedAccount "contoso\Administrator"

New-SPWebApplication -Name "Demo Gateway" -ApplicationPool "DemoGatewayPool"
-ApplicationPoolAccount $adminManagedAccount -Port $webAppPort -AuthenticationProvider
$authProvider

Install-SPFeature -AllExistingFeatures -Force # Active all required Farm Features
```

## Creating Your Root Site Collection

You are almost there! All that is left is to create is a root site collection in the SharePoint web application that you created in the previous section. SharePoint exposes several templates for creating new site collections out-of-the-box. For the purpose of simplicity, use the Blank Site template, which will create a new site with the minimum set of features activated by default.

```
$blankSiteTemplate = Get-SPWebTemplate STS#1
New-SPSite -Url "http://localhost/" -Name "Home" -Template $blankSiteTemplate -OwnerAlias
"contoso\administrator"
```

This script should only take a few seconds to execute. Once it is finished, open a new Internet Explorer window and navigate to http://localhost/ to ensure that your new site collection was properly created, as shown in Figure 4-12.

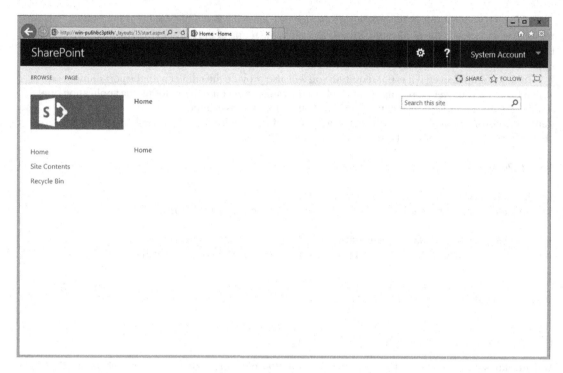

*Figure 4-12.* *New SharePoint 2016 team site*

## Granting Users Access

Remember how you created five users and five security groups at the beginning of this chapter? Well, now is the time to set their permissions in our newly created SharePoint environment. You will be granting permissions to the Active Directory groups instead of granting permissions to the users directly. The permission list will look like Table 4-3.

*Table 4-3.* *Your Active Directory Groups and Permissions*

| Group Name | Permission |
|---|---|
| Administration | Design |
| Finance | Contribute |
| Human Resources | Contribute |
| Directors | Read |
| Tech Support | Full Control |

For a full description of what each role does and what privileges are granted with each one, we recommend that you read the following Microsoft article: http://technet.microsoft.com/en-us/library/cc288074(v=office.14).aspx.

The following lines of PowerShell will automatically add the security groups you created earlier and will take care of granting the appropriate permission level to our site. In SharePoint, before you can grant permission on a site to a user, you need to ensure that this user is registered against that site first. The SPWeb.EnsureUser() method ensures that a user is registered against a specific site and returns a reference to the user object.

```
$web = Get-SPWeb http://localhost
$user = $web.EnsureUser("Contoso\Administration")
Set-SPUser -Identity $user -web $web -AddPermissionLevel "Design"

$user = $web.EnsureUser("Contoso\Finance")
Set-SPUser -Identity $user -web $web -AddPermissionLevel "Contribute"

$user = $web.EnsureUser("Contoso\Human Resources")
Set-SPUser -Identity $user -web $web -AddPermissionLevel "Contribute"

$user = $web.EnsureUser("Contoso\Directors")
Set-SPUser -Identity $user -web $web -AddPermissionLevel "Read"

$user = $web.EnsureUser("Contoso\Tech Support")
Set-SPUser -Identity $user -web $web -AddPermissionLevel "Full Control"
```

Figure 4-13 shows the different SharePoint groups that have been created.

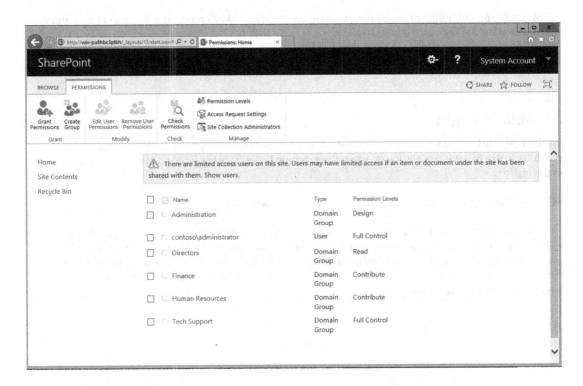

**Figure 4-13.** *List of users and groups and their associated permissions in SharePoint*

# Putting It All Together

Throughout the previous sections of this chapter, you have learned how to configure different aspects of your SharePoint 2016 farm environment using PowerShell. Now, wouldn't it be awesome if we could put it all together and simply start our script on a fresh installation of the operating system and let it run automatically, without requiring interaction at all? Simply putting all the lines of code together in a single PowerShell script file is not going to work. The installation requires the machine to reboot several times, so how do you ensure that PowerShell knows to restart its execution where it left off before the reboot? Also, because your machine will be joining a domain, how do you have the machine log on automatically after rebooting? You don't want to have to monitor the installation all the time and have to input your credentials to log on every time the machine starts.

Luckily, there is an old Windows trick that you can use to ensure that you can create a fully unattended installation script. You can use PowerShell to write reboot instructions to the registry, and Windows will automatically read from these entries on rebooting.

## Writing to the Registry

PowerShell provides a very simple way of creating and modifying properties of registry keys in Windows. The Set-ItemProperty cmdlet takes as parameters the registry path of the key to add/modify, the name of the property, and its value.

```
Set-ItemProperty -Path <KeyPath> -Name "<PropertyName>" -Value "<PropertyValue>"
```

As you've probably figured out by now, the cmdlet to remove a key's property is Remove-ItemProperty, which only takes the key's path and its name:

```
RemoveItemProperty -Path <KeyPath> -Name "<KeyName>"
```

## Automatic Login

The first registry key that you will need is the WinLogon key, which allows you to specify credentials for Windows to use to automatically log on when the machine boots. This key is found at the following location in the registry:

```
HKLM:\SOFTWARE\Microsoft\Windows NT\CurrentVersion\WinLogon
```

Remember that while this key is set, the computer will always attempt to log in as the specified user. If you want to get the default login screen prompting you for your credentials, you will need to clear this key's properties first, or you can limit the number of times the automatic logon will happen by specifying the AutoLogonCount property. There are several properties, shown in Table 4-4, that you will need to set for the automatic logon to work properly.

**Table 4-4.** *Properties Needed for Automatic Logon*

| Property's Name | Description |
| --- | --- |
| DefaultUserName | User name to use to automatically logon |
| DefaultPassword | Password for the associated user account |
| AutoAdminLogon | 0 = Disabled<br>1 = Enabled |
| AutoLogonCount | Number of times to automatically log on. Upon each login, the counter will be decreased by 1. |
| DefaultDomainName | Domain name for the user account to use. |

To achieve a fully unattended installation of SharePoint, encapsulate the code that sets the automatic logon key in a method for reusability. Each time you need the installation to reboot, you will make a call to this method to have the credentials set automatically on reboot. The method that you will use will look like the following:

```
Function AutoLogonAfterReboot
{
    $WinLogonKey = "HKLM:\SOFTWARE\Microsoft\Windows NT\CurrentVersion\WinLogon"

    Set-ItemProperty $WinLogonKey "DefaultUserName" "Administrator"
    Set-ItemProperty $WinLogonKey "DefaultPassword" "pass@word1"
    Set-ItemProperty $WinLogonKey "AutoAdminLogon" "1"
    Set-ItemProperty $WinLogonKey "AutoLogonCount" "1"
    Set-ItemProperty $WinLogonKey "DefaultDomainName" "Contoso"
}
```

# Script Orchestrator

A piece of software or code that is used to determine what other piece of code to execute next is what we refer to as an *orchestrator*. In our case, an orchestrator will need to be developed to allow our installation to decide what to execute next on restarting. Our code will need to set a registry key containing instructions for what to execute next after rebooting. On rebooting, Windows will look at this registry key to determine whether it needs to execute a command or not. The registry key to tell Windows what command to execute next on rebooting is the following:

```
HKLM:\SOFTWARE\Microsoft\Windows\CurrentVersion\Run
```

The orchestrator will break your installation down into several logical execution steps (configure domain controller, install SQL Server, install the SharePoint prerequisites, and so on). It will allow users to specify, through a parameter, which step of execution they would like to call next, and it will execute the appropriate piece of code based on this parameter.

Each execution step that requires the machine to reboot after completion will need to call your orchestrator to set the registry key, passing it the name of the next execution step. After the reboot is completed, PowerShell will automatically launch, call your installation script, and pass it the name of the next logical execution step to execute. The orchestrator's logical flow is summarized in Figure 4-14.

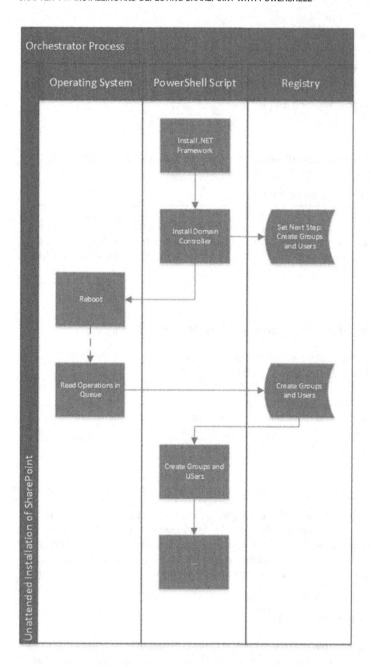

***Figure 4-14.*** *Orchestrator flow of logic*

The orchestrator's code will need to have two main methods defined. One method will verify whether an execution step is the one that you should execute next, and the other will store the value of the next command to execute in the registry.

```
# Receives the name of a step and determines if it's the next logical step to execute;
Function IsCurrentStep($nextStep)
{
    if ($global:startingStep -eq $nextStep -or $global:isStarted) {
        $global:started = $TRUE
    }
    return $global:started}

# Set the next command to execute upon rebooting in the registry key.
Function SetNextStep($script, $step)
{
    Set-ItemProperty $runKey $global:restartKey "$global:powershell $script -Step $step"
    Restart-Computer
    exit
}
```

The SetNextStep method will store the path to the PowerShell executable as the next command to execute, and will pass it the path for your script as well as the name of the next logical execution step to run as parameters (see Figure 4-15).

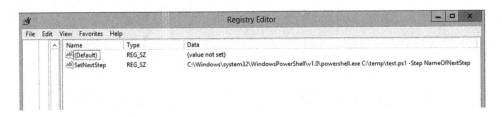

*Figure 4-15.* *Registry key used by the orchestrator*

With the orchestrator in place, all that is left to do is to wrap each execution step in our PowerShell script in if statements and call the IsNextStep method on each one to decide whether or not to execute it.

```
if (IsCurrentStep "ASP.NET")
{
    ...
}

if (IsCurrentStep "DomainController")
{
    SetNextStep $script "GroupsAndUsers" # Computer will reboot after this line;
}

if (IsCurrentStep "GroupsAndUsers")
{
    ... # Execution will restart here after reboot;
    SetNextStep $script "NextStepName" # Computer will reboot after this line;
}
...
```

You should consult the electronic resources offered with this book to get your hands on the full script. The script will ask you to fill in certain details regarding your environment, such as what port to install SharePoint Central Administration on, your administrator's account password, and so on. It will then start its execution and configure everything as expected. The script takes about an hour to execute. Once finished, it will automatically open a new Internet Explorer window and navigate to your new SharePoint 2016 homepage.

# Summary

In this chapter, you have learned how you can automate the configuration of your SharePoint environment using PowerShell. The various demos have enabled you to familiarize yourself with the SharePoint 2016 PowerShell cmdlets, as well as how to use them to interact with the SharePoint 2016 object model. In the next chapter, we will build on this newly acquired knowledge and will dig into the various aspects of SharePoint that you can control using PowerShell.

■ ■ ■

# CHAPTER 5

# Managing SharePoint with PowerShell

We are now ready to take on the core of the subject of this book: how to interact with your SharePoint environment using PowerShell. In this chapter, we will make various analogies to compare how PowerShell relates to classic .NET interactions using the SharePoint object model. Throughout the following sections you will learn how you can write PowerShell scripts to manage and interact with different levels of SharePoint artifacts such as site collections, sites, lists, items, and so on. By the end of this chapter, you will have been exposed to the different components of SharePoint, and to their methods and properties that are made available through the object model. As mentioned earlier in this book, we assume that by now you have had some level of exposure to some version of SharePoint, and that you understand the different hierarchies of entities that exist within it.

Users who have previously done .NET development for SharePoint will recognize many concepts used in the examples that follow. Remember, PowerShell is built on the .NET Common Language Runtime (CLR), and therefore it can be used to interact with any .NET artifact, just as you could do if you were using C# or Visual Basic. And just as with any good piece of software, special care needs to be paid to object disposition in PowerShell. SharePoint objects tend to take a lot of resources in memory, and it is important to free those resources once you are done working with the objects in question. We will dedicate an entire section of this chapter to managing resources and memory properly.

By the end of this chapter, you will be able to write, test, and deploy PowerShell scripts that will allow you to perform large and repetitive operations on your SharePoint farms. You will be familiar with the various cmdlets available to you through the Microsoft.SharePoint.PowerShell snap-in that comes with SharePoint 2016, and you will be able to create your own reusable modules. You will learn how to modify configuration settings, create new objects, and interact with them using scripts. Several real-life scenarios will be given to help you understand how the various examples presented could apply to your work environment.

We will start by describing how to interact with high-level objects such as site collections and webs, and will slowly make our way down to lower-level objects such as list items and users. Farm administration and monitoring will be covered in later chapters.

## Interacting with Objects

PowerShell in the context of SharePoint is all about interacting with the various artifacts made available by the server platform. SharePoint objects expose properties and methods just like any .NET object. For example, a list item exposes a property that indicates the date it was last modified. It also exposes a method that can induce a checkout operation on it. All of these properties and methods are available in PowerShell, and you can make direct calls to them, as long as you obtain a reference to the object that you wish to modify

© Nikolas Charlebois-Laprade and John Edward Naguib 2017                                        67
N. Charlebois-Laprade and J. E. Naguib, *Beginning PowerShell for SharePoint 2016*,
DOI 10.1007/978-1-4842-2884-5_5

using a retriever method. We refer to methods as being retrievers when their sole purpose is to return a single or an array of objects. For example, the Get-SPSite cmdlet that returns a site collection object is a retriever method.

---

■ **Note** Remember, you can always get a list of all available methods and properties for a specific object by passing it as a pipe operator to the Get-Member cmdlet.

---

PowerShell can also be used to execute long-lasting and repetitive operations against a farm. In many cases, PowerShell has been proven to be faster to execute administrative operations than its predecessor, the Stsadm command-line utility.

The following sections provide a quick overview of the most important PowerShell cmdlets that you'll need to remember in your daily work as a SharePoint administrator. This chapter should serve as a quick reference when you need to perform a specific operation against your SharePoint farm. Content in the next few pages will be presented as a cookbook, listing various operations with a short description that explains what each one does and what you should be using them for. The cmdlets are grouped by the level of objects that they affect or with which they interact. All examples listed here will use the SharePoint environment that you built in the previous chapter.

## Site Collections

Site collections in the SharePoint world represent the highest level of concrete objects with which your end users will interact. A site collection represents a set of websites that are logically linked together. Each site collection has its own set of permissions, solutions gallery, and other types of resource libraries dedicated to it. In the SharePoint object model, site collections are represented by the SPSite class.

## Get-SPSite

The Get-SPSite cmdlet returns a list of site collections matching the specified criteria. You can use this cmdlet along with a URL for a specific site. There are also different parameters that can be used to retrieve different sets of site collections, but these are outside the scope of this chapter. Just know that you could, as an example, retrieve all site collections belonging to a specific content database:

```
$siteCol = Get-SPSite http://localhost
```

This PowerShell line will return the site collection associated with the `http://localhost` URL and will assign it to variable `$siteCol` (see Figure 5-1).

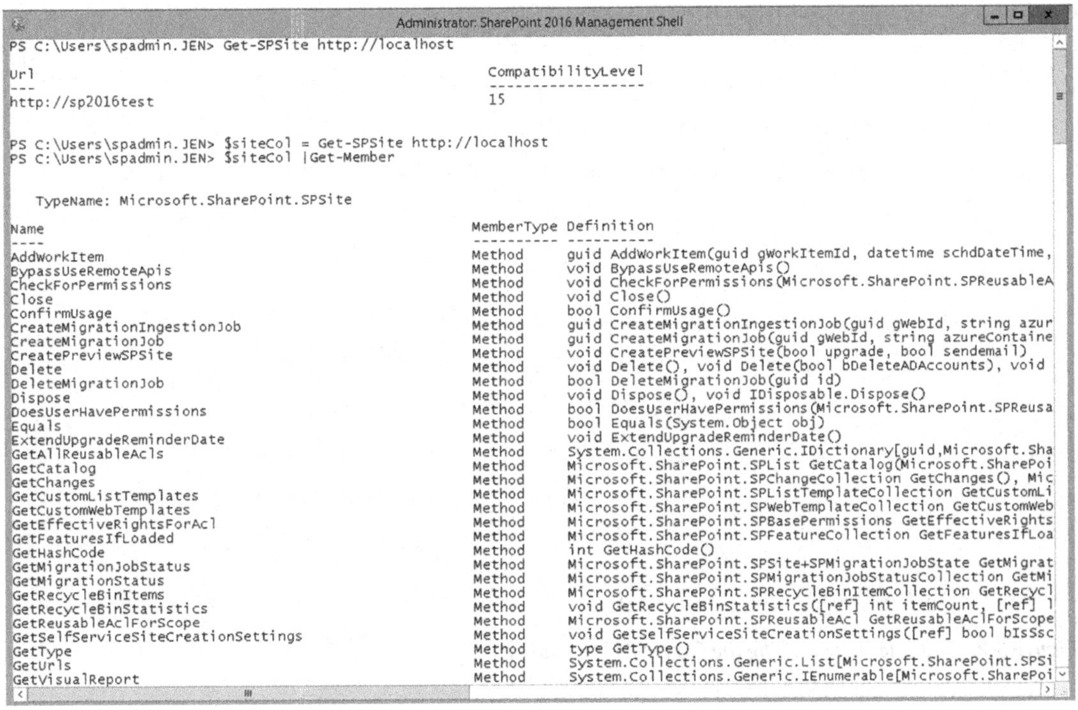

**Figure 5-1.** *Example of* `Get-SPSite`

## Move-SPSite

`Move-SPSite` lets you move an existing site collection from one content database to another. It can be useful to regroup together various site collections for backup purposes. The following example assumes that the `NewContentDB` database already exists and that you are trying to move the specified site collection to it:

```
Move-SPSite http://localhost -DestinationDatabase NewContentDB
```

## Copy-SPSite

The `Copy-SPSite` cmdlet makes a copy of an existing site collection. The copy can be made in the same content database or in a different one. You also can use this cmdlet to copy a site collection from one web application to another one, as shown in Figure 5-2.

```
Copy-SPSite http://localhost http://localhost/sites/destination
```

*Figure 5-2.* *New site created using the* Copy-SPSite *cmdlet*

## New-SPSite

New-SPSite creates a new site collection under a SharePoint web application. You have the option of specifying under what content database to have it created. If no content databases are specified, SharePoint automatically determines where to store it. Take note that if you don't specify a template type when creating your new site collection, you will get a prompt asking you to select a template when you'll first try to access it through the SharePoint interface. To specify a default web template, you can add the -Template parameter to the cmdlet call and pass it the name of the template to use. You can find a full list of all template names that are available in SharePoint 2016 by using the Get-SPWebTemplate cmdlet. Figure 5-3 shows the creation of a new site collection using PowerShell.

```
New-SPSite http://localhost/sites/test -OwnerAlias "Jen\spadmin"
```

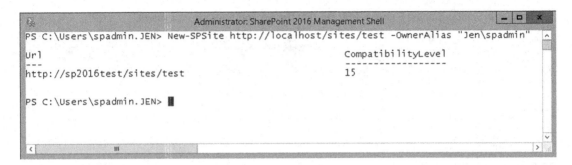

*Figure 5-3.* *New site created using the New-SPSite cmdlet*

## Set-SPSite

Set-SPSite applies the specified configuration parameters to a specific site collection. Note that you can also get a reference to your site and directly modify the properties you want. Set-SPSite is what we consider to be a "shortcut" cmdlet:

```
Set-SPSite http://localhost/sites/test -MaxSize 2000
```

This example sets a specific quota for the http://localhost/sites/test site collection. The same results could have been achieved by calling the following code:

```
$siteCol = Get-SPSite http://localhost/sites/test
$siteCol.Quota.StorageMaximumLevel = 2000
```

The PowerShell snippet in Figure 5-4 proves that the two methods are equivalent.

***Figure 5-4.*** *Changing a site collection's quota using PowerShell*

## Remove-SPSite

The Remove-SPSite cmdlet does exactly what you think it does. It deletes a specific site collection from a web application (see Figure 5-5). The only required parameter for this operation is the URL or GUID of the site collection to delete.

```
Remove-SPSite http://localhost/sites/test
```

***Figure 5-5.*** *Removing a site collection using the Remove-SPSite cmdlet*

## Get-SPDeletedSite

Get-SPDeletedSite is a retriever method that returns a list of site collections that have been deleted, based on specific research criteria. For example, you could get a list of all site collections that have been deleted (see Figure 5-6).

```
$colSiteCol = Get-SPDeletedSite
$colSiteCol.Length
$colSiteCol[0].Path
$colSiteCol[0] | get-member
```

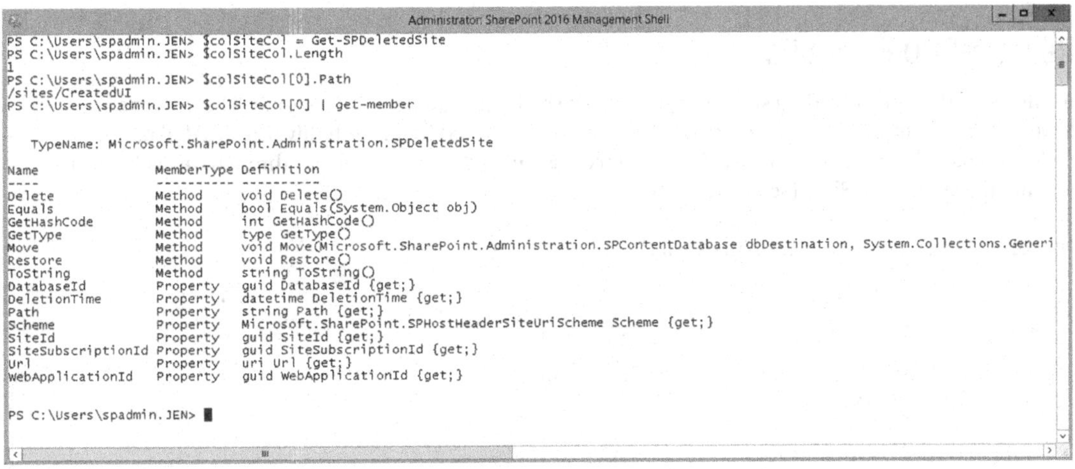

*Figure 5-6.* *Retrieving a deleted site collection using PowerShell*

---

■ **Note**    This cmdlet returns only site collections that have been deleted via the SharePoint interface. The site collection we deleted using PowerShell in our previous example is long gone and cannot be retrieved.

---

## Remove-SPDeletedSite

As you've just seen, a special type of site collection object in SharePoint exists, called the *deleted site collection*. This object is in limbo between life and death. Think of it as being a file in the Recycle Bin, which is given a second chance. From that state on, a site collection can either be permanently deleted or restored back. Of course, it can be moved over another content database, but nothing more.

The Remove-SPDeletedSite cmdlet receives the identity of the deleted site collection you want to permanently delete and deletes it. You can either specify a specific site collection by its GUID, or specify a server-relative URL. Based on the Get-SPDeletedSite example in the preceding section, if we would like to remove the /sites/CreatedUI collection, we could execute the following line of PowerShell, as shown in Figure 5-7.

```
Remove-SPDeletedSite /sites/CreatedUI
```

```
Administrator: SharePoint 2016 Management Shell
PS C:\Users\spadmin.JEN> Remove-SPDeletedSite /sites/CreatedUI

Confirm
Are you sure you want to perform this action?
Performing the operation "Remove-SPDeletedSite" on target "http://sp2016test/sites/CreatedUI".
[Y] Yes  [A] Yes to All  [N] No  [L] No to All  [S] Suspend  [?] Help (default is "Y"): y
PS C:\Users\spadmin.JEN>
```

*Figure 5-7. Removing a deleted site collection from the Recycle Bin using PowerShell*

## Restore-SPDeletedSite

As mentioned in the preceding section, a deleted site collection also can be restored. The Restore-SPDeletedSite cmdlet does the opposite of Remove-SPDeletedSite and actually brings a deleted site collection back from the dead into its former glory, assuming that it was deleted through the web interface and not through PowerShell (see Figure 5-8).

Restore-SPDeletedSite /sites/CreatedUI

```
Administrator: SharePoint 2016 Management Shell
PS C:\Users\spadmin.JEN> Restore-SPDeletedSite /sites/CreatedUI

Confirm
Are you sure you want to perform this action?
Performing the operation "Restore-SPDeletedSite" on target "http://sp2016test/sites/CreatedUI".
[Y] Yes  [A] Yes to All  [N] No  [L] No to All  [S] Suspend  [?] Help (default is "Y"): y
PS C:\Users\spadmin.JEN>
```

*Figure 5-8. Restoring a deleted site collection from the Recycle Bin using PowerShell*

## Putting It Together: Creating a Site Collection Structure

Now that you have learned how easily we can interact with SharePoint site collections using PowerShell, we will continue building the environment begun in the previous chapter and will create a new site collection for every business unit identified in our fictive company, called Contoso. You will remember that when you created users in your domain, you also created five different security groups, each representing a different business unit. Those were:

- Administration

- Finance

- Human Resources

- Directors

- Tech Support

What you will want to do first is call the New-SPSite cmdlet and let it create these new business site collections. You could just call the cmdlet five times in a row with different parameters, but you've learned to do better. Put your newly acquired PowerShell skills to work and write something a bit more creative and reusable. What you are trying to achieve here can actually be achieved as a one-liner using a pipe operation. Start by declaring an array containing the name of each business unit, and then pipe each of these names into your New-SPSite cmdlet. Then use the $_ operand to insert the names into the new site collection's URL as follows (see Figure 5-9):

```
"Administration", "Finance", "Human Resources", "Directors", "Tech Support" |
%{New-SPSite http://localhost/sites/$_ -OwnerAlias contoso\administrator -Template "STS#0"}
```

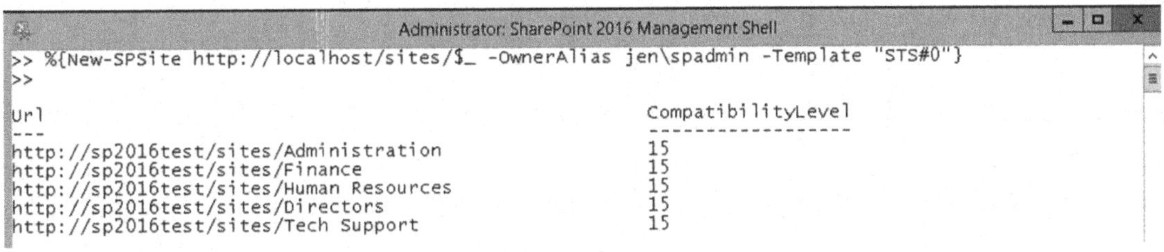

*Figure 5-9.* *Creating site collections in a batch using PowerShell*

It doesn't get any simpler than that. You are now ready to dig deeper into the SharePoint object model and start looking at the various ways PowerShell can help you interact with webs.

## Webs

Some of you may refer to webs as being SharePoint sites. we tend to prefer using "webs," just because it doesn't make it ambiguous as to whether we are talking about site collections (SPSite) or about an actual website. Microsoft identifies webs as being SPWeb objects in the SharePoint object model. A web in the context of SharePoint is what your users will be interacting with. It is something more tangible to end users than the concept of a site collection. It is important to note that, in SharePoint 2016, every site collection needs at least one web in it. This web needs to exist directly at the root of its site collection and is referred to as the root web for the collection. By default, when you execute the New-SPSite cmdlet, PowerShell will automatically create a new root web inside the new site collection.

The following sections will give you an overview of the different cmdlets available for interacting with SharePoint webs. You will see several similarities in the naming and in the functionality to the ones made available for interacting with site collections.

## Get-SPWeb

Get-SPWeb is the main retriever method to get a reference to an SPWeb object. It only requires you to specify the direct URL for the web you are trying to retrieve (see Figure 5-10).

```
Get-SPWeb "http://localhost/sites/HumanResources"
```

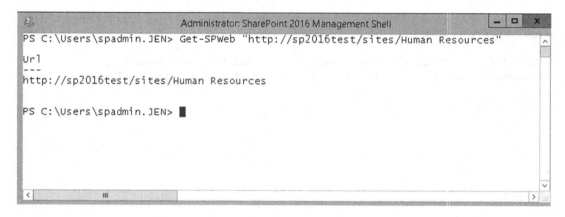

*Figure 5-10.* *Using the Get-SPWeb cmdlet to obtain a reference to a web*

## New-SPWeb

The New-SPWeb cmdlet lets you create a new web under a specified site collection. Table 5-1 lists the different templates that can be used to create new SharePoint 2016 webs and their short names to use with PowerShell.

*Table 5-1.* *List of Available SharePoint 2016 Web Templates*

| Short Name | Title |
|---|---|
| GLOBAL#0 | Global template |
| STS#0 | Team Site |
| STS#1 | Blank Site |
| STS#2 | Document Workspace |
| MPS#0 | Basic Meeting Workspace |
| MPS#1 | Blank Meeting Workspace |
| MPS#2 | Decision Meeting Workspace |
| MPS#3 | Social Meeting Workspace |
| MPS#4 | Multipage Meeting Workspace |
| CENTRALADMIN#0 | Central Admin Site |
| WIKI#0 | Wiki Site |
| BLOG#0 | Blog |
| SGS#0 | Group Work Site |
| TENANTADMIN#0 | Tenant Admin Site |
| APP#0 | App Template |
| APPCATALOG#0 | App Catalog Site |
| ACCSRV#0 | Access Services Site |

*(continued)*

***Table 5-1.*** (*continued*)

| Short Name | Title |
|---|---|
| ACCSVC#0 | Access Services Site Internal |
| ACCSVC#1 | Access Services Site |
| BDR#0 | Document Center |
| TBH#0 | In-Place Hold Policy Center |
| DEV#0 | Developer Site |
| EDISC#0 | eDiscovery Center |
| EDISC#1 | eDiscovery Case |
| OFFILE#0 | (obsolete) Records Center |
| OFFILE#1 | Records Center |
| OSRV#0 | Shared Services Administration Site |
| PPSMASite#0 | PerformancePoint |
| BICenterSite#0 | Business Intelligence Center |
| PWA#0 | Project Web App Site |
| PWS#0 | Microsoft Project Site |
| POLICYCTR#0 | Compliance Policy Center |
| SPS#0 | SharePoint Portal Server Site |
| SPSPERS#0 | SharePoint Portal Server Personal S |
| SPSPERS#2 | Storage And Social SharePoint Porta |
| SPSPERS#3 | Storage Only SharePoint Portal Serv |
| SPSPERS#4 | Social Only SharePoint Portal Serve |
| SPSPERS#5 | Empty SharePoint Portal Server Pers |
| SPSPERS#6 | Storage And Social SharePoint Porta |
| SPSPERS#7 | Storage And Social SharePoint Porta |
| SPSPERS#8 | Storage And Social SharePoint Porta |
| SPSPERS#9 | Storage And Social SharePoint Porta |
| SPSPERS#10 | Storage And Social SharePoint Porta |
| SPSMSITE#0 | Personalization Site |
| SPSTOC#0 | Contents area Template |
| SPSTOPIC#0 | Topic area template |
| SPSNEWS#0 | News Site |
| CMSPUBLISHING#0 | Publishing Site |
| BLANKINTERNET#0 | Publishing Site |
| BLANKINTERNET#1 | Press Releases Site |
| BLANKINTERNET#2 | Publishing Site with Workflow |

(*continued*)

***Table 5-1.*** (*continued*)

| Short Name | Title |
| --- | --- |
| SPSNHOME#0 | News Site |
| SPSSITES#0 | Site Directory |
| SPSCOMMU#0 | Community area template |
| SPSREPORTCENTER#0 | Report Center |
| SPSPORTAL#0 | Collaboration Portal |
| SRCHCEN#0 | Enterprise Search Center |
| PROFILES#0 | Profiles |
| BLANKINTERNETCONT… | Publishing Portal |
| SPSMSITEHOST#0 | My Site Host |
| ENTERWIKI#0 | Enterprise Wiki |
| PROJECTSITE#0 | Project Site |
| PRODUCTCATALOG#0 | Product Catalog |
| COMMUNITY#0 | Community Site |
| COMMUNITYPORTAL#0 | Community Portal |
| GROUP#0 | Group |
| POINTPUBLISHINGHUB#0 | PointPublishing Hub |
| POINTPUBLISHINGPE… | PointPublishing Personal |
| POINTPUBLISHINGTO… | PointPublishing Topic |
| SRCHCENTERLITE#0 | Basic Search Center |
| SRCHCENTERLITE#1 | Basic Search Center |
| visprus#0 | Visio Process Repository |
| GLOBAL#0 | Global template |
| STS#0 | Team Site |
| STS#1 | Blank Site |
| STS#2 | Document Workspace |
| MPS#0 | Basic Meeting Workspace |
| MPS#1 | Blank Meeting Workspace |
| MPS#2 | Decision Meeting Workspace |
| MPS#3 | Social Meeting Workspace |
| MPS#4 | Multipage Meeting Workspace |
| CENTRALADMIN#0 | Central Admin Site |
| WIKI#0 | Wiki Site |
| BLOG#0 | Blog |
| SGS#0 | Group Work Site |

(*continued*)

***Table 5-1.*** (*continued*)

| Short Name | Title |
|---|---|
| TENANTADMIN#0 | Tenant Admin Site |
| ACCSRV#0 | Access Services Site |
| ACCSRV#1 | Assets Web Database |
| ACCSRV#3 | Charitable Contributions Web Database |
| ACCSRV#4 | Contacts Web Database |
| ACCSRV#6 | Issues Web Database |
| ACCSRV#5 | Projects Web Database |
| BDR#0 | Document Center |
| OFFILE#0 | (obsolete) Records Center |
| OFFILE#1 | Records Center |
| OSRV#0 | Shared Services Administration Site |
| PPSMASite#0 | PerformancePoint |
| BICenterSite#0 | Business Intelligence Center |
| PWA#0 | Project Web App Site |
| PWS#0 | Microsoft Project Site |
| SPS#0 | SharePoint Portal Server Site |
| SPSPERS#0 | SharePoint Portal Server Personal Site |
| SPSMSITE#0 | Personalization Site |
| SPSTOC#0 | Contents area Template |
| SPSTOPIC#0 | Topic area template |
| SPSNEWS#0 | News Site |
| CMSPUBLISHING#0 | Publishing Site |
| BLANKINTERNET#0 | Publishing Site |
| BLANKINTERNET#1 | Press Releases Site |
| BLANKINTERNET#2 | Publishing Site with Workflow |
| SPSNHOME#0 | News Site |
| SPSSITES#0 | Site Directory |
| SPSCOMMU#0 | Community area template |
| SPSREPORTCENTER#0 | Report Center |
| SPSPORTAL#0 | Collaboration Portal |
| SRCHCEN#0 | Enterprise Search Center |
| PROFILES#0 | Profiles |
| BLANKINTERNETCONT... | Publishing Portal |
| SPSMSITEHOST#0 | My Site Host |

(continued)

***Table 5-1.*** (*continued*)

| Short Name | Title |
| --- | --- |
| ENTERWIKI#0 | Enterprise Wiki |
| SRCHCENTERLITE#0 | Basic Search Center |
| SRCHCENTERLITE#1 | Basic Search Center |
| SRCHCENTERFAST#0 | FAST Search Center |
| visprus#0 | Visio Process Repository |

The following example shows how to create a new web using the Blank Site template. If you don't specify a template for it, you'll be prompted to select one the first time you access it through the SharePoint interface.

```
New-SPWeb http://localhost/NewWeb -Template "STS#1"
```

## Remove-SPWeb

Remove-SPWeb lets you delete an existing web by specifying its URL. Note that deleting a web using PowerShell deletes it permanently, unless you specify the -Recycle parameter:

```
Remove-SPWeb http://localhost/NewWeb
```

If a web is deleted through the SharePoint interface, it becomes an SPDeletedSite object! Yes, you've heard us; just as in the case of a deleted site collection, a deleted web becomes the same object. Why is that? Because when you delete a site collection, all you're actually doing is deleting the webs contained in it. When you restore at least one web in the site collection, you're automatically restoring the site collection itself. There is such a thing as a SPDeletedSiteCollection object, but it does not expose any methods to remove or to restore itself.

The sad part, however, is that you cannot use the Get-SPDeletedSite cmdlet to retrieve webs that have been deleted in a site collection that still exists. To get a reference to such a web, you'll need to get a reference to the site collection's recycle bin, and then obtain a reference to the deleted web by iterating through the list of deleted objects. The example in Figure 5-11 shows how you can retrieve a list of deleted webs from the Recycle Bin, and restore them using PowerShell.

*Figure 5-11.* *Restoring all deleted webs from the Recycle Bin using PowerShell*

## Set-SPWeb

Just like the Set-SPSite cmdlet, Set-SPWeb is a shortcut command that allows you to configure a specified web. It allows you to specify a new URL, a new name, or a new description, or lets you apply a new template for the web. Again, just as is the case with the site collection level method, you could easily accomplish the same operation by getting a reference to the object using its retriever method, and by assigning values to its properties directly. The following example shows how you can change the URL of a web using this PowerShell cmdlet (see Figure 5-12).

```
Set-SPWeb http://localhost/NewWeb -RelativeUrl ModifiedWeb
```

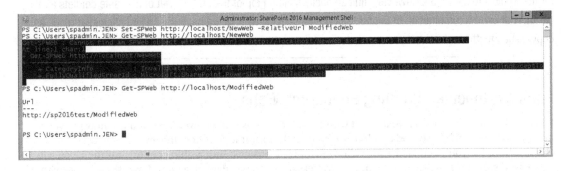

*Figure 5-12.* *Change a web's URL using PowerShell*

## Export-SPWeb

Export-SPWeb lets you export a web along with all of its lists and libraries and their contents. The operation creates the backup file locally on disk and generates an associated backup log. If you do not wish to have an export log generated on disk, you can simply use the -NoLogFile parameter. It is also important to note that this cmdlet will not preserve permissions for lists with broken inheritance or item-level permissions.

```
Export-SPWeb http://localhost/ModifiedWeb -Path "C:\ExportedWeb.cmp"
```

## Import-SPWeb

Peanut butter is to jam what Import-SPWeb is to Export-SPWeb: they just go along together. Cheesy analogy, we know, but what can you do with a backup of something if you don't have a means to restore it? This cmdlet lets you import a web along with all of its lists, libraries, and items. Just as in the case of the export method, it creates an operation log on disk. You can restore the backup on top of the existing site, or you could make a copy of it by creating a new site and restoring it at this new location, as shown in the following example (see Figure 5-13).

```
New-SPWeb https://localhost/MyImportedWeb
Import-SPWeb http://localhost/MyImportedWeb -Path "C:\ExportedWeb.cmp"
```

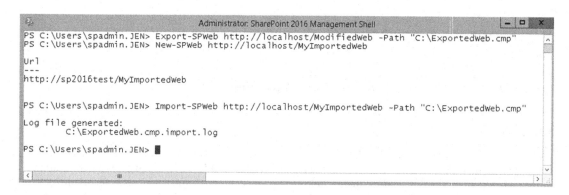

*Figure 5-13. Importing a web using the Import-SPWeb PowerShell cmdlet*

---

■ **Note** There are no Copy-SPWeb cmdlets available by default in SharePoint 2016, but there is CopySPSite for the whole site collection. However, you can easily build on top of the existing set of available cmdlets and create your own. A combination of Export/Import on a specific web would have the same anticipated result as a Copy-SPWeb method.

---

## Putting It Together: Creating Supporting Webs

You have learned how easy it is to interact with SharePoint webs using PowerShell. You will now put your new knowledge to good use, and continue to build on the example started in the previous section of this chapter. Now that you've created a site collection for each business unit within your organization, you will create workspaces for each team within the business unit. You will declare a multidimensional array with two dimensions: one representing the unit and one that will contains its associated teams. The logic will then loop through each row and create the new webs using the Team Site template (STS#0, as seen earlier in Table 5-1). To make things more exciting, each business unit will see their webs use a different theme to make sure that they can be easily differentiated. We begin by declaring the array as follow:

```
$team = @{}
$team["Finance"] = @("Payroll", "Financial Systems", "Procurement")
$team["Human Resources"] = @("Training", "Staff Services", "Recruiting")
$team["Administration"] = @("Executive Assistants", "Planification")
$team["Directors"] = @("CIO", "CEO", "COO")
$team["Tech Support"] = @("Help Desk", "Applications", "Infrastructure")
```

Your next step is to define what the theme will be for each of these team sites. In SharePoint 2016, themes are now referred to as *composed looks*. However, the ApplyTheme method is what you need to use to apply custom theming. A composed look is made up of three important parts: a color palette, a font scheme, and a background image. You will declare a second multidimensional array to keep track of which composed look will be applied to which web. The array contains the name of the SharePoint theme that you want to apply. The array will be declared as follows:

```
$theme = @{}
$theme["Finance"] = "Sea Monster"
$theme["Human Resources"] = "Sketch"
$theme["Administration"] = "Characters"
$theme["Directors"] = "Wood"
$theme["Tech Support"] = "Nature"
```

To get a reference to the appropriate color palette, font scheme, and background image, you need to get a reference to the composed look based on its name, as specified in the previous array. In order to achieve this, you need to get a reference to the site collection's design catalog. This can be achieved by getting a reference to the site collection and calling the .GetCatalog(<name>) method. Once you have obtained the reference to the catalog, all that's left to do is to query it based on the composed look's name. You could get a reference to the Sea Monster theme for the Finance unit by using the following PowerShell code (see Figure 5-14):

```
$site = Get-SPSite "http://localhost/sites/Finance"
$catalog= $site.GetCatalog("Design")
$theme = $catalog.Items | Where {$_.Name -eq "Sea Monster"}

$color = $theme["ThemeUrl"].Split(',')[1].Trim()
$font = $theme["FontSchemeUrl"].Split(',')[1].Trim()
$image = $theme["ImageUrl"].Split(',')[1].Trim()
write-host $color
write-host $font
write-host $image
```

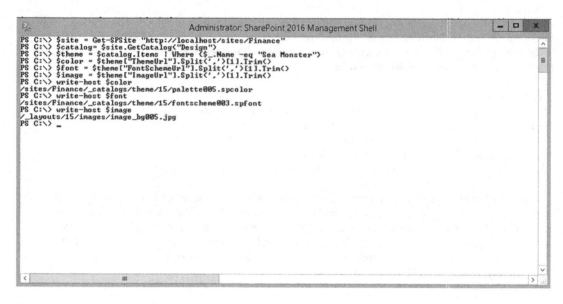

**Figure 5-14.** *Creating webs in a batch and applying custom themes using PowerShell*

Now that both of our hashtables have been properly declared and initialized, you can loop through each of the entries and make calls to the New-SPWeb cmdlet for each one. You will need to loop through each of the team array's keys and use its key value to determine what the associated team is for a given business array:

```
foreach($businessUnit in $teamArray.Keys) # this returns a list of business units
{
    foreach($team in $teamArray[$businessUnit]
    {
        # At this point we have access to the teams' names, and we can dynamically
        # build the urls for the composed looks using that information    }
}
```

If you now try to put it all back together, your script will look like the following. You can use a unique set of foreach loops to access both the team and theme arrays. The script should take about five minutes to execute, at the end of which all of your webs will have been properly created:

```
#Declaring the various components of composed look for each team
$themeArray = @{}
$themeArray["Finance"] = "Sea Monster"
$themeArray["Human Resources"] = "Sketch"
$themeArray["Administration"] = "Characters"
$themeArray["Directors"] = "Wood"
$themeArray["Tech Support"] = "Nature"

foreach($businessUnit in $teamArray.Keys)
{
    $site = Get-SPSite "http://localhost/sites/$businessUnit"
    $catalog = $site.GetCatalog("Design")
    $theme = $catalog.Items | Where {$_.Name -eq $themeArray[$businessUnit]}
```

```
foreach($team in $teamArray[$businessUnit])
{
    $web = New-SPWeb "http://localhost/sites/$businessUnit/$team " -Template STS#0 -Name
    $team

    $color = $theme["ThemeUrl"].Split(',')[1].Trim()
    $font = $theme["FontSchemeUrl"].Split(',')[1].Trim()
    $image = $theme["ImageUrl"].Split(',')[1].Trim()
    write-host $color
    $web.ApplyTheme($color, $font, $image, $true)
    write-host $team -backgroundcolor green

    $web.Dispose()
}
$site.Dispose()
}
```

To ensure that everything worked as expected, navigate to `http://localhost/sites/Finance/Payroll/`. Your team site should have been created with the Sea Monster composed look, which is made up of an orange suite bar at the top (where you see the name SharePoint), along with green tiles and icons.

We are now ready to dig deeper into the SharePoint object model and start playing with lists and libraries.

# Lists

A list is probably the most widely used type of object in SharePoint . Almost any out-of-the-box "app" (remember that in 2016 everything is an app or addin) uses lists in the backend. A document library, as an example, is just a SharePoint list with a special SharePoint content type associated with it. Just like the other types of artifacts we already touched on in this chapter (site collections and webs), SharePoint lists can have unique permissions or inherit permissions from their parent web. Since SharePoint 2010, lists also have a feature called *throttling*, which prevents large lists from bringing a server down to its knees. Users have a maximum number of items they can have in a list before SharePoint stops trying to render its content on screen.

A list in the SharePoint object model is represented by the `SPList` object. It represents a set of items that have different properties associated with them. We tend to think of a list in the SharePoint context as being a data table with columns and rows, like a table you would find in an Excel spreadsheet, for example. The rows would be the list's items, and the columns would be represented by the properties associated with the items. These properties are also referred to as *fields*. Each field has a data type associated with it, which represents the type of data that the field can accept as input value.

A list can also have a predefined set of filters, sorting options, and display fields. These are referred to as *views*. Think of a SharePoint view just like you would think of a view in the database world. It is a way to present data from a specific source in a format and in a fashion that makes sense to the end user. For example, assume that you are a regional manager in charge of managing a store for the city of Ottawa. Your organization keeps track of every transaction made across all the different stores in the region into a single SharePoint list. It may not make sense for you to view the transactions for the city of Toronto, for example. What you want to do is to create for yourself a view on the list so that the data display shows only records for the store you are managing. You could also decide to hide certain fields that you may judge are not necessary to display. Creating such a view does not affect the data source; it simply changes its presentation layer.

Throughout the following sections, you will learn how you can use PowerShell to interact with the structure and the configuration properties of SharePoint lists. we will not be discussing list items at this point. This will be addressed in a later section. Unlike site collections and webs, there aren't any cmdlets that deal directly with lists. Instead, you need to obtain your own instance of a list and manipulate it through its methods and properties.

## Getting a List Instance

SharePoint lists are contained at the web level. Every SPWeb object has a property called Lists that represents an array of all the lists contained in that specific web. In order to get a reference to a specific list, you'll need to get it from that list array using either its name or its GUID. Another option would be to use the GetList method, which expects the list's relative URL as a parameter. The following example shows how to get a reference to the Style Library located at the root of our site collection on http://localhost:

```
$web = Get-SPWeb http://localhost
$list = $web.Lists["Style Library"]
$fields = $list.Fields.InternalName
$fields | Where {$_ -like '*workflow*'}
```

This gets a list of all the internal names of the fields contained in the Style Library list. Think of internal names as being unique IDs. Each field has two names, an internal one and a display one. There is nothing preventing a list from having two fields with the same display names, but you cannot have two fields with the same internal name being part of the same list. Once you've retrieved a list of all internal names, you can query it using the pipeline operator, to retrieve only the field names that contain the word "workflow" (see Figure 5-15).

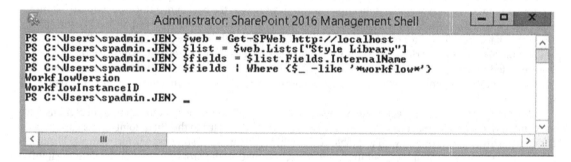

***Figure 5-15.*** *Obtaining a list of all fields' names in a SharePoint list using PowerShell*

## Creating a New List

To create a new list instance, you will need to first obtain a reference to the web in which you want to add the list. After the reference is obtained, the new list can be created by calling the .Add() method on the Lists properties of the web object. In most cases, you will be calling the Add() method using three parameters: a title, a description, and the list template associated with your list. To get a full list of all available list templates, as shown in Figure 5-16, you can simply run the following PowerShell command:

```
$web = Get-SPWeb http://localhost
$web.ListTemplates.Name
```

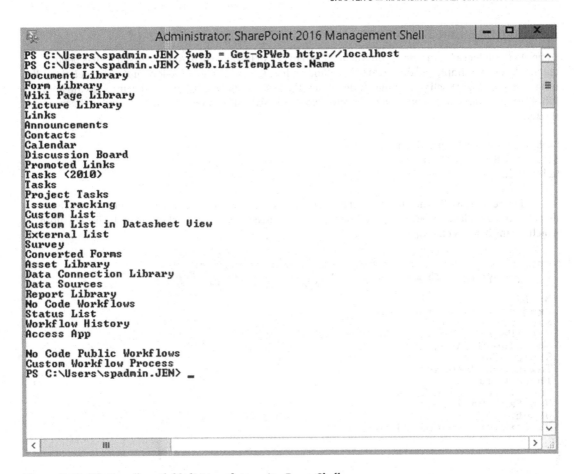

*Figure 5-16.* *Listing all available list templates using PowerShell*

Once you have determined which list template to use for your new list, you can call the following commands to have your list created (see Figure 5-17). Note that the Add() method returns a GUID associated with your newly created list, not an SPList object. You will need to get an instance of your new list using either the list's name or obtained GUID to interact with it further.

```
$web = Get-SPWeb http://localhost
$ID = $web.Lists.Add("My List", "My Description", $web.ListTemplates["Custom List"])
$ID
```

*Figure 5-17.* *Creating a new SharePoint list using PowerShell*

## Removing a List Instance

To be able to delete a list instance, you will first need to get an instance of it. After an instance has been obtained, you can simply call the Delete() method on it. Just as with site collections and webs, deleting a list instance using PowerShell will permanently remove the list, and it won't be recoverable through the Recycle Bin. The following code example shows how to delete the "My List" instance that was created in the previous section:

```
$web = Get-SPWeb http://localhost
$list = $web.Lists["My List"]
$list.Delete()
```

In Figure 5-18, we list the titles of all of the lists that exist at the specified web level. You can clearly see that after you've called the Delete() method on your list's instance, it doesn't show up in the list anymore, which means it has been properly deleted.

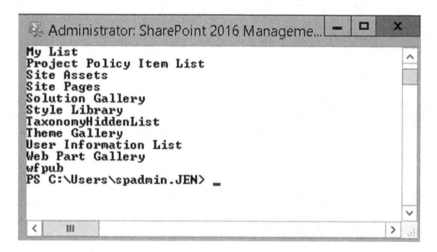

***Figure 5-18.*** *Listing all existing lists from a web using PowerShell*

## Restoring a List Instance

A SharePoint list that is deleted from the interface and not by the delete() PowerShell command makes it into the Recycle Bin before being deleted from the server for good. You then have the option of restoring it by getting a reference to the current site's Recycle Bin object, and by iterating through its items. Once you have obtained a reference to the appropriate item in the Recycle Bin, simply call the Restore() method on it (see Figure 5-19). To have the list deleted permanently, you should call the Delete() method instead.

```
$spsite = Get-SPSite http://localhost
$bin = $spsite.RecycleBin
$myList = $bin | Where{$_.ItemType -eq "List"}
$myList
$myList.Restore()
```

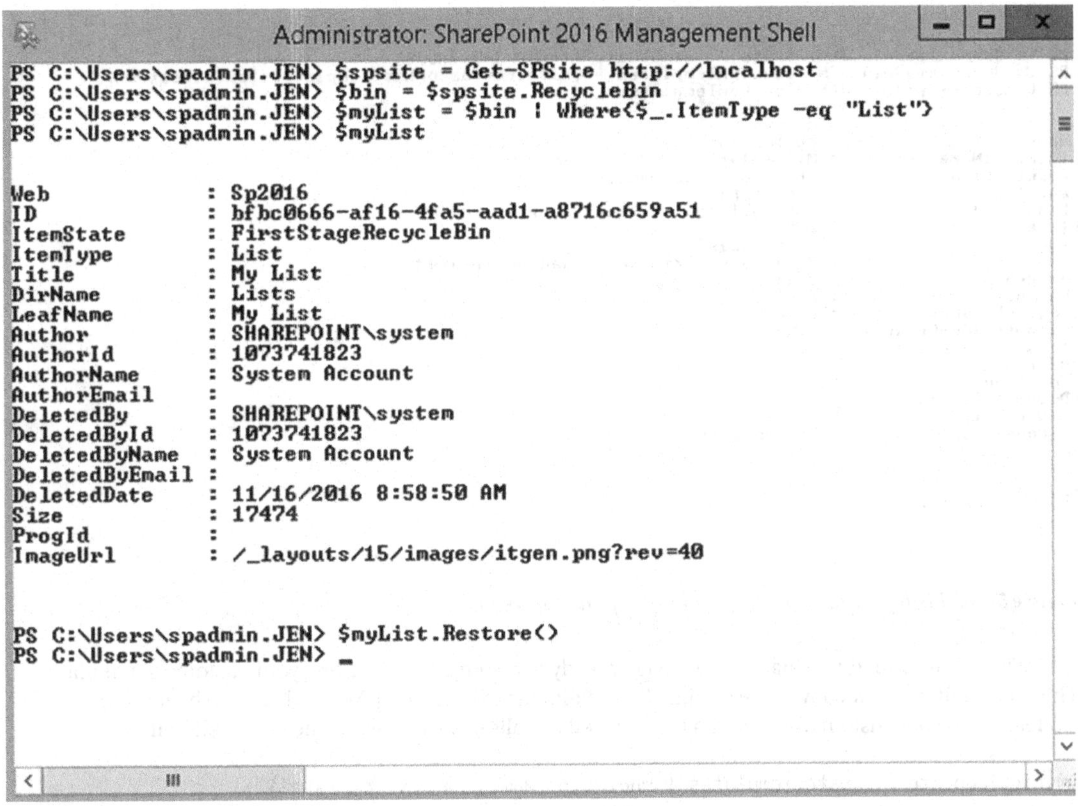

**Figure 5-19.** *Restoring a deleted list from the Recycle Bin using PowerShell*

## Copying a List Instance

Sadly, there are no direct ways to copy a SharePoint list using PowerShell. You can, however, copy an existing list along with all of its data using a combination of two operations. To be able to copy a SharePoint list instance using PowerShell, you will need to first save your list as a list template and then create a new copy of the list using that template. Saving a list as a template is as simple as calling the SaveAsTemplate() method on a SharePoint list instance. This method requires you to specify a name for the resulting .stp (template) file, a title for your template, and a description, and it lets you specify whether to save the list's content and data as part of the template:

```
$web = Get-SPWeb http://localhost
$list = $web.Lists["My List"]
$list.SaveAsTemplate("MyTemplate", "My Template", "This is my custom list", $true)
```

Custom list templates in SharePoint are stored at the site collection level. To get a list of available custom list templates, you'll need to call the GetCustomListTemplates() method on the site collection object (see Figure 5-20):

```
$site = Get-SPSite http://localhost
$customTemplates = $site.GetCustomListTemplates($site.RootWeb)
$customTemplates
```

```
Administrator: SharePoint 2016 Management Shell                    _  □  X
PS C:\Users\spadmin.JEN> $site = Get-SPSite http://localhost
PS C:\Users\spadmin.JEN> $customTemplates = $site.GetCustomListTemplates($site.RootWeb)
PS C:\Users\spadmin.JEN> $customTemplates


Name                  : My Template
InternalName          : MyTemplate.stp
Description           : This is my custom list
BaseType              : GenericList
FeatureId             : 00bfea71-de22-43b2-a848-c05709900100
Type_Client           : 100
Type                  : GenericList
ImageUrl              : /_layouts/15/images/itgen.png?rev=40
Hidden                : False
Unique                : False
OnQuickLaunch         : True
AllowsFolderCreation  : True
IsCustomTemplate      : True
NewPage               :
EditPage              :
DocumentTemplate      :
SchemaXml             :
CategoryType          : CustomLists


PS C:\Users\spadmin.JEN> _
```

*Figure 5-20.* *Listing custom SharePoint list templates using PowerShell*

With this information in hand, you are now ready to create a new list using your custom list template. This will result in a new copy of the original SharePoint list to be created. You will need to begin by obtaining a reference to your custom list. This can be achieved by calling the following line of PowerShell:

```
$myListTemplate = $customTemplates | Where {$_.Name -eq "My Template"}
```

To create the copy of your list, you will need to call the Add() method on a specific web list collection, as you did in the "Creating a New List" section. This time, however, you will call an overload of the method, meaning that you will call the method using a different set of parameters as input. In order to create a list based on a custom list template, you need to call the method using the six parameters shown here:

```
$web.Lists.Add("My Copy", # Title
      "Description", # List Description
      "Lists/MyCopy", # Relative URL
      $myListTemplate.FeatureId, # Feature Id of custom template
      100, # List Type - 100 is for none
      "101") # Document Template Type - 101 is for none
```

Remember that there is an opportunity to create your own cmdlet to automate these two operations into a single one. You could easily create a new Copy-SPList cmdlet taking the source list and its destination title as input parameters.

## Putting It Together: Creating Common Lists

We will now continue to build upon this demo environment, and put your latest acquired knowledge to use. In real-life scenarios, business units often share similar processes. For example, every business unit in an organization will be subject to a set of policies, procedures, and guidelines. It would be considered best practice to keep all documents related to these in a SharePoint document library under each business unit workspace. Another important feature that each business unit may also want to have is a task list to allow various tasks assigned to their employees to be tracked.

Here you will create a new PowerShell script that will iterate through all the various sites created earlier, and that will create a new document library at its root named "Business Documents" as well as a new task list named "Unit Tasks." The following script will allow you to do just that, but this time you'll add a little twist to it. In the previous demo ("Putting it Together: Creating Support Webs"), you had obtained references to each site collection by generating their URLs dynamically. This time around, you will delve into some of the material covered in the next chapters to obtain a reference to the SharePoint web application that you've created on port 80. Remember, a web application can be thought of as a container for site collections. All site collections that are hosted on port 80 logically belong to the same web application. By obtaining a reference to this object, you will be able to iterate through all of its contained site collections, and then in turn iterate through the set of webs they each contain:

```
$webApp = Get-SPWebApplication http://localhost

foreach($site in $webApp.Sites)
{
    foreach($web in $site.AllWebs)
    {
        $web.Lists.Add("Business Documents", "",
            $web.ListTemplates["Document Library"]);
        $web.Lists.Add("Unit Tasks", "", $web.ListTemplates["Tasks"]);
    }
}
```

As you can see from this example, in order to get a reference to a SharePoint web application, you can call the Get-SPWebApplication PowerShell cmdlet.

## List Items

The next logical level in the SharePoint object model hierarchy is a *list item*. A list item in the SharePoint world represents a logical unit that contains pertinent information. For example, a Word document stored in a SharePoint library would be considered to be a list item, as would a new project task stored in a task list. Descriptive data associated with list items is referred to as *metadata*. Think of metadata as being a field in the list. Each field captures different information about each list item. You will learn more about fields in the next section. List items are also the lowest level of objects in the hierarchy that can have unique permissions applied. SharePoint permissions will also be covered later in the chapter.

This section focuses on explaining the basics of list items and how we can interact with them using PowerShell. As with SharePoint lists, the SharePoint modules provided for PowerShell don't include cmdlets that let you interact directly with list items. You will need to obtain them manually by drilling down into the object model.

## Getting List Items

To obtain a reference to a list item, you need to obtain a reference to the list that contains it. Once the reference has been obtained, you can get access to a collection of all list items contained in the list by calling the Items property on it. Other than accessing an item directly by its position in the list (for example, $list.Items[2] where 2 is the position in the list) there is no way to obtain a reference to a single list item in SharePoint. The best you can do to get a reference to a specific item is to query a collection of items back based on certain criteria, and hope that there is only one item contained in it.

To get a collection of items back, you could either write a CAML query and use it to get a specific set of items back from a list, or you could simply use PowerShell to iterate through the collection of returned items and find the item based on a specific property's value. Both options are explained in the following example. Figure 5-21 shows the SharePoint list used for the example.

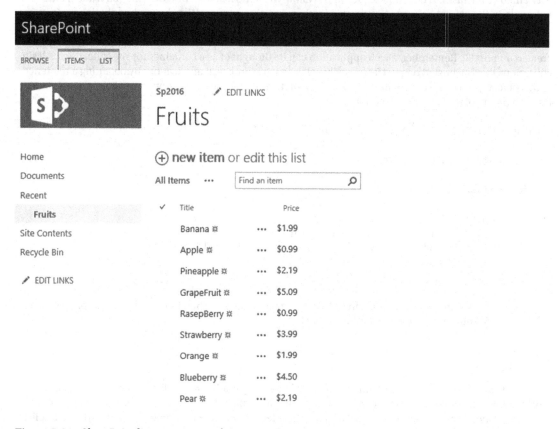

**Figure 5-21.** *SharePoint list containing information about various fruits and their associated unit prices*

```
# Assuming a SharePoint List that contains a list of fruits and their unit price.

$web = Get-SPWeb http://localhost
$fruitsList = $web.Lists["Fruits"]

# Scenario A - Get a reference to the apple item

# Option 1 - Write a CAML Query
$query = "<Where><Eq><FieldRef Name='Title' /><Value Type='Text'>Apple</Value></Eq></Where>";
$spQuery = New-Object Microsoft.SharePoint.SPQuery
$spQuery.Query = $query

$items = $fruitsList.GetItems($spQuery)
$items[0].Title
```

```
# Option 2 - Use PowerShell to query by property
$items = $fruitsList.Items | Where {$_.Title -eq "Apple"}
$items.Title
```

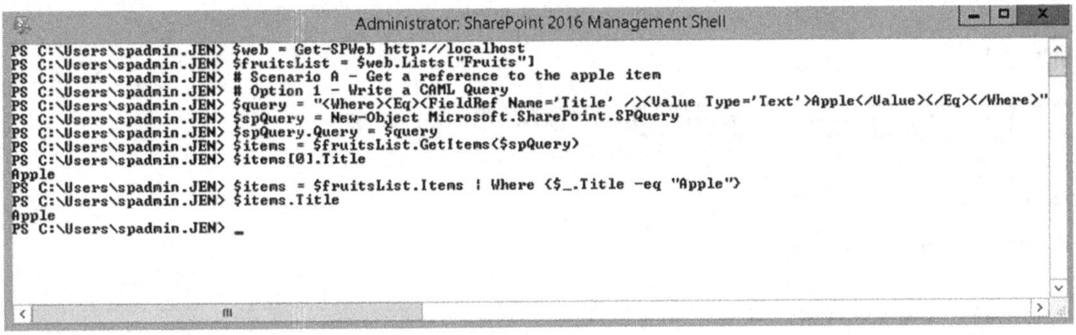

```
Administrator: SharePoint 2016 Management Shell                          _ □ X
PS C:\Users\spadmin..JEN> $web = Get-SPWeb http://localhost
PS C:\Users\spadmin..JEN> $fruitsList = $web.Lists["Fruits"]
PS C:\Users\spadmin..JEN> # Scenario A - Get a reference to the apple item
PS C:\Users\spadmin..JEN> # Option 1 - Write a CAML Query
PS C:\Users\spadmin..JEN> $query = "<Where><Eq><FieldRef Name='Title' /><Value Type='Text'>Apple</Value></Eq></Where>"
PS C:\Users\spadmin..JEN> $spQuery = New-Object Microsoft.SharePoint.SPQuery
PS C:\Users\spadmin..JEN> $spQuery.Query = $query
PS C:\Users\spadmin..JEN> $items = $fruitsList.GetItems($spQuery)
PS C:\Users\spadmin..JEN> $items[0].Title
Apple
PS C:\Users\spadmin..JEN> $items = $fruitsList.Items | Where ($_.Title -eq "Apple")
PS C:\Users\spadmin..JEN> $items.Title
Apple
PS C:\Users\spadmin..JEN> _
```

*Figure 5-22.* *Comparing two option to get specific items from a SharePoint list using PowerShell*

Here is a second example using the same list, to obtain a list of all items that have a unit price of $4.00 or more:

```
# Scenario B - Get items that are $4 and over

# Option 1 - Write a CAML Query
$query = "<Where><Gt><FieldRef Name='Price' /><Value Type='Currency'>4</Value></Gt></Where>"
$spQuery = New-Object Microsoft.SharePoint.SPQuery
$spQuery.Query = $query

$expItems = $fruitsList.GetItems($spQuery)
$ expItems | select Title

# Option 2 - Use PowerShell to query by property
$expItems = $fruitsList.Items | Where{$_["Price"] -gt 4}
$ expItems | select Title
```

```
Administrator: SharePoint 2016 Management Shell                          _ □ X

PS C:\Users\spadmin.JEN> # Scenario B - Get items that are 4$ and over
PS C:\Users\spadmin.JEN> # Option 1 - Write a CAML Query
PS C:\Users\spadmin.JEN> $query = "<Where><Gt><FieldRef Name='Price' /><Value Type='Currency'>4</Value></Gt></Where>"
PS C:\Users\spadmin.JEN> $spQuery = New-Object Microsoft.SharePoint.SPQuery
PS C:\Users\spadmin.JEN> $spQuery.Query = $query
PS C:\Users\spadmin.JEN> $expItems = $fruitsList.GetItems($spQuery)
PS C:\Users\spadmin.JEN> $expItems | select Title

Title
-----
GrapeFruit
Blueberry


PS C:\Users\spadmin.JEN> # Option 2 - Use PowerShell to query by property
PS C:\Users\spadmin.JEN> $expItems = $fruitsList.Items | Where($_["Price"] -gt 4)
PS C:\Users\spadmin.JEN> $expItems | select Title

Title
-----
GrapeFruit
Blueberry


PS C:\Users\spadmin.JEN> _
```

***Figure 5-23.*** *Getting a list of items based on a specific property using PowerShell*

## Removing a List Item

The operation to delete a list items is fairly simple. All you need to do is obtain the ID of the object that you wish to delete, and then call the Delete() method on the list's item collection, passing the item's position in the list as a parameter. As with webs and lists, a deleted list item makes it into the site's Recycle Bin and can be restored or deleted from there. As always, remember that only list items that have been deleted through the SharePoint interface are given a second chance in the Recycle Bin. Those deleted through PowerShell are deleted permanently.

You need to pay special attention when deleting an item from a SharePoint list. The index you're passing to the Delete() method is actually referencing the position of the item to delete in the list. Simply getting the ID position of the object may not end up deleting the proper object. IDs assigned to items in a list are automatically incremented. Once an item has been deleted, its ID stays reserved, and no other items in that list can have the same ID. This could prove to be very confusing, and often results in catastrophic results when forgotten.

For example, assume that you have a list of five different items, say user names. When the list is first created, all items are given a unique number from 1 to 5; this is their ID property. In addition, items in a list are also assigned a relative position in the list, based on the order in which they were added. In the beginning, our five users are all assigned a position number that matches their ID. The next user to be added to the list will automatically be granted an ID of 6, with a position value of 6. Now, let's assume that user #2 is deleted; what happens to the position values? User #3 will now be shifted down one position in the list, and so will the other three users. Only user #1 will keep its original position. With this in mind, if you were to call the Delete() method passing a position value of 4 as a parameter, user #5 is the user that would actually be deleted.

To make sure that you delete the appropriate item in your list, you need to loop through the list of items and get their exact positions. Then you can call the Delete() method on the collection to have the proper item deleted. To illustrate this, see the SharePoint list in Figure 5-24. We've used the following PowerShell code to display each item in the list along with its current position:

```
$web = Get-SPWeb http://localhost
$fruitsList = $web.Lists["Fruits"]
$position = 0
foreach($fruit in $fruitsList.Items)
{
     Write-Host "Position $position :"  $fruit.Title - ID:   $fruit.Id
$position++
}
```

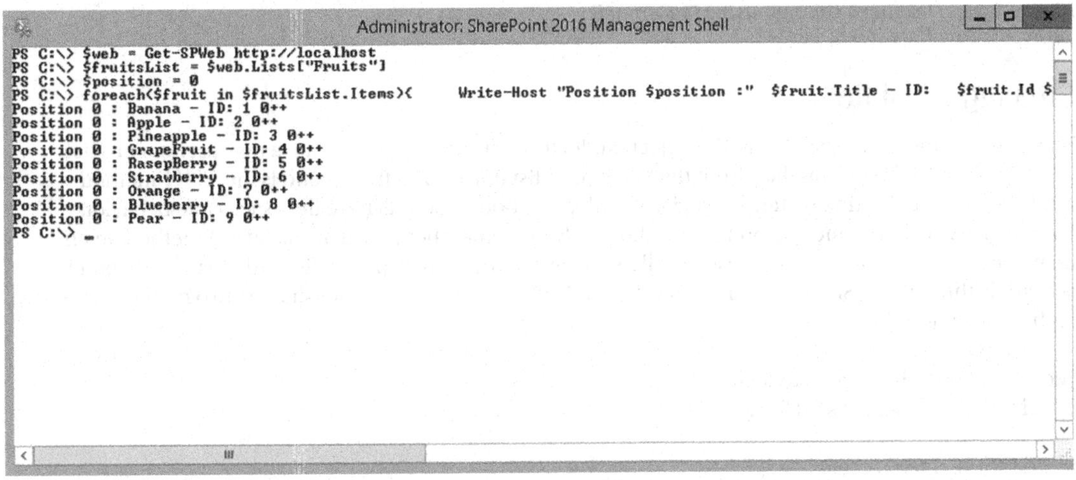

*Figure 5-24.* *Listing item positions and IDs from a SharePoint list using PowerShell*

The following lines will loop through the entire collection of items and compare each item's ID to that of the apple item. If a match is found, then the item at the current position (the apple item) will be removed from the collection (see Figure 5-25):

```
$web = Get-SPWeb http://localhost
$fruitsList = $web.Lists["Fruits"]
$appleItem = $fruitsList.Items | Where {$_.Title -eq "Apple"}
$appleId = $appleItem.ID

$position = 0;
foreach($fruit in $fruitsList.Items)
{
    if($fruit.ID -eq $appleId)
    {
        $fruitsList.Items.Delete($position)
    }
    $position++ # Increases the current position
}
```

```
Administrator: SharePoint 2016 Management Shell                    _  □  X

PS C:\> $web = Get-SPWeb http://localhost
PS C:\> $fruitsList = $web.Lists["Fruits"]
PS C:\> $appleItem = $fruitsList.Items | Where {$_.Title -eq "Apple"}
PS C:\> $appleId = $appleItem.ID
PS C:\> $position = 0;
PS C:\> foreach($fruit in $fruitsList.Items)
>> {
>> if($fruit.ID -eq $appleId)
>> {
>>          $fruitsList.Items.Delete($position)
>> }
>>     $position++ # Increases the current position
>> }
>>
PS C:\>
```

***Figure 5-25.*** *Deleting a list item using PowerShell*

## Creating a List Item

There are two methods available in the object model that will allow you to create a new list item in a list. The first is the AddItem() method from the SharePoint list object, and the second is the Add() method available on the collection of items associated with a list. Both methods have the exact same behavior. You can use whichever one you prefer. You should always remember to use the Update() method on an item once you've created it; otherwise, it will not be registered with its parent list and, therefore, won't be accessible through the SharePoint interface. Figure 5-26 shows the results of using the two methods included in the following code:

```
$web = Get-SPWeb http://localhost
$fruitsList = $web.Lists["Fruits"]

$fruitsList.Items.count

$newItem1 = $fruitsList.AddItem()
$newItem1["Title"] = "Kiwi";
$newItem1["Price"] = 6.99;
$newItem1.Update()

$fruitsList.Items.count

$newItem2 = $fruitsList.Items.Add()
$newItem2["Title"] = "Grapes"
$newItem2["Price"] = 5.99
$newItem2.Update()

$fruitsList.Items.count
```

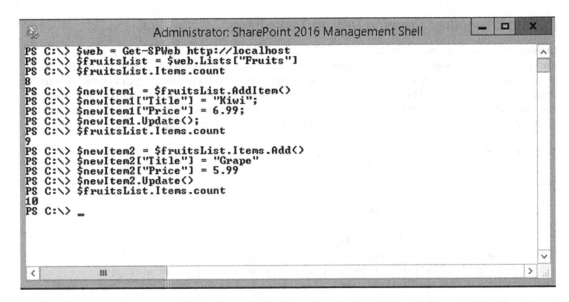

*Figure 5-26. Creating a new list item using PowerShell*

## Updating a List Item

Just like any good artifacts supporting CRUD (create, read, update, and delete) operations, list items in SharePoint allow you to update an existing item's properties. You'll first need to get a reference to the item you wish to update, and then modify the value of the property you wish to change by accessing it directly in the fields' collection. In the current example, a common scenario may be to update the unit price of a specific fruit on a regular basis. The following lines of PowerShell script provide more details on how you could achieve this update, which is then shown in Figure 5-27. Note that once you've modified a list item's property, you do need to call the Update() method on it for the changes to be reflected.

```
$web = Get-SPWeb http://localhost
$fruitsList = $web.Lists["Fruits"]

$bananaItem = $fruitsList.Items | Where {$_.Title -eq "Banana"}
$bananaItem["Price"] = 0.99
$bananaItem.Update()
```

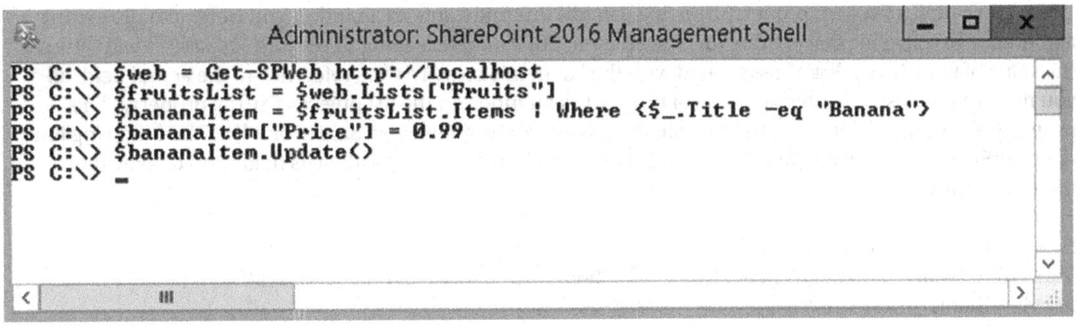

```
Administrator: SharePoint 2016 Management Shell                    _  □  x
PS C:\> $web = Get-SPWeb http://localhost
PS C:\> $fruitsList = $web.Lists["Fruits"]
PS C:\> $bananaItem = $fruitsList.Items | Where {$_.Title -eq "Banana"}
PS C:\> $bananaItem["Price"] = 0.99
PS C:\> $bananaItem.Update()
PS C:\> _
```

*Figure 5-27. Updating an existing list item using PowerShell*

## Putting It Together: Creating Default Tasks Items

In this section, you'll continue building on your SharePoint organizational workspaces. The goal of this exercise is to loop through all the various business unit sites that you have and add a default task in each team's "Unit Tasks" list. The default task will be called "Get familiar with your unit's SharePoint workspace," and it will have a deadline scheduled a week from today. The key thing to take from this exercise is that you will have to use objects that are of the SharePoint scope, and use objects that are built in the core .NET Framework. In this case, you will be using the .NET DateTime object to get next week's date.

```
$webApp = Get-SPWebApplication http://localhost

foreach($site in $webApp.Sites)
{
    foreach($web in $site.AllWebs)
    {
        $list = $web.Lists["Unit Tasks"]
        $newTask = $list.AddItem();
        $newTask["Title"] = "Get familiar with your unit's SharePoint workspace"
        $today = [System.DateTime]::Now
        $nextWeek = $today.AddDays(7)
        $newTask["DueDate"] = $nextWeek
        $newTask.Update()
    }
}
```

## List Fields

We've already briefly touched on the subject of List Fields in this chapter. We've explained that a field contains a specific type of information about a list item contained in a list. List fields can have many types, such as text, number, currency, choice, data, and so on. Each field is given two name properties, an internal name and an external name. These two names can be the same, but the internal name has to be unique within the list. This internal name is used by SharePoint to reference a field. Think of it as being the unique identifier for a specific field in a list. In this section, you will learn how to interact with fields in a SharePoint list using PowerShell.

## Getting an Instance of a Field

You've already seen how to get a reference to a specific field's value, in the previous section's examples. When you called a list item property by using a field's internal name as an index, you were actually getting a reference to a specific field's value for a given item. For example, calling $item["FieldName"] will return the value of field "FieldName" associated with the list item $item. To get a reference to the actual field, all you need to do it use the internal name of the field as an index on the list object's Fields property. This property represents an array containing all of the fields associated with a SharePoint list. The following lines of PowerShell script will create a new SharePoint list and iterate through all of its fields and display their internal names:

```
$web = Get-SPWeb http://localhost
$listID = $web.Lists.Add("DemoList", "", $web.ListTemplates["Custom List"])
$list = $web.Lists[$listID]
foreach($field in $list.Fields)
```

```
{
    write-host $field.InternalName" - Hidden:" $field.Hidden" - ReadOnly:" field.
ReadOnlyField
}
```

You will see that some fields listed by the script in Figure 5-28 look familiar (such as title, author, and attachments). Others, however, aren't recognizable. These are most likely hidden fields that are required by SharePoint. In addition to having a data type defining the type of value that they can accept, fields can have two other properties that can be set to determine their behaviors: the ReadOnlyField and the Hidden properties. One of these two properties set to true on a field will normally indicate that the field is reserved by SharePoint.

*Figure 5-28. Listing information related to a list's fields using PowerShell*

## Creating a New Field

Fields are created by calling the Add() method on the array of fields associated with a SharePoint list instance. When calling this method, you will need to specify a title for the field, the type of data this field should be accepting, and whether the field is required or not.

```
$web = Get-SPWeb http://localhost
$demoList = $web.Lists["DemoList"]
$fieldID = $demoList.Fields.Add("HairColor", [Microsoft.SharePoint.SPFieldType]::Choice,
$true)
$myNewChoiceField = $demoList.Fields["HairColor"]

$myNewChoiceField.Choices.Add("Brown")
$myNewChoiceField.Choices.Add("Blond")
```

```
$myNewChoiceField.Choices.Add("Red")
$myNewChoiceField.Choices.Add("Black")
$myNewChoiceField.Choices.Add("Grey")
$myNewChoiceField.Choices.Add("None")

#
```

Now you need to call the `Update()` method in order for the choices to appear on the interface:

```
$myNewChoiceField.Update()
```

As you can see in Figure 5-29, the new field has been created in SharePoint with all the values that you provided in PowerShell.

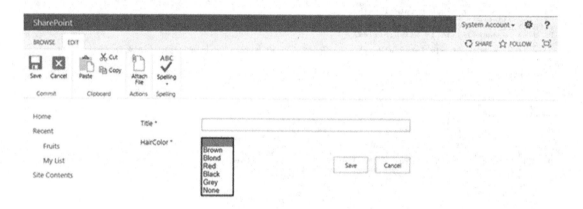

***Figure 5-29.*** *New item form showing a list field created by PowerShell*

## Removing a Field

To remove a field, simply get a reference to the field in question and call the `Delete()` method on it. The operation of deleting a field is permanent and cannot be recovered. Once a field has been deleted, all of the data that was contained in it is removed as well.

```
$web = Get-SPWeb http://localhost
$demoList = $web.Lists["DemoList"]
$field = $demoList.Fields["HairColor"]
$field.Delete()
```

# Permissions

Up to this point, you've learned about how you can interact with various types of artifacts in your SharePoint environment using PowerShell. We have now arrived at the most important topic: permissions. With the exception of fields, specific permissions can be applied on all the types of artifacts that we've covered in this chapter. By default, permissions are applied at a site collection's root web and inherited down to every web, every list, and every list item contained within it, which means they all use the same set of permissions.

For example, if a list inherits its permissions from its parent web, changes to the permissions on that parent web will automatically be reflected in the list's permissions, as well. You do have the option, if you want, to break the permission inheritance on any object that inherits permissions from a parent.

For example, if we have a web that contains a document library storing information about salaries for our employees, we would probably want to prevent unauthorized users from seeing the information in the library. One way of achieving this could be to break the inheritance at the document library level and only grant access to those authorized. This way, users that are not authorized to see the information contained in the library would not even see the library at all.

Another option may be to break the inheritance at the document level. For example, if each user is entitled to see their own salary information, we could break the inheritance on each document in the library and simply grant access to each employee to their own files. This will result in each employee seeing the library, but only being able to view one document in it. Documents for which they are not granted permissions would be hidden and made inaccessible to them.

In the context of SharePoint, permissions are made up of two pieces of information: a role definition that specifies what privileges a permission entry is granting, and a role assignment that specifies who is assigned to the role definition entry. In this section, you will learn how easy it is to interact with SharePoint permissions using PowerShell. For the sake of simplicity, we will keep our explanations of permissions at the list level. To interact with permissions at a web or a list-item level, the same methods and operations apply.

## List Permissions on an Object

The following request is something that always comes back: given a specific artifact in SharePoint, we want to know who has access to it. Using PowerShell, it becomes extremely easy to get such information about an object. To illustrate how to obtain information about permissions for a list, we will start by creating a new SharePoint list using PowerShell:

```
$web = http://localhost
$newListId = $web.Lists.Add("Secure", "", $web.ListTemplates["Custom List"])
$secureList = $web.Lists[$newListId]
```

By default, using the Add() method with the signature we used here will create the new list and inherit permissions from its parent web. If you want to list the permissions that are applied to it by default, you can simply get access to the RoleAssignments properties of your new list. Doing this will return a list of all users that have some level of access to your list, along with information about what their role definition is (see Figure 5-30):

```
$newListId = $web.Lists.Add("Secure", "", $web.ListTemplates["Custom List"])
$secureList = $web.Lists[$newListId]
$secureList.RoleAssignments
```

```
PS C:\temp> $newListId = $web.Lists.Add("Secure", "", $web.ListTemplates["Custom List"])
PS C:\temp> $secureList = $web.Lists[$newListId]
PS C:\temp> $secureList.RoleAssignments

Member                          RoleDefinitionBindings           Parent
--------                        -----------------------          --------
i:0#.w|contoso\administrator    {Full Control, Limited Acc...    Secure
c:0+.w|s-1-5-21-1561338869...   {Contribute}                     Secure
c:0+.w|s-1-5-21-1561338869...   {Design}                         Secure
c:0+.w|s-1-5-21-1561338869...   {Contribute}                     Secure
c:0+.w|s-1-5-21-1561338869...   {Read}                           Secure
c:0+.w|s-1-5-21-1561338869...   {Full Control}                   Secure


PS C:\temp>
```

*Figure 5-30.* *Listing all role assignments on a specific list using PowerShell*

## Breaking Permission Inheritance

The concept of *breaking inheritance* describes the scenario in which we want to stop permissions on an object from being inherited from its parent container. When breaking inheritance on a container, we are given the choice to copy the parent permissions down to the object's permissions, or to start fresh. Once the permission inheritance has been broken on an object, modifying the permissions for its parent will not have any impact on it, and vice versa. Permission inheritance from the parent container can be restored at any time by calling the ResetRoleInheritance() method on the object. The following example shows how to break inheritance for your list and start fresh with no role assignments (see Figure 5-31):

```
$web = Get-SPWeb http://localhost
$secureList = $web.Lists["Secure"]
$secureList.BreakRoleInheritance($false)
```

```
PS C:\temp> $web = Get-SPWeb http://localhost
PS C:\temp> $secureList = $web.Lists["Secure"]
PS C:\temp> $secureList.RoleAssignments.Count
6
PS C:\temp> $secureList.BreakRoleInheritance($false)
PS C:\temp> $secureList.RoleAssignments.Count
0
PS C:\temp>
```

*Figure 5-31.* *Breaking permission inheritance on a SharePoint list using PowerShell*

## Granting New Permissions

In order to be able to grant new permissions on a SharePoint artifact, you'll need to start by determining which role definition you want to map the user to and obtain a reference to it. A role definition instance can be obtained at the web level, as shown with the following example code and in Figure 5-32:

```
$web = Get-SPWeb http://localhost
$fullControlRoleDefinition = $web.RoleDefinitions["Full Control"]
```

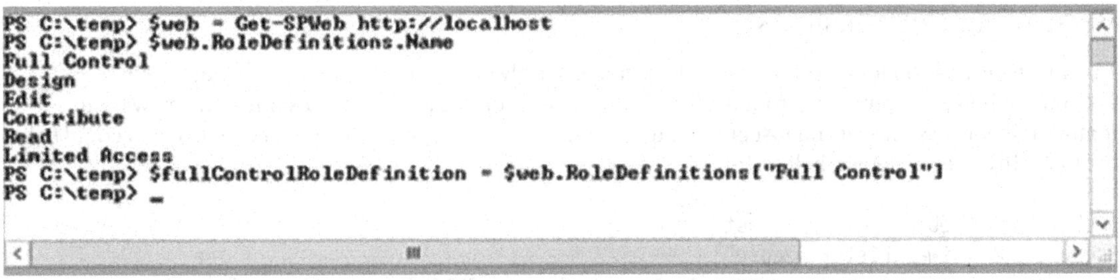

```
PS C:\temp> $web = Get-SPWeb http://localhost
PS C:\temp> $web.RoleDefinitions.Name
Full Control
Design
Edit
Contribute
Read
Limited Access
PS C:\temp> $fullControlRoleDefinition = $web.RoleDefinitions["Full Control"]
PS C:\temp> _
```

***Figure 5-32.*** *Declaring a new role definition using PowerShell*

Once a reference has been obtained, you will need to declare a new `RoleAssignment`variable as follows:

```
$roleAssignment = New-Object Microsoft.SharePoint.SPRoleAssignment("DOMAIN\
UserName","username@domain.com ","Display_Name","Notes about the assignment");
```

Now comes the tricky part: linking the role definition you've obtained previously with the newly created SPRoleAssignment object. In order to achieve this, you need to declare a new object of type SPRoleDefinitionBindingCollecton, and associate both entities through it:

```
$bindings = $roleAssignment.RoleDefinitionBindings
$bindings.Add($fullControlRoleDefinition)
```

Once the linkage has been created, you are now ready to add your new role assignment definition to your list:

```
$secureList.RoleAssignments.Add($roleAssignment)
```

This will automatically grant Full Control permission on your secure list to the administrator account, as shown in Figure 5-33.

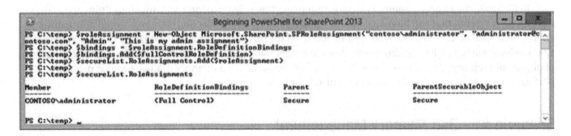

***Figure 5-33.*** *Creating a new role assignment on a SharePoint list using PowerShell*

## Removing Permissions

To remove permission for a user on a specific artifact, simply get a reference to the associated role assignment item, and remove it from the list of assignments on the artifact. For example, if you want to remove the permission that you just granted to the administrator account on your secure list, you could call the following lines of PowerShell script:

```
$web = Get-SPWeb http://localhost
$secureList = $web.Lists["Secure"]
$secureList.RoleAssignments.Remove($web.EnsureUser("CONTOSO\Administrator"))
```

## Updating Permissions

The most straightforward way to update a permission would be to remove the existing one and add a completely new one. Normally, you would update only the role definition portion of an assignment; otherwise, you'd be changing the user associated with a permission entry, which really amounts to creating a new entry altogether. There are no ways of updating an existing role assignment without first removing the existing one and adding a new one instead.

## Objects Disposal

SharePoint is a beast when it comes to memory consumption. For the sake of performance, when dealing with large objects such as site collections and webs, the .NET Framework keeps entire SharePoint objects in memory. The responsibility for properly disposing of SharePoint objects in memory once they are done with them comes back to the user that deals with them. Many large objects in the SharePoint world implement the IDisposable interface behind the scene, meaning that they all expose a Dispose() method to force the removal of objects from memory.

Most of the examples provided throughout this chapter did not properly dispose of objects. Almost all of them have declared a web object without implicitly calling the dispose method on it. In these scenarios, the impact of not properly disposing of items was minimal, but imagine a scenario in which there are thousands of site collections, each having a few hundred sites under it. If you iterate through all these site collections and webs using PowerShell without properly disposing of them, you risk bringing the server to its knees.

To illustrate the effects of memory disposition using PowerShell to interact with SharePoint artifacts, we have created a demo that will loop 10,000 times through all the site collections in a web application and get an instance of all of its webs. The web application used for this demo has about a dozen site collections, with 1,000 webs in each. The first scenario will showcase what happens to the server if you don't properly dispose of objects in memory, and the second will show what happens when memory management is properly performed. We have monitored the memory usage for both scenarios.

## Scenario #1 - Bad Memory Management

The following PowerShell code example shows a scenario in which memory is not being freed up and objects not disposed of properly:

```
$webApp = Get-SPWebApplication http://localhost

for($i = 0; $i -le 10000; $i++)
{
    foreach($site in $webApp.Sites)
```

```
{
    foreach($web in $site.AllWebs)
    {
        Write-host $web.Title
    }
}
}
```

In Figure 5-34, you can see that the memory usage of our PowerShell script keeps increasing as time goes by without ever releasing it in a significant way. This is because all of the webs and site collection objects used by our script are kept in memory.

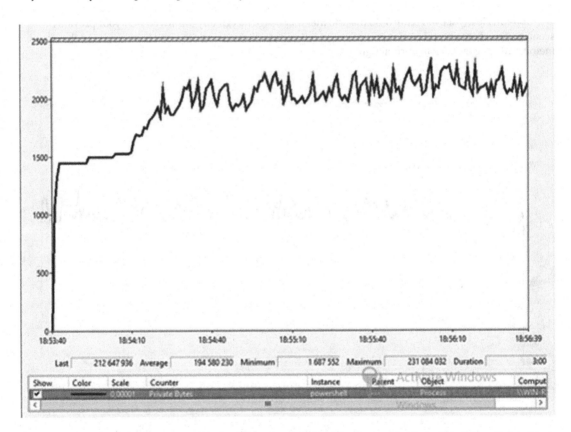

***Figure 5-34.*** *Performance Monitor window for code running without properly disposing of SharePoint objects in memory*

## Scenario #2 - Good Memory Management

The following lines of PowerShell code ensure that you dispose of objects in memory after you are done using them:

```
$webApp = Get-SPWebApplication http://localhost
for($i = 0; $i -le 10000; $i++)
```

```
{
    foreach($site in $webApp.Sites)
    {
        foreach($web in $site.AllWebs)
        {
            Write-host $web.Title
            $web.Dispose()
        }
        $site.Dispose()
    }
}
```

You can clearly see in Figure 5-35 that the memory usage has greatly improved over your previous scenario. Yes, there are spikes of memory usage, but as objects are being disposed from memory, the overall memory usage goes back to normal right away.

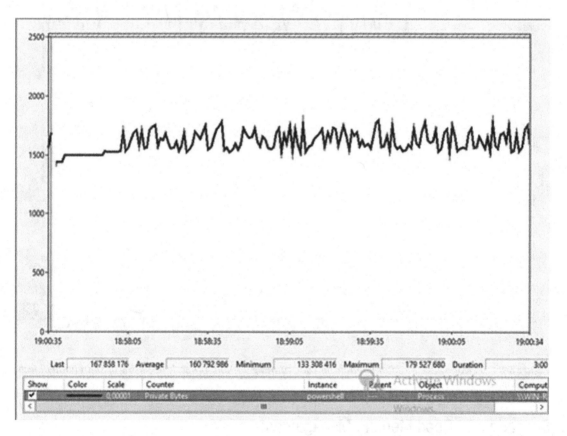

***Figure 5-35.*** *Performance Monitor window for code running that properly disposes of SharePoint objects in memory*

# Summary

In this chapter, you've learned how you can interact with SharePoint objects using PowerShell. To a certain extent, the objects that you've been dealing with in this chapter are what we consider to be front-end artifacts: normally tangible objects with which end users can interact, such as list items and webs. In the traditional scenario, automating operations on these types of objects has always been done by developers. However, this reality has changed drastically in the past few years. Administrators are now given the ability to write scripts of their own using PowerShell, without ever having to "open code." We consider PowerShell to be a gray zone when it comes to governance and responsibility. Even if your organization decides that PowerShell scripts are to be handled by the development team, the fact that these are actually written in plain text and use an administrative scripting language will allow your administrators to at least take a peek at the code and understand what is being executed.

In the next two chapters, we will show you how to use PowerShell to monitor and manage the administrative side of SharePoint, something that the end users don't see. This chapter has given you an overview of how you can interact with objects that you'll see in the SharePoint interface, and Chapter 6 will give you an overview of how to use PowerShell to interact with objects that are normally managed through the Central Administration interface.

# CHAPTER 6

■ ■ ■

# Monitoring SharePoint with PowerShell

This chapter is where most of you will get the biggest bang for your buck. It is full of IT pro goodness and will really get into the guts of SharePoint administration. As mentioned earlier in this book, there used to be a time when SharePoint administrative tasks all had to be done using a command-line tool called STSAdm. This legacy tool came from the time when the SharePoint product as we know it today was called SharePoint Team Sites (therefore the STS prefix in the tool's name). This tool was good, but it was extremely slow to execute heavy operations against the server, and it was difficult for administrators to really know what its methods were really doing in the background.

The story has changed dramatically with the appearance of PowerShell. Now administrators can easily automate long-lasting operations against their SharePoint farms, and have full control over what steps are being executed as part of it. This chapter will cover various aspects of SharePoint administration using PowerShell. It will include several real-life examples and will provide multiple code samples that can be reused in your own organizations to assist you in your day-to-day jobs. Topics covered will include the automation of backups and restores, the monitoring of timer jobs, and the management of services, as well as monitoring the overall SharePoint 2016 farm's well-being using the Health Analyzer.

Most of the things we will cover in this chapter are things that can be achieved manually by using the SharePoint Central Administration web interface. However, if you add PowerShell to the mix, you can create new reusable and repeatable scripts that can improve performance and avoid a lot of headaches. By the end of this chapter, you will have learned the basics of everything a SharePoint farm administrator has to do in order to be successful in his or her role.

## Features

In this section, you will learn how to use PowerShell to interact with SharePoint 2016 features. More specifically, you will learn how to enable and disable features on site collections and webs. A *feature*, in the context of SharePoint, represents a self-contained set of elements that can be made available at various levels of a SharePoint environment. A SharePoint solution (.wsp package) can contain one or many features, each associated with a different deployment scope (farm, web application, site collection, or web).

When creating custom SharePoint solutions, developers can choose against which scope they wish to associate their features. For example, assume that you have a custom farm solution that contains a web part that you wish to deploy to your environment. The web part will be associated with a feature, and this feature is scoped at the site-collection level. The simple fact of deploying your farm solution will not automatically make that web part available to end users to use in all site collections. In order for the web part to become available, the feature will need to be activated for every site collection on which you wish to use the web part. The process of activating a feature against a specific scope is called *feature stapling*.

© Nikolas Charlebois-Laprade and John Edward Naguib 2017
N. Charlebois-Laprade and J. E. Naguib, *Beginning PowerShell for SharePoint 2016*,
DOI 10.1007/978-1-4842-2884-5_6

## Getting a Reference to an Existing Feature

The Get-SPFeature PowerShell cmdlet lets you get a reference to the list of all features deployed in your local SharePoint environment, no matter what the scope. Each feature is given a unique identifier, a name, and an associated scope. Figure 6-1 shows how to get a list of all existing features in your SharePoint environment using PowerShell. It also shows how you can get a reference to a specific feature using only its name—in this case, the ExcelServer farm feature:

```
$excelServer = Get-SPFeature | Where{$_.DisplayName -eq "ExcelServer"}
$excelServer
```

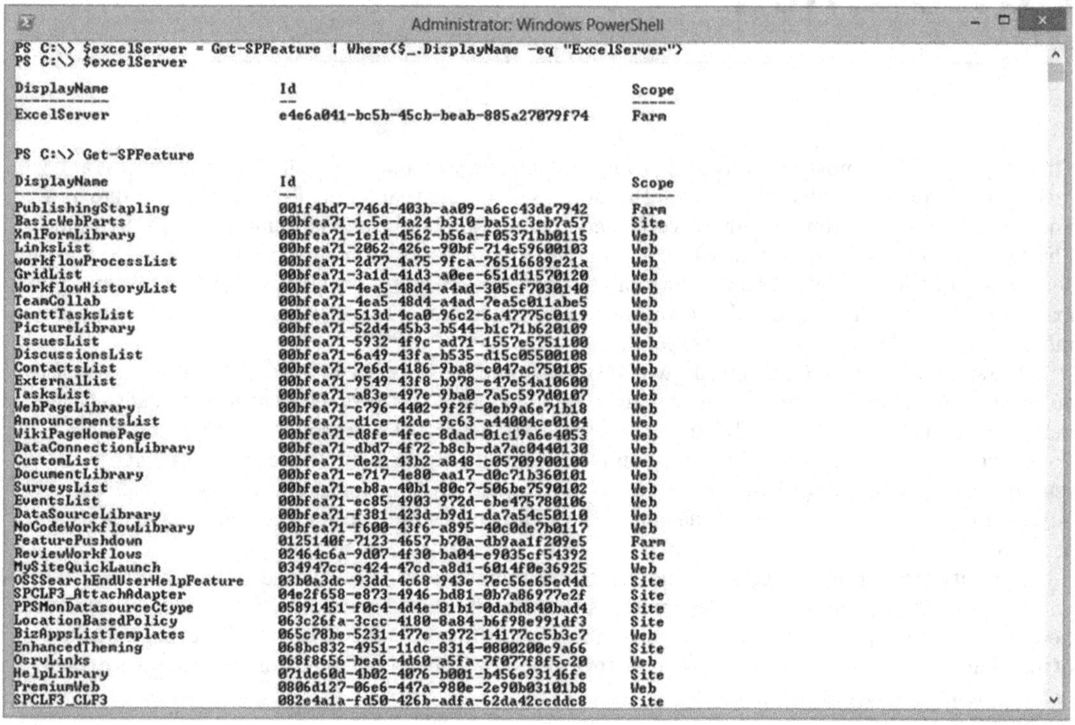

*Figure 6-1.* *Getting a reference to SharePoint features using PowerShell*

# Activating a Feature

To activate a SharePoint feature using PowerShell, you need to use the Enable-SPFeature cmdlet and pass it a reference to the feature that you wish to activate. Note that you cannot decide the scope against which to activate a specific feature. Each feature is already preassociated with a specific scope, and this cannot be changed using PowerShell. Figure 6-2 shows how to activate the web-scoped GroupWork feature against your root web.

```
$groupWork = Get-SPFeature | Where{$_.DisplayName -eq "GroupWork"}
Enable-SPFeature -URL http://localhost -Identity $groupWork
```

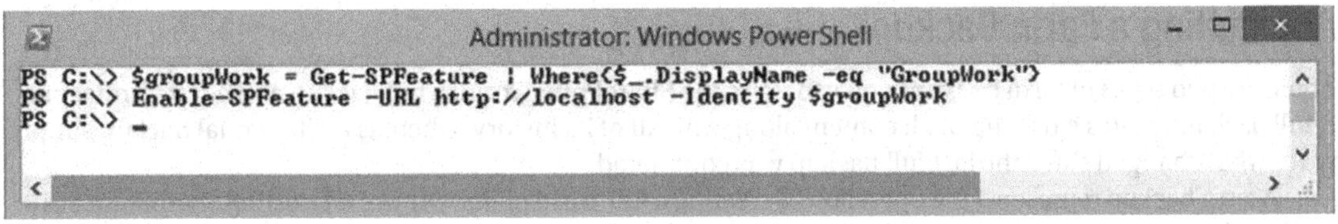

```
Administrator: Windows PowerShell                                    _ □ ×

PS C:\> $groupWork = Get-SPFeature | Where{$_.DisplayName -eq "GroupWork"}
PS C:\> Enable-SPFeature -URL http://localhost -Identity $groupWork
PS C:\> _
```

*Figure 6-2. Enabling a SharePoint feature using PowerShell*

■ **Note**    While running the previous commands you may get two GroupWork features, so you will need to select which one you will enable.

## Disabling a Feature

To use PowerShell to disable a SharePoint feature that has previously been activated, use the Disable-SPFeature cmdlet. This method requires you to pass a reference to the feature that you wish to disable. Figure 6-3 shows how to use PowerShell to disable the GroupWork feature we activated in the previous section.

```
$groupWork = Get-SPFeature | Where{$_.DisplayName -eq "GroupWork"}
Disable-SPFeature -URL http://localhost -Identity $groupWork -Confirm:$false
```

```
Administrator: Windows PowerShell                                    _ □ ×

PS C:\> $groupWork = Get-SPFeature | Where{$_.DisplayName -eq "GroupWork"}
PS C:\> Disable-SPFeature -URL http://localhost -Identity $groupWork -Confirm:$false
PS C:\> _
```

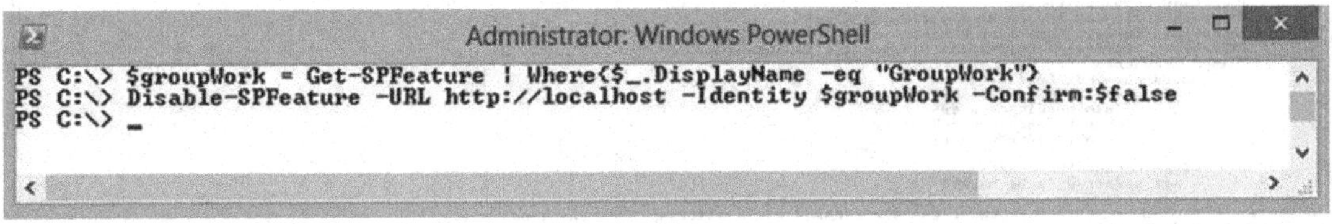

*Figure 6-3. Disabling a SharePoint feature using PowerShell*

## Backups

In the SharePoint world, there are several types of backups available. When backing up entities, SharePoint creates .bak files. These files are essential when trying to restore a SharePoint instance to a previous state. It is important to note that you can also use the built-in SharePoint backup mechanism to assist in transferring site collections or web applications from one SharePoint farm to another, as long as the destination server has exactly the same product version as the source server.

You can back up any SharePoint entities from any level of the hierarchy (farm, web application, or site collection). By default, PowerShell provides four main cmdlets to interact with SharePoint 2016 backups: one for backing up the configuration database, one for backing up the enterprise search index, another one for backing up the entire farm or specific content databases, and one for backing up site collections. In this section, you will learn how to use PowerShell to automate backups of different architectural components of a SharePoint farm (content databases, web applications, site collections, and so on) using PowerShell. Content related to backing up the enterprise search content of SharePoint 2016 is outside the scope of this book.

# Automating a Farm Backup

There are two types of farm backups you can do in the SharePoint world: a full backup and a differential one. A full backup creates a backup of all content along with all of its history, whereas a differential backup simply saves what changed since the last full backup was completed.

A farm backup represents the operation of creating a full-trust, offline copy of an existing SharePoint 2016 farm, and storing it elsewhere on a shared location. Farm backups can be automated with PowerShell using the Backup-SPFarm cmdlet. As mentioned previously, you can choose what level of SharePoint artifacts you wish to back up. In order to determine the different artifacts you can back up, you can call this cmdlet passing it the –ShowTree switch. This will automatically display all available items for backup on the screen (see Figure 6-4).

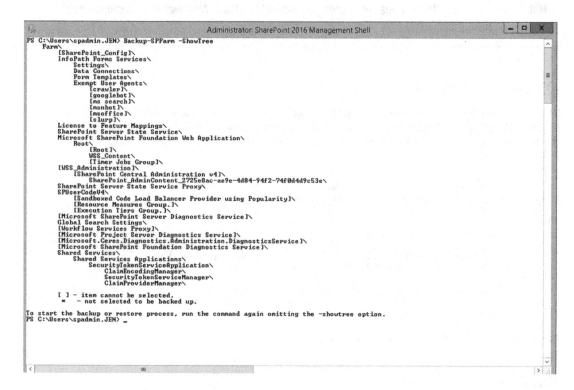

***Figure 6-4.*** *Listing all SharePoint 2016 artifacts available for backup using PowerShell*

Once you've determine the type of backup (full or differential), and the artifacts you wish to back up, you can proceed with the backup process. The following code will initiate a full farm backup. The backup files will be stored in a local share you've created at C:\Backups\. To perform a differential backup, you simply replace Full with Differential.

```
Backup-SPFarm -Directory \\localhost\Backups\ -BackupMethod Full
```

Executing this code can take several minutes depending on the size of your farm. PowerShell will initiate a backup process and wait for the process to finish before returning the results to screen. Don't be fooled; you might think that nothing is happening while the execution goes on, but, in reality, timer jobs related to the backup process are busy at work. Figure 6-5 shows the result of navigating to the Backup and Restore Job Status screen in Central Administration. This page will give you a live overview of what is actively going on in the backup process.

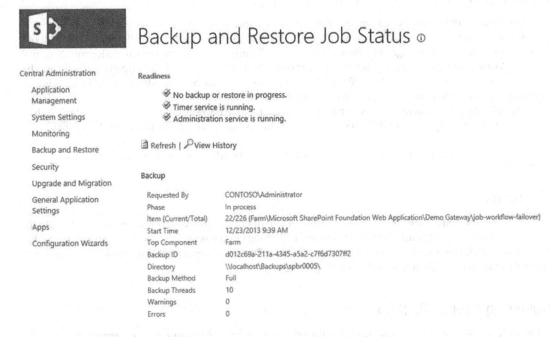

*Figure 6-5.  Viewing an ongoing backup status through Central Administration*

## Viewing Backup History

Once a SharePoint backup process is completed, it is inserted into the history list of its associated backup folder. A history list is nothing more than an XML file on disk that contains a record of all backup processes that have been sent to the folder. If you navigate to any backup folder, you should see a file named spbrtoc.xml. This is the file that keeps track of all backups. Using PowerShell, you can get a list of all completed backups for a specific folder using the Get-SPBackupHistory cmdlet. Figure 6-6 shows the execution of this cmdlet against a backup folder in which multiple backup processes were initiated. You pipe the resulting output into the generic PowerShell Format-List method to get more details out of the operation.

```
Get-SPBackupHistory -Directory \\localhost\Backups\ | Format-List
```

```
Administrator: SharePoint 2016 Management Shell
PS C:\Users\spadmin.JEN> Get-SPBackupHistory -Directory \\localhost\Backups\ | Format-List

BackupMethod       : Full
RestoreMethod      : None
IsBackup           : True
ConfigurationOnly  : False
FailureMessage     :
StartTime          : 12/12/2016 8:30:15 AM
EndTime            : 12/12/2016 8:40:30 AM
SelfId             : 37ba9dab-020c-4b93-9820-386aa2125e9c
RestoreId          : 00000000-0000-0000-0000-000000000000
ParentId           : 00000000-0000-0000-0000-000000000000
Name               :
TopComponent       : Farm
TopComponentId     : 3931a225-677a-452c-a5b2-07eb302932f8
Directory          : \\localhost\Backups\spbr0000\
DirectoryName      : spbr0000
RequestedBy        : JEN\spadmin
WarningCount       : 0
ErrorCount         : 0
IsFailure          : False
T                  : B
S                  : Y
Method             : Full
```

*Figure 6-6.  Retrieving a list of all backups for a specific shared folder using PowerShell*

## Automating a Site-Collection Backup

The second flavor of backups we can do in SharePoint is what we call a *site-collection backup.* As you've probably guessed by the name, this type of backup is aimed at a single specific site collection. The result of such an operation will be a single .bak file containing all information related to that site collection. Note that compared to a farm backup, site-collection backups don't keep a history list of all completed processes. The PowerShell cmdlet for backing up SharePoint site collections is Backup-SPSite. All this method takes is a parameter that specifies into which shared folder to put the resulting .bak file.

The following code will initiate a site-collection backup of the root site collection of your default web application. You specify to PowerShell that the name of the resulting .bak file should be RootSite.bak:

```
Backup-SPSite -Identity http://localhost -Path \\localhost\Backups\RootSite.bak
```

## Restores

In the SharePoint context, a restore operation is the action of bringing the content of backup files back to life, either on the same server from which the backups are coming or on a separate SharePoint environment. Just as with the backup operations, there are two types of SharePoint restores: a farm restore and a site-collection restore. Both can be easily automated using PowerShell.

## Restoring a Farm Backup

When restoring from a farm backup, you have the option to restore the content as a new environment, or to overwrite the existing one; these are called the restore methods. To initiate the restore process, you'll need to use the Restore-SPFarm PowerShell cmdlet. This cmdlet will expect you to pass it the location of the shared folder where the backup files are located, the restore method (new or overwrite), and the farm credentials.

The following PowerShell code will initiate a farm restore using the latest full backup files from our environment, and overwriting the current files and configuration. Note that this script will prompt you to enter the password for the farm account:

```
$farmAccount = Get-Credential Contoso\Administrator
Restore-SPFarm -Directory \\localhost\Backups\ -RestoreMethod Overwrite -FarmCredentials
$farmAccount
```

If you had wanted to restore the content to a new location, you would have needed to specify the value New for the -RestoreMethod parameter. Doing so will initiate PowerShell to prompt you to specify additional parameters such as a URL for the new web application and a new name for each of the databases (content, administration, and configuration). Figure 6-7 shows an example of trying to restore a farm backup to a new location.

```
PS C:\Users\Administrator> $farmAccount = Get-Credential Contoso\Administrator
PS C:\Users\Administrator> Restore-SPFarm -Directory \\localhost\Backups\ -RestoreMethod New -FarmCredentials $farmAccou
nt

Confirm
Are you sure you want to perform this action?
Performing operation "Restore-SPFarm" on Target "WIN-RBRR22MRAOR".
[Y] Yes  [A] Yes to All  [N] No  [L] No to All  [S] Suspend  [?] Help (default is "Y"): Y
Change location/name for: Farm\SharePoint Server State Service\State Service\StateService_901de73876804b179ae0602c83b44
1c2
        New directory name: (default: C:\Program Files\Microsoft SQL Server\MSSQL11.MSSQLSERVER\MSSQL\DATA):
MyNewDirectory
        New database name: (default: StateService_901de73876804b179ae0602c83b441c2):
MyNew database
        New database server name: (default: WIN-RBRR22MRAOR):

Change location/name for: Farm\Microsoft SharePoint Foundation Web Application\Demo Gateway
        New web application name: (default: Demo Gateway):
NewWebApplication
        New web application URL: (default: http://win-rbrr22mraor/):
http://win-rbrr22mraor:77
Change location/name for: Farm\Microsoft SharePoint Foundation Web Application\Demo Gateway\WSS_Content
        New directory name: (default: C:\Program Files\Microsoft SQL Server\MSSQL11.MSSQLSERVER\MSSQL\DATA):
```

*Figure 6-7. Restoring a SharePoint farm backup to a new location using PowerShell*

## Restoring a Site Collection Backup

The process of restoring content from a site collection backup file using PowerShell is very similar to the process of restoring a farm backup. The cmdlet used in this case is `Restore-SPSite`, and it requires you to specify the URL to which you wish to restore the site collection's content, as well as the path to the .bak file that contains the content. To restore a site collection's backup to an existing location (that is, overwrite a site collection), pass the `-Force` parameter to the cmdlet.

The following PowerShell code example shows how to restore the site collection backup file created earlier and overwrite its current location. This will replace the content that has changed since the moment we took the backup and revert it back to what it was. For those familiar with the concept of Virtual Machine snapshots in Hyper-V, this process is similar to rolling back a Virtual Machine's snapshot back to an earlier instance:

```
Restore-SPSite http://localhost -Path \\localhost\Backups\RootSite.bak -Force
```

## Timer Jobs

Timer jobs in SharePoint are comparable to scheduled tasks in the context of the Windows operating system. They are, more often than not, repeatable activities set to execute at specific times. The SharePoint object model allows for the development of custom timer jobs, which can help expand the set of default jobs we have to help maintain our SharePoint farm. Timer jobs are associated with schedules that determine the time lapse between two executions of its related activities. Schedules can be of any of the following types: Minutes, Hourly, Daily, Weekly, and Monthly.

SharePoint timer jobs are responsible for activities such as the installation of SharePoint apps, the creation of variation pages in the context of publishing, the removal of deleted site collections, and so on. These are essentials to the well-being of your SharePoint environment. Using PowerShell, there are several ways for users to interact with them. We can use PowerShell to disable timer jobs completely, to enable them, to set their schedule, or to force their immediate execution.

## Getting a Reference to an Existing Timer Job

There are various reasons why you may want to get a reference to an existing timer job using PowerShell. To get a list of all the existing timer jobs in your SharePoint environment, you can use the Get-SPTimerJob cmdlet. Figure 6-8 shows the result of obtaining a list of all timer jobs that have a schedule set to daily.

```
$dailyJobs = Get-SPTimerJob | Where{$_.Schedule -like "daily*"}
```

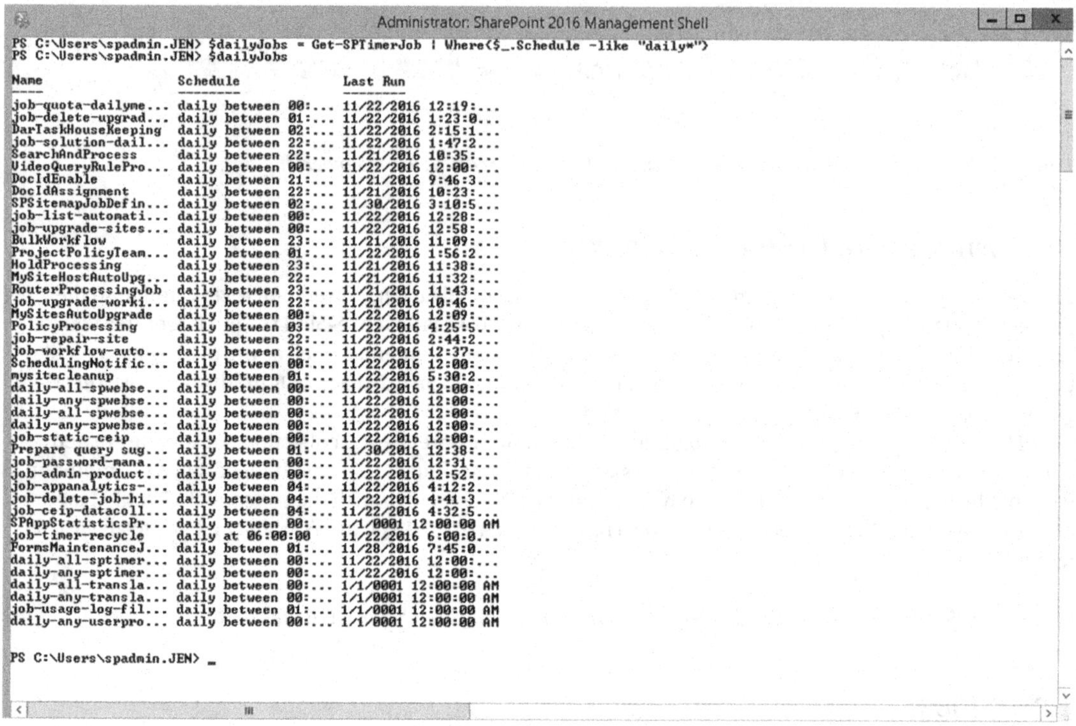

*Figure 6-8.* Listing all timer jobs with a daily schedule using PowerShell

## Disabling a Timer Job

There might be cases in which you wish to prevent a SharePoint timer job completely from running; for example, if you wish to prevent the app diagnostics timer job from running and gathering information because it can somehow affect the performance of your server. Using PowerShell, you can disable a timer job by calling the Disable-SPTimerJob cmdlet. This method expects to receive a reference to the timer job you wish to disable. The following PowerShell script will get a reference to a specific timer job (apps diagnostics), and disable its execution:

```
$appDiagnosticsJob = Get-SPTimerJob | Where{$_.DisplayName -eq "Diagnostic Data Provider:
App Usage"}
Disable-SPTimerJob $appDiagnosticsJob
```

If you navigate to the Jobs Definition page in Central Administration on the server, you should now see that the instance of the timer job specified in this script is marked as Disabled (see Figure 6-9).

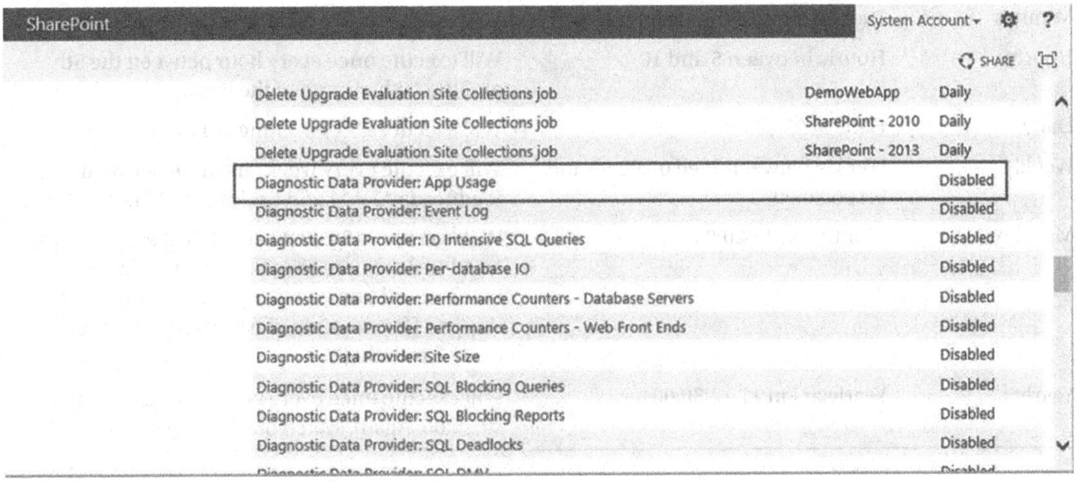

*Figure 6-9.* *Viewing a disabled timer job in Central Adminsitration*

## Enabling a Timer Job

To enable a timer job in SharePoint using PowerShell, use the Enable-SPTimerjob cmdlet. Just like the method for disabling a timer job, this method expects you to pass it a reference to the timer job object you wish to enable. The following PowerShell code will re-enable the timer job you disabled in the previous section:

```
$appDiagnosticsJob = Get-SPTimerJob | Where{$_.DisplayName -eq "Diagnostic Data Provider:
App Usage"}
Enable-SPTimerJob $appDiagnosticsJob
```

## Changing a Timer Job's Schedule

Another very common operation is to change the schedule for your timer jobs. A very common scenario is to change the frequency of the timer job that automatically creates upgrade evaluation site collections for testing upgrades. By default, this timer job is set to run once every day. During a migration project, you may want to bring this interval down so it's an hourly process to allow your users to test their upgrades more rapidly. The PowerShell cmdlet to use to modify a timer job's schedule is the Set-SPTimerJob method. This cmdlet expects you to pass it the identity of the timer job to modify as well as its new schedule in the form of free text. The schedule parameter can be a little tricky to figure out. Table 6-1 gives you a list of all possible types of schedules as well as an example for each.

***Table 6-1.*** *Timer Job Schedules and Their Uses*

| Schedule Type | Example | Description |
| --- | --- | --- |
| Minutes | Every 2 minutes between 0 and 59 | Will execute every 2 minutes in the hour. |
| Hourly | Hourly between 5 and 10 | Will execute once every hour between the 5th and the 10th minute of the hour. |
| Daily | Daily at 23:00:00 | Will execute every evening at 11 PM. |
| Weekly | Weekly between Wed 07:00:00 and Fri 06:30:00 | Will execute every week, any time between Wednesday 7 AM and Friday 6:30 AM. |
| Monthly | Monthly at 17 20:00:00 | Will execute at 20:00:00 the 17th of every month. Need to watch out to make sure the date exists in the month; otherwise the execution will be skipped (for example, the 31st only exists for every 2 months). |
| Yearly | Yearly at Jan 17 12:30:00 | Will execute once every year on January 17th at 12:30:00. Again, watch out for leap years. |

The following PowerShell code will change the schedule for the creation of upgrade evaluation site collection as discussed earlier. You will be using an hourly schedule to have the job execute every hour between the 5th and the 10th minutes of the hour. One thing to watch out for here is that if you have multiple web applications created in your farm, the first line of script that gets a reference to the timer job instance will actually return one instance per web application. You need to make sure that you are modifying the instance that is associated with the web application you want to impact. Figure 6-10 shows the result of viewing the modified timer job's schedule through the SharePoint Central Administration web interface.

```
$upEvalCreation = Get-SPTimerJob | Where{$_.DisplayName -eq "Create Upgrade Evaluation Site
Collections job"}

Set-SPTimerJob -Identity $upEvalCreation[0] -Schedule "Hourly between 5 and 10"
```

■ **Note** The expression $upEvalCreation[0] uses the variable with an index of 0 to be sure it returns a value of 1.

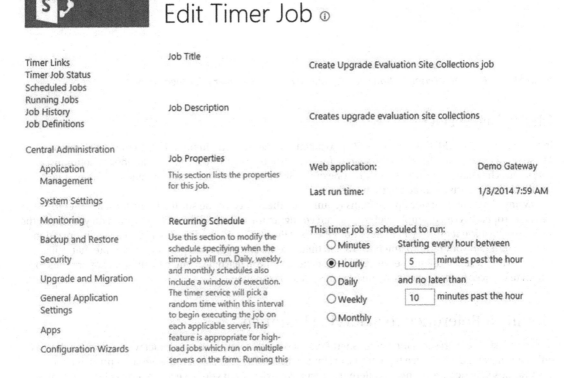

*Figure 6-10.* *Viewing a modified timer job's schedule through the SharePoint 2016 Central Administration web interface*

## Starting a Timer Job

The last operation left for timer jobs that PowerShell lets you automate is the initiation of a timer job's execution. This lets you bypass a timer job's schedule and execute its associated actions right away. This is basically the equivalent of clicking the Run Now button on the Edit Timer Job screen in Central Administration. The PowerShell cmdlet that lets you achieve this is Start-SPTimerJob. All this method expects is the identity of the timer job that you wish to execute.

To demonstrate this method, we will use PowerShell to trigger the immediate execution of a SharePoint timer job, called "Delete Job History," which is set to execute on a weekly basis. The following code will automate this process. Figure 6-11 shows that the timer job executed properly.

```
$DeleteJobHistory = Get-SPTimerJob | Where{$_.DisplayName -eq "Delete Job History"}
Start-SPTimerJob -Identity $DeleteJobHistory
```

*Figure 6-11.* *Central Administration showing the execution of a timer job triggered by PowerShell*

## Managing Services

In the SharePoint world, there are over 30 associated services that run in parallel with the environment. These services control things like the search, the user profile synchronization, the sandboxed solutions, and so on. They can either run directly on one of the SharePoint web front-end servers or on a separate application server that is attached to the farm.

Many SharePoint service applications require that these services be started in the farm in order to execute properly. As an example, before you can configure the user profile synchronization on your farm, the service application requires you to have both the User Profile Service and the User Profile Synchronization Service started in your farm. Using PowerShell, there are several operations you can automate that will interact with these SharePoint services. In this section, you will learn how you can automate operations to obtain references to these services, and how to start and stop them.

## Getting a Reference to a Service Instance

A service instance represents the actual SharePoint service that you wish to interact with. Although there is only one entry for each service type in a farm (for example, only one User Profile Service entry), there can exist various instances, running on different servers. For example, if you have three servers in your farm, say servers A, B, and C, you can have both servers B and C run the Distributed Cache Service. There is, however, a maximum of one instance of a specific service running on each server at any given point. It is just that multiple servers can be used to run a service in a SharePoint farm.

To get a reference to a specific instance using PowerShell, we can use the Get-SPServiceInstance cmdlet. You will need to pass it either a GUID for your instance or the name of the server you wish to retrieve the instances from. In the latter case, you will be getting a list of all services on a specific server. The following code example will show you how you can use PowerShell to retrieve a list of all services instances that have been started in your SharePoint farm, no matter the server on which they are running. Figure 6-12 shows the result of running this line of code in the PowerShell Console, in a tabular format to make sure we view all information on the screen:

```
Get-SPServiceInstance | Where{$_.Status -eq "Online"} | Format-Table
```

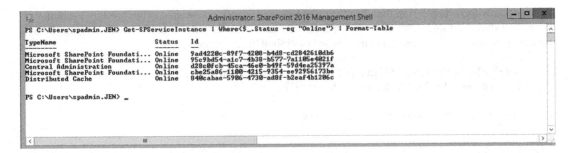

**Figure 6-12.** *Listing all enabled timer jobs in the SharePoint farm using PowerShell*

## Starting a SharePoint Service Instance

Once you've obtained a reference to a service instance using PowerShell, there are really only two main operations that you can perform on them. You can either enable them or disable them on a specific server. The PowerShell cmdlet used to enable a service instance on a SharePoint server is Start-SPServiceInstance. All this cmdlet expects as parameter is the identity of the instance to start. Remember that a service instance is unique to a server, meaning that the instance reference you obtain using the Get-SPServiceInstance already contains information about what server in the farm it's associated with. This means that there are no ways for you to specify to the Start-SPServiceInstance cmdlet what server to start a service on.

The following lines of PowerShell code will get a reference to the Visio Graphics Service on our main SharePoint Web Front-End (WIN-RBRR22MRAOR) and will start its instance. Figure 6-13 shows that the service instance has been properly started via the SharePoint 2016 Central Administration web interface.

```
$visioServiceInstance = Get-SPServiceInstance -Server "WIN-RBRR22MRAOR"
|Where{$_.TypeName -Eq "Visio Graphics Service"}

Start-SPServiceInstance $visioServiceInstance
```

| | | |
|---|---|---|
| SharePoint Server Search | Started | Stop |
| User Profile Service | Started | Stop |
| User Profile Synchronization Service | Started | Stop |
| Visio Graphics Service | Started | Stop |
| Word Automation Services | Stopped | Start |
| Work Management Service | Stopped | Start |

**Figure 6-13.** *Viewing the status of the Visio Graphics Service in Central Administration*

## Stopping a SharePoint Service Instance

The opposite process, the one in which you want to stop a service instance from running on a specific server, is in all respects similar to the process of starting it. The only different is that you need to call the Stop-SPServiceInstance cmdlet instead.

The following code will stop the Visio Graphics Service instance you started in the previous section. Figure 6-14 shows, through Central Administration, that the service instance is in the process of going back to its original stopped state after executing these PowerShell lines of code:

```
$visioServiceInstance = Get-SPServiceInstance -Server "WIN-RBRR22MRAOR" |
Where{$_.TypeName -Eq "Visio Graphics Service"}

Stop-SPServiceInstance $visioServiceInstance
```

| | | |
|---|---|---|
| User Profile Service | Started | Stop |
| User Profile Synchronization Service | Started | Stop |
| Visio Graphics Service | Stopping | |
| Word Automation Services | Stopped | Start |
| Work Management Service | Stopped | Start |

*Figure 6-14.* *Viewing a service instance in the process of being stopped*

# SharePoint Health Analyzer

The 2010 version of SharePoint has the concept of a health analyzer built into it. What this component does is run frequent checks on the farm's components to detect common issues that can impact the performance and the overall well-being of a SharePoint environment. These checks are called Health Analyzer rules, and they contain information about what to check in the SharePoint farm to detect anomalies and can even contain information about what corrective measures to take automatically if issues are detected. By default, SharePoint 2016 comes with several predefined Health Analyzer rules. You can define your own custom rules if you wish, but this topic is outside the scope of this book.

Health Analyzer rules, just like timer jobs, have an associated schedule. For example, the rule that checks to see if the databases indexes' statistics are out of date runs on a daily basis. Depending on the type of schedule a Health Analyzer rule is given, it will get executed by a specific timer job. Figure 6-15 shows a list of all timer jobs that are dedicated to the Health Analyzer engine of SharePoint. In this section, you will learn how to use PowerShell to interact with the SharePoint 2016 Health Analyzer component.

Health Analysis Job (Daily, Central Administration, All Servers)

Health Analysis Job (Daily, Central Administration, Any Server)

Health Analysis Job (Daily, Microsoft SharePoint Foundation Timer, All Servers)

Health Analysis Job (Daily, Microsoft SharePoint Foundation Timer, Any Server)

Health Analysis Job (Daily, Microsoft SharePoint Foundation Web Application, All Servers)

Health Analysis Job (Daily, Microsoft SharePoint Foundation Web Application, Any Server)

*Figure 6-15.* *A list of all Health Analyzer-related timer jobs viewed in Central Administration*

## Getting References to Health Analyzer Rules

You're probably starting to see a pattern here. The first topic we will cover in this section is how to get a reference to a Health Analyzer rule object so that you can extract information out of it. The PowerShell cmdlet you need to use to get such a reference is the Get-SPHealthAnalysisRule method. This cmdlet returns a list of all existing rules in your SharePoint farm.

The following PowerShell line of code will get that list and display the rule's name and its description in a tabular format on screen. Figure 6-16 shows a portion of the resulting table.

```
Get-SPHealthAnalysisRule | Format-Table -Property Name, Summary
```

*Figure 6-16.* *A list of all SharePoint Health Analysis rules returned by PowerShell*

## Disabling a SharePoint Health Analyzer Rule

To disable a Health Analyzer rule using PowerShell, you need to use the `Disable-SPHealthAnalysisRule` cmdlet. This method simply requires you to pass it a reference to the rule you wish to disable. Figure 6-17 shows the result of disabling the "Missing server side dependencies" rule.

```
# The code below uses the name of the rule, instead of the display name.
# These very often vary from one another.
$rule = Get-SPHealthAnalysisRule | Where{$_.Name -eq "ContentDatabaseCorruption"}

Disable-SPHealthAnalysisRule $rule
```

| | | | |
|---|---|---|---|
| BROWSE ITEMS LIST | | | |
| Application pools recycle when memory limits are exceeded. | Weekly | Yes | No |
| Databases used by SharePoint have fragmented indices. | Daily | Yes | Yes |
| Databases exist on servers running SharePoint Foundation. | Weekly | Yes | No |
| The paging file size should exceed the amount of physical RAM in the system. | Weekly | Yes | No |
| Databases used by SharePoint have outdated index statistics. | Daily | Yes | Yes |
| The timer service failed to recycle. | Weekly | Yes | No |
| Search - One or more crawl databases may have fragmented indices. | Daily | Yes | Yes |
| ◢ Category : **Configuration** (38) | | | |
| Alternate access URLs have not been configured. | Daily | Yes | No |
| The Application Discovery and Load Balancer Service is not running in this farm. | Hourly | Yes | No |
| Automatic Update setting inconsistent across farm servers. | Daily | Yes | No |
| Built-in accounts are used as application pool or service identities. | Weekly | Yes | No |
| Missing server side dependencies. | Weekly | No | No |
| Databases require upgrade or not supported. | Daily | Yes | No |
| Databases running in compatibility range, upgrade recommended. | Daily | Yes | No |
| One or more categories are configured with Verbose trace logging. | Daily | Yes | No |
| Outbound e-mail has not been configured. | Weekly | Yes | No |
| Product / patch installation or server upgrade required. | Daily | Yes | No |

*Figure 6-17. Viewing a disabled Health Analyzer rule in Central Administration*

## Enabling a SharePoint Health Analyzer Rule

The opposite operation, to enable a disabled rule, is simple enough: use the `Enable-SPHealthAnalysisRule` PowerShell cmdlet and pass it a reference to the rule object as a parameter. The following code will re-enable the "Missing server side dependencies" rule that you disabled in the previous section:

```
$rule=Get-SPHealthAnalysisRule|Where{$_.Name -eq "ContentDatabaseCorruption"}
Enable-SPHealthAnalysisRule $rule
```

# Summary

In this chapter, you have learned how to interact with the administrative components of a SharePoint 2016 farm using PowerShell. You learned how to use the scripting language to monitor certain aspects of your environment, and how to perform backups of your content and configurations. You have now covered all aspects of on-premises SharePoint management using PowerShell.

# CHAPTER 7

∎ ∎ ∎

# Upgrading from SharePoint 2013 to 2016 with PowerShell

Suppose your organization has a previous SharePoint farm version, and you would like to move the data to a new SharePoint 2016 farm. You have two paths:

- Upgrade your farm.

- Use a third-party tool.

This chapter will demonstrate the first approach, given that you have a 2013 farm.

The upgrade story has been a changing one between versions of SharePoint for the last decade. If you take a look back at SharePoint Portal Server 2003, you had three options for upgrading to SharePoint 2007. The first option was to do an in-place upgrade, which simply required you to put in the installation media, start the upgrade wizard, and pray for the best. Unfortunately, this didn't work well for customized SharePoint environments. The second option, called the gradual update, allowed you to run both SharePoint 2003 and 2007 side by side. The last option was to do what Microsoft calls a database attach. This basically involved starting by creating a new SharePoint farm running the desired version of SharePoint, in this case 2007, and attaching copies of your previous environment's content databases. In many cases, the third option was the preferred one. People often decided while upgrading the software that they might as well upgrade the hardware as well. From SharePoint 2007 to 2010, Microsoft dropped the option to do gradual upgrades, and decided to allow only database-attach and in-place upgrades. With SharePoint 2016, the only option left to upgrade from a previous version is to attach a database to a new SharePoint 2016 server and upgrade it from there using PowerShell.

In Table 7-1 you will find migrations paths.

*Table 7-1.* *Migration Paths*

| Steps | Source | Target | Upgrade approach |
|-------|--------|--------|------------------|
| 1 | MOSS 2007/WSS 3.0 | SharePoint 2010 | In Place upgrade or database attach upgrade or both |
| 2 | SharePoint 2010 | SharePoint 2013 | Database attach upgrade only |
| 3 | SharePoint 2013 | SharePoint 2016 | Database attach upgrade only |

© Nikolas Charlebois-Laprade and John Edward Naguib 2017
N. Charlebois-Laprade and J. E. Naguib, *Beginning PowerShell for SharePoint 2016*,
DOI 10.1007/978-1-4842-2884-5_7

Of course, there is no way to automate the upgrade process from beginning to end using PowerShell; however, you can use several cmdlets provided by SharePoint to help achieve your goal. This chapter is intended to be used as a quick reference guide for automating portions of your upgrade process. With the use of PowerShell, you will learn how to detect missing features in the new SharePoint 2016 farm, convert content databases to SharePoint 2016, create evaluation site collections to preview what the upgrade will look like, and finally, upgrade a site collection.

At the end of this chapter you will have learned how to create a PowerShell script to automate as much as possible the upgrade process of a SharePoint 2013 farm to SharePoint 2016.

Throughout this chapter we will use a demo environment that was built especially for demonstrating the upgrade process.

# Why Should I Upgrade?

This is an excellent question; each case has its business justifications. If your current environment is satisfying your business objectives, then it is good for you, but if you are lacking capabilities that could enhance your business and you are looking for more, then you should look into SharePoint 2016. Following are some of the main enhancements; if you need more details, see the following link:

```
https://technet.microsoft.com/en-us/library/mt346121%28v=office.16%29.aspx?f=255&MSPPErr
or=-2147217396
```

- Large file support: SharePoint Server 2016 now supports uploading and downloading files larger than 2,047 MB.

- Min Role: This new feature in SharePoint Server 2016 allows a SharePoint farm administrator to define each server's role in a farm topology.

- Zero down time while patching.

- Mobile Experience: SharePoint Server 2016 offers an improved mobile navigation experience.

- Hybrid: This feature in SharePoint Server 2016 enables you to integrate your on-premises farm with Office 365 productivity experiences, allowing you to adopt the cloud at your own pace.

- Durable links: Resource-based URLs now retain links when documents are renamed or moved in SharePoint.

# The Upgrade Process

The upgrade consists of the following broad steps :

1. Create a new SharePoint 2016 farm.

2. Make sure that your 2013 farm is updated as required to the SP2013+ service pack 1.

3. Copy databases to the new farm.

4. Upgrade service applications (in our example we will omit this stage).

5. Upgrade content databases and site collections.

# Overview of the Source Environment

For demonstration purposes, the SharePoint 2013 environment we are using is a simple one that has one content database. In almost any real-life scenario, your source 2013 environment will have more than one content database and various types of service applications.

You should note that only six types of service applications in SharePoint 2013 have an upgrade option for 2016. Those are:

- Business Data Connectivity

- Managed Metadata

- PerformancePoint Services

- Secure Store

- User Profile

- Search

For more information about upgrading existing service applications to SharePoint 2016, please refer to the following TechNet article:

```
https://technet.microsoft.com/en-us/library/ee731990(v=office.16).aspx
```

# Copying the Database to the New Farm

The simplest approach is to go to the SQL Server for the SharePoint 2013 farm and start making a backup of the database, and then copy it to the SharePoint 2016 farm as shown in Figure 7-1.

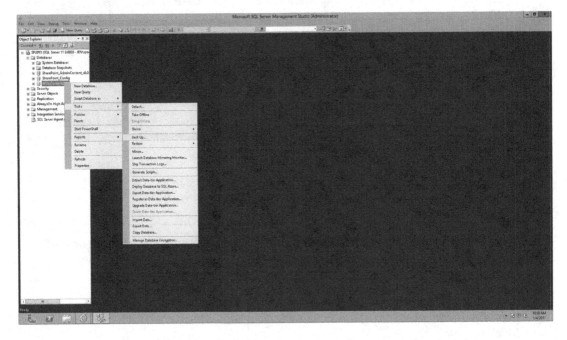

*Figure 7-1. SQL Server task to back up the database*

Then a dialog box will be opened, as shown in Figure 7-2.

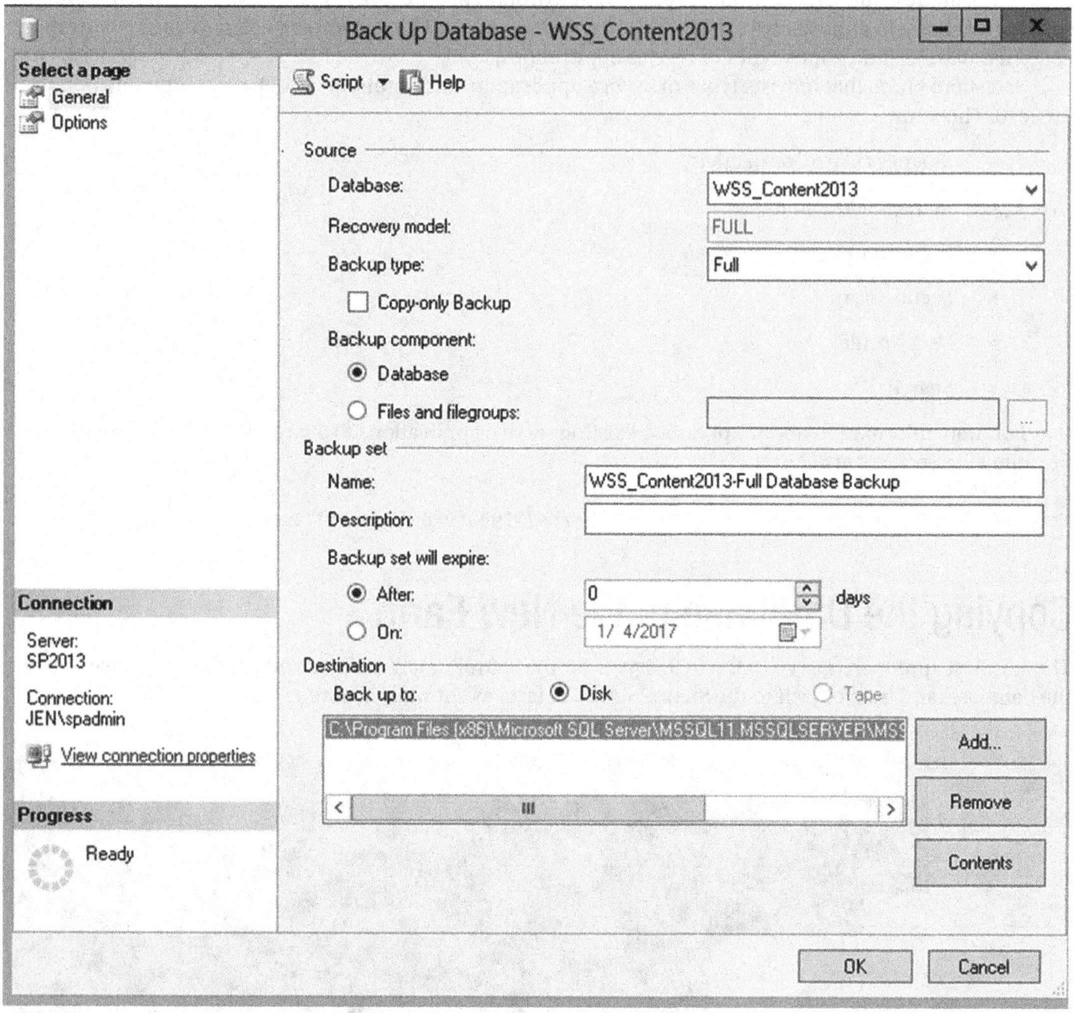

***Figure 7-2.*** *Backing up the database that will be migrated*

Then copy the files to the SharePoint 2016 SQL Server.

---

**Note**   It is better to set the database to read-only from the database properties and, when you restore it on the new farm, return to read/write to guarantee that nothing has changed.

---

# Restoring the Database to the New Farm

Open the SQL Server 2014 Management Studio on the SQL Server for the SharePoint 2016 Farm and then right -click Databases and select Restore Database as shown in Figure 7-3.

***Figure 7-3.*** *Restoring the database that will be migrated*

Then, as shown in Figure 7-4, select Device, click the ellipsis button to select the backup file, and then click OK.

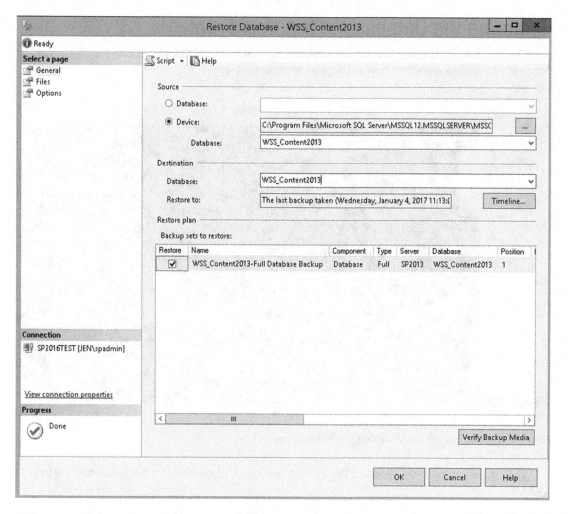

***Figure 7-4.*** *Restoring the the database that will be migrated from restore dialog*

The database is now available on SQL Server.

Notes:

- Make sure that the account you use to copy the databases has access to SQL Server Management Studio on both the SharePoint Server 2013 with Service Pack 1 (SP1) and SharePoint Server 2016 environments and has access to a network location that can be accessed from both environments to store the copies of the databases.

- Make sure that the account you use to set the databases to read-only and read/write is a member of the db_owner fixed database role for the content databases that you want to upgrade.

# Upgrading the Content Database

We have completed the database copy/restore process and attached to the new SharePoint 2016 farm. You now need to tell your new SharePoint 2016 about the new database and that it actually contains SharePoint content databases. To do so, call the `Mount-SPContentDatabase` PowerShell cmdlet. This cmdlet requires you to pass in the URL of a web application to link the content databases. For the purpose of this demonstration, create a new SharePoint web application on port 8333 (port number chosen randomly) using PowerShell, and attach the content databases to it. The following PowerShell script will automate this process:

```
$ap = New-SPAuthenticationProvider
$admin = Get-SPManagedAccount domain\admin

$webApp = New-SPWebApplication -Name "DemoWebApp" -URL "http://localhost:8333"
-ApplicationPool"DemoAppPool" -ApplicationPoolAccount $admin -AuthenticationProvider $ap

Mount-SPContentDatabase "ContentDB1" -webApplication http://localhost:8333
```

When you start running those commands, you will see a percentage of the database migrated until it reaches 100% as in Figure 7-5.

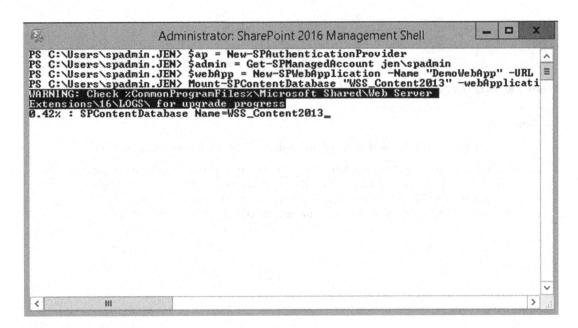

***Figure 7-5.*** *Mount migrated database to SharePoint 2016*

In Figure 7-6 the migration is completed and you can see that the new web application now contains one site collection that was migrated from SharePoint 2013.

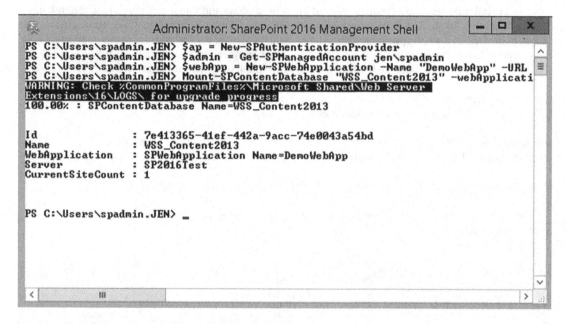

***Figure 7-6.*** *The database is migrated to SharePoint 2016.*

Notes:

- If you have a custom solution, make sure to deploy it before you mount the database.

- If you get error messages, to obtain more information related to what the actual error really is, you can have a look at the log file generated in the 16 hive. Another option is to use the `Test-SPContentDatabase` PowerShell cmdlet that will take a look at your partially mounted database and write the associated upgrade errors on screen.

Now if we browse to the `http://localhost:8333` we will get the site that was in the old SharePoint 2013 farm as shown in Figure 7-7.

**Figure 7-7.**  *The migrated site*

If you would like to test to be sure that no content database requires upgrade, you can run this command as shown in Figure 7-8.

```
Get-SPContentDatabase | ft -Auto Name, NeedsUpgradeIncludeChildren
```

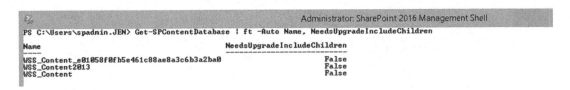

**Figure 7-8.**  *Testing whether the content databases need upgrade*

---

■ **Note**    You can Also use `Format-Table` instead of `FT`.

---

So now your farm has a migrated content database with one site collection as shown in Figure 7-9.

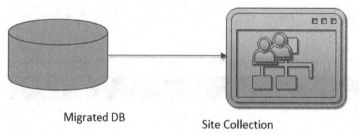

Migrated DB          Site Collection

***Figure 7-9.*** *Migrated content database and associated site collection*

You can also test the site collection upgrade status from Site Collection Administration by going to the site collection settings and clicking Site Collection Upgrade as shown in Figure 7-10.

***Figure 7-10.*** *Site collection settings*

This will open the screen shown in Figure 7-11.

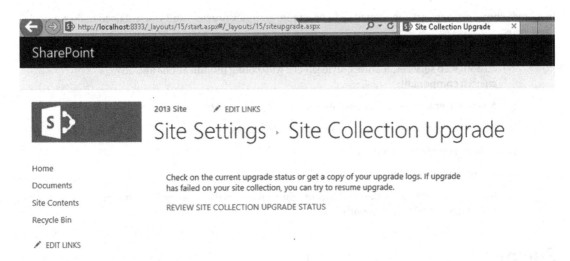

***Figure 7-11.*** *Site collection upgrade*

Then click Review Site Collection Upgrade Status to open the screen shown in Figure 7-12.

***Figure 7-12.*** *Site collection Upgrade status*

You will see that there are no errors, and upgrade completed successfully.

# Additional Steps

In a production environment, the upgrade will be a more complex process, and you will need to do some extra steps;

1.  Migrate customizations, like custom solution files, web parts, site definitions, custom web services, features, style sheets, web.config modifications and any custom component.

2.  Migrate user accounts to claims authentication if necessary.

3.  Update links that are used by InfoPath form templates.

4.  Migrate service applications.

5.  Perform a full crawl so that search will start working.

6.  It is also a good time to start looking into the app model if you are going to further customize or redevelop applications.

# Summary

This is it: you are now qualified to upgrade your organization's SharePoint 2013 environment to a brand-new shiny SharePoint 2016 one. You are now a PowerShell rock star! In this chapter, you learned how to upgrade to 2016 and you have automated its creation using PowerShell. It is important to remember that when you implement these upgrades, your users testing the upgraded environment should not put any business-critical information in them. Then, when the official upgrade process is initiated, only data contained in the original site collection will be brought over.

# CHAPTER 8

■ ■ ■

# Managing Office 365 SharePoint Online with PowerShell

As the title says, this chapter is about teaching you how to use PowerShell to manage your SharePoint Online instance in Office 365. We will not be covering the Exchange and Lync aspects of Office 365 in this chapter. It is assumed that readers have already had some level of exposure to the maintenance of site collections in Office 365. In October 2010, Microsoft announced a new wave of online products that was going to be taking their Office suite to the cloud. This new service was going to let users manage their own SharePoint 2010 instances in a multitenant environment. For the sake of clarity, we will use the term SharePoint Online to refer to the SharePoint offering side of Office 365.

Microsoft had attempted in early 2009 to launch the ancestor of SharePoint Online, called Business Productivity Online Services (BPOS). This is one author's opinion (one that we know is shared by all of our SharePoint colleagues), but BPOS was a disaster. The service offered highly restrictive SharePoint 2007 environments to users, who could not do any significant level of customization to their site collections. Of course, Microsoft offered users the choice to buy a license for a dedicated online server instance, but the prices for those licenses were just ridiculous. Things got a lot better with Office 365. For barely $10 a month per user, you could create both a hosted collaborative SharePoint 2010 environment for your organization and also have a public site collection to expose to the outside world as your corporate web site. On top of this, for a few additional dollars monthly came all the Office client license benefits, which, for us, was simply icing on the cake.

Then, at the beginning of 2013, Microsoft announced that it was going to upgrade all SharePoint online farms to run SharePoint 2013, or to whatever the latest version of SharePoint was. We say this because even today, if you look at the configuration link files on the Office 365 servers, you see that they are running SharePoint version 16 dot something, and SharePoint 2013 was always labelled version 15. The important point is that with this new cloud offering, Microsoft ensures that users will always be running the latest and greatest version of its platform.

In summer of 2012, Microsoft announced something called the SharePoint Online Management Shell, which allowed users to configure and interact with their SharePoint online instances remotely using PowerShell. Of course, Microsoft could not make all the same cmdlets that you have on premises to interact with SharePoint available on the cloud. Remember that SharePoint Online is a multitenant environment and that there are several users on the same farm. Therefore, they needed to ensure that whatever cmdlets they made available were not able to go over the site-collection boundaries. This chapter will be all about using the SharePoint Online Management Shell to interact with your SharePoint Online environment.

© Nikolas Charlebois-Laprade and John Edward Naguib 2017
N. Charlebois-Laprade and J. E. Naguib, *Beginning PowerShell for SharePoint 2016*,
DOI 10.1007/978-1-4842-2884-5_8

# Overview of the Environment

Throughout this chapter, we will be using an Office 365 trial account that we've created. The trial account uses the Microsoft Office 365 E3 plan, which offers 30 days of free use. The account that we've created uses a custom subdomain that one of us registered when creating his trial registration. The domain that we will use in this chapter is PoShSP2016.onmicrosoft.com. The environment has been created from scratch and contains only the default SharePoint site collections created by Microsoft on provision of a new Office 365 account. Figure 8-1 shows the site collection made available by default using the SharePoint admin center of Office 365.

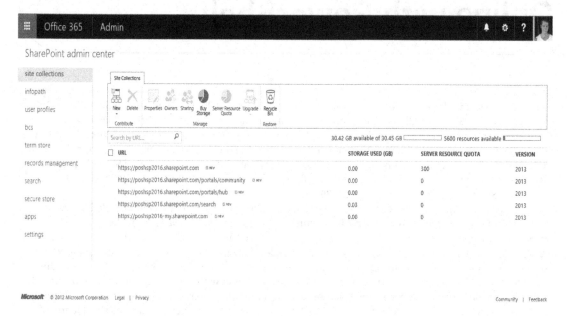

***Figure 8-1.*** *Default site collections viewed in the Office 365 SharePoint admin center*

# SharePoint Online Management Shell

As mentioned earlier in this chapter, Microsoft released a tool to help to manage SharePoint Online instances remotely using PowerShell. To be able to use it, you will need to go to Microsoft's site and download and install it locally. The tool can be downloaded from http://www.microsoft.com/en-us/download/details.aspx?id=35588. On the site, upon trying to download the tool, you will be prompted to choose between the 32--and 64-bit versions of the tool. Choose the appropriate version for your machine. In our case we are using a 64-bit operating system to run the tool. Upon running the installation executable, you will be prompted to accept the License Agreement. Simply check the "I accept the terms in the License Agreement" option and click Install (see Figure 8-2).

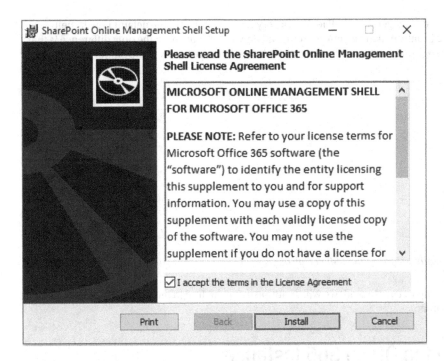

*Figure 8-2. SharePoint Online Management Shell Setup*

The installation process should take about 30 seconds to complete on most computers. Once the installation is completed, simply click Finish to close the executable.

Once the tool is installed on your system, you can open a new instance of it. The easiest way to identify where the tool is located on your computer is to do a search. Assuming you have installed the tool on a desktop operating system running Windows 8 or higher (this trick also works for Windows Server 2012 R2), simply press the Windows key on your keyboard and start typing **SharePoint Online Management Shell**. A shortcut to the application should be returned by your search. If you are not able to find the application using this method, you can simply launch a new PowerShell console (or in our case the Integrated Script Editor) and input the following line of PowerShell code to load the SharePoint Online Management module within your new PowerShell session (see Figure 8-3):

```
Import-Module Microsoft.Online.SharePoint.PowerShell -DisableNameChecking
```

*Figure 8-3. Loading the Microsoft.Online.SharePoint.PowerShell module using PowerShell*

The SharePoint Online Management Shell looks in every respect similar to the default PowerShell console. It uses the same profile, making it generic across all PowerShell consoles; the only difference is that you're not allowed to change the console's title. Figure 8-4 shows the default view of the SharePoint Online Management Shell.

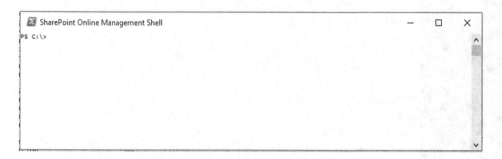

**Figure 8-4.** *SharePoint Online Management Shell console*

To keep the code examples easy to read, we will continue using the Integrated Script Editor throughout the remainder of this chapter.

# Connecting to the Office 365 Instance

The first thing to do once you have the management shell set up is, obviously, to connect to your remote Office 365 instance. The management shell offers a new cmdlet named Connect-SPOService that allows you to connect remotely to the Office 365 SharePoint Online service. Every PowerShell session that wants to interact with Office 365 must first authenticate using this method. In this example, you will use this cmdlet to connect to your environment with the following PowerShell line:

```
Connect-SPOService -URL https://PoShSP2016-admin.sharepoint.com -Credential  PoShSP2016@
PoSHSP2016.onmicrosoft.com
```

In this line, the URL parameter is the root of the SharePoint admin center for your Office 365 account, in which the credentials used are the credentials of a user with administrator rights on the SharePoint Online instance. Calling this PowerShell code will automatically prompt the user for their credentials (see Figure 8-5).

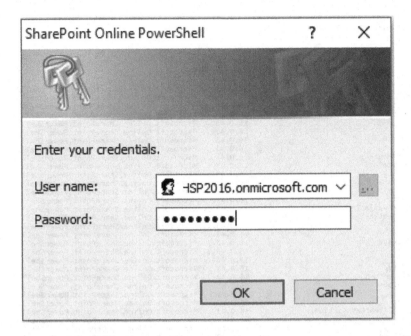

***Figure 8-5.*** *SharePoint Online Management Shell prompting for user's credentials upon authenticating*

Enter your credentials as requested, and click OK. It may take a few seconds for the management shell to properly authenticate you with Office 365. Once the authentication has been successful, you will be returned to the management shell and allowed to type in new commands.

# Listing Available Commands

This is more of a refresher, but just as you did for on-premises PowerShell, you can generate a list of all available cmdlets in the online shell by using the Get-Command cmdlet. However, simply calling this command without any filters will return a list of well over 1,000 items, including all the basic PowerShell cmdlets that are not specific to SharePoint. What you want to do is filter this list to show only the cmdlets that pertain to SharePoint. The module that contains all of the SharePoint Online PowerShell cmdlets is named Microsoft.Online.SharePoint.PowerShell. Using this information, you can produce a query that will filter the list of all commands to only return the ones related to what you want. The following lines of PowerShell will allow us to achieve just that:

```
$spo = Get-Command |
Where{$_.ModuleName -eq "Microsoft.Online.SharePoint.PowerShell"}
```

With this command, you've captured all SharePoint Online–related cmdlets into a PowerShell variable named $spo. Getting the Count property of this variable will tell you that there are currently 41 cmdlets available to manage SharePoint Online. Note that because this is a cloud environment, this number is subject to change at any time given that Microsoft has frequent releases for the online platform. The rest of this chapter will give you an overview of each of these 41 online cmdlets. To display a list of all available cmdlets in the SharePoint Online Management Shell, simply make a call into the $spo variable we've just obtained values for (see Figure 8-6).

```
PS C:\> $spo = Get-Command |
Where{$_.ModuleName -eq "Microsoft.Online.SharePoint.PowerShell"}

PS C:\> $spo

CommandType    Name                                        Version   Source ·
-----------    ----                                        -------   ------
Cmdlet         Add-SPOUser                                 16.0.43... Microsoft.Online.SharePoint.PowerShell
Cmdlet         Connect-SPOService                          16.0.43... Microsoft.Online.SharePoint.PowerShell
Cmdlet         ConvertTo-SPOMigrationTargetedPackage       16.0.43... Microsoft.Online.SharePoint.PowerShell
Cmdlet         Disconnect-SPOService                       16.0.43... Microsoft.Online.SharePoint.PowerShell
Cmdlet         Get-SPOAppErrors                            16.0.43... Microsoft.Online.SharePoint.PowerShell
Cmdlet         Get-SPOAppInfo                              16.0.43... Microsoft.Online.SharePoint.PowerShell
Cmdlet         Get-SPODeletedSite                          16.0.43... Microsoft.Online.SharePoint.PowerShell
Cmdlet         Get-SPOExternalUser                         16.0.43... Microsoft.Online.SharePoint.PowerShell
Cmdlet         Get-SPOMigrationJobProgress                 16.0.43... Microsoft.Online.SharePoint.PowerShell
Cmdlet         Get-SPOMigrationJobStatus                   16.0.43... Microsoft.Online.SharePoint.PowerShell
Cmdlet         Get-SPOSite                                 16.0.43... Microsoft.Online.SharePoint.PowerShell
Cmdlet         Get-SPOSiteGroup                            16.0.43... Microsoft.Online.SharePoint.PowerShell
Cmdlet         Get-SPOTenant                               16.0.43... Microsoft.Online.SharePoint.PowerShell
Cmdlet         Get-SPOTenantLogEntry                       16.0.43... Microsoft.Online.SharePoint.PowerShell
Cmdlet         Get-SPOTenantLogLastAvailableTimeInUtc      16.0.43... Microsoft.Online.SharePoint.PowerShell
Cmdlet         Get-SPOTenantSyncClientRestriction          16.0.43... Microsoft.Online.SharePoint.PowerShell
Cmdlet         Get-SPOUser                                 16.0.43... Microsoft.Online.SharePoint.PowerShell
Cmdlet         Get-SPOWebTemplate                          16.0.43... Microsoft.Online.SharePoint.PowerShell
Cmdlet         New-SPOMigrationPackage                     16.0.43... Microsoft.Online.SharePoint.PowerShell
Cmdlet         New-SPOSite                                 16.0.43... Microsoft.Online.SharePoint.PowerShell
Cmdlet         New-SPOSiteGroup                            16.0.43... Microsoft.Online.SharePoint.PowerShell
Cmdlet         Remove-SPODeletedSite                       16.0.43... Microsoft.Online.SharePoint.PowerShell
Cmdlet         Remove-SPOExternalUser                      16.0.43... Microsoft.Online.SharePoint.PowerShell
Cmdlet         Remove-SPOMigrationJob                      16.0.43... Microsoft.Online.SharePoint.PowerShell
Cmdlet         Remove-SPOSite                              16.0.43... Microsoft.Online.SharePoint.PowerShell
Cmdlet         Remove-SPOSiteGroup                         16.0.43... Microsoft.Online.SharePoint.PowerShell
Cmdlet         Remove-SPOTenantSyncClientRestriction       16.0.43... Microsoft.Online.SharePoint.PowerShell
Cmdlet         Remove-SPOUser                              16.0.43... Microsoft.Online.SharePoint.PowerShell
Cmdlet         Repair-SPOSite                              16.0.43... Microsoft.Online.SharePoint.PowerShell
Cmdlet         Request-SPOPersonalSite                     16.0.43... Microsoft.Online.SharePoint.PowerShell
Cmdlet         Request-SPOUpgradeEvaluationSite            16.0.43... Microsoft.Online.SharePoint.PowerShell
Cmdlet         Restore-SPODeletedSite                      16.0.43... Microsoft.Online.SharePoint.PowerShell
Cmdlet         Set-SPOMigrationPackageAzureSource          16.0.43... Microsoft.Online.SharePoint.PowerShell
Cmdlet         Set-SPOSite                                 16.0.43... Microsoft.Online.SharePoint.PowerShell
Cmdlet         Set-SPOSiteGroup                            16.0.43... Microsoft.Online.SharePoint.PowerShell
Cmdlet         Set-SPOTenant                               16.0.43... Microsoft.Online.SharePoint.PowerShell
Cmdlet         Set-SPOTenantSyncClientRestriction          16.0.43... Microsoft.Online.SharePoint.PowerShell
Cmdlet         Set-SPOUser                                 16.0.43... Microsoft.Online.SharePoint.PowerShell
Cmdlet         Submit-SPOMigrationJob                      16.0.43... Microsoft.Online.SharePoint.PowerShell
Cmdlet         Test-SPOSite                                16.0.43... Microsoft.Online.SharePoint.PowerShell
Cmdlet         Upgrade-SPOSite                             16.0.43... Microsoft.Online.SharePoint.PowerShell

PS C:\> |
```

*Figure 8-6.* *Listing all PowerShell cmdlets in the SharePoint Online Management Shell*

# SharePoint Online Cmdlets

The following section details the main cmdlets that are available to you in the cloud and provides some examples of real-life scenarios in which you may have to use them to manage your SharePoint Online instances. They are grouped by the type of SharePoint artifacts they interact with. PowerShell cmdlets that are related to the Office 365 Migration API are omitted from this chapter and will be covered in Chapter 10.

## Site Collections

PowerShell has a total of 11 cmdlets that are available to interact with SharePoint Online site collections. In the context of SharePoint Online, the PowerShell object that represents a site collection is called an SPOSite object.

# Get-SPOSite

The Get-SPOSite cmdlet returns a reference to a SharePoint Online site collection. As mentioned earlier, the object returned by this method is an SPOSite object as opposed to an SPSite object for an on-premises site collection. Because this object exposes a different type of SharePoint artifact than the on-premises object, the properties exposed by it are also different. The following short PowerShell script loops through each property of a SPOSite object and prints its value on screen. The script will prompt the user to enter the URL to one of its SharePoint Online site collections, will get a reference to it, and will query its members to obtain the list of available properties. The script then loops through each of these properties obtained, and prints both its name and its value on screen. Figure 8-7 shows the execution of this PowerShell script against our public-facing site collection.

```
$url = Read-Host "What is your Site's Url"
$site = Get-SPOSite $url

$members = $site | Get-Member | Where{$_.MemberType -eq "Property"}
for($i = 0; $i -lt $members.Count; $i++)
{
        $name = $members[$i].Name
        Write-Host $name":" $site.$name
}
```

```
PS C:\> $url = Read-Host "What is your Site's Url"
$site = Get-SPOSite $url

$members = $site | Get-Member | Where{$_.MemberType -eq "Property"}
for($i = 0; $i -lt $members.Count; $i++)
{|
    $name = $members[$i].Name
    Write-Host $name":" $site.$name
}

What is your Site's Url: https://PoShSP2016.SharePoint.com
AllowSelfServiceUpgrade: False
CompatibilityLevel: 0
DenyAddAndCustomizePages: Unknown
DisableSharingForNonOwnersStatus:
LastContentModifiedDate: 0001-01-01 00:00:00
LocaleId: 1033
LockIssue:
LockState: UnLock
Owner:
PWAEnabled: Unknown
ResourceQuota: 300
ResourceQuotaWarningLevel: 255
ResourceUsageAverage: 0
ResourceUsageCurrent: 0
SandboxedCodeActivationCapability: Unknown
SharingCapability: ExternalUserAndGuestSharing
Status: Active
StorageQuota: 1000
StorageQuotaWarningLevel: 0
StorageUsageCurrent: 0
Template: EHS#1
Title:
Url: https://poshsp2016.sharepoint.com/
WebsCount: 0

PS C:\>
```

*Figure 8-7. SPOSite properties and their values for your SharePoint Online public-facing site collection*

By default, Office 365 creates five site collections for each Enterprise-level account. Table 8-1 shows the site collection template ID used for each of these four site collections for your demo account.

***Table 8-1.*** *Default SharePoint Online Site Collections and Their Associated Site Template IDs*

| Site Collection | URL | Template ID |
| --- | --- | --- |
| **Intranet** | `https://PoShSP2016.sharepoint.com` | EHS#1 |
| **Search Center** | `https://PoShSP2016.sharepoint.com/search` | SRCHCEN#0 |
| **My Site Host** | `https://PoShSP2016-my.sharepoint.com` | SPSMSITEHOST#0 |
| **Community Portal** | `https://PoShSP2016.sharepoint.com/portals/community` | POINTPUBLISHINGTOPIC#0 |
| **Portal Hub (Office 365 Video)** | `https://PoShSP2016.sharepoint.com/hub` | POINTPUBLISHINGHUB#0 |

It is important to note that although the Search Center and My Site Host templates are also available on-premises, the two site-collection templates used for the SharePoint Online Intranet site collections are new templates that are exclusive to Office 365.

# New-SPOSite

The `New-SPOSite` cmdlet lets you create a new SharePoint Online site collection. This PowerShell cmdlet takes three mandatory parameters to execute: a URL for the new site collection, the username of the Office 365 user that will be its owner, and a storage quota. You're probably wondering why you're not passing the site collection's template ID as a parameter. Actually, although this is not a mandatory parameter, you can still pass it to the cmdlet. If you omit it, your SharePoint Online will force you to select a template the first time you try to access your new site collection. Figure 8-8 shows the prompt that a user gets the first time he or she accesses a site collection in SharePoint Online for which no default site collection template has been chosen.

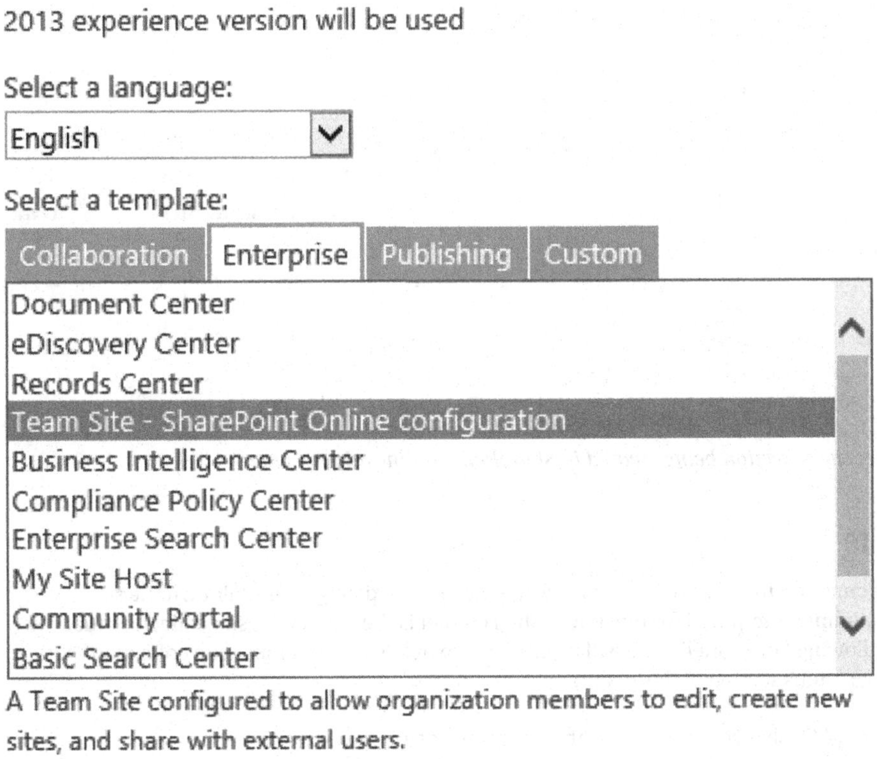

2013 experience version will be used

Select a language:

| English ⌄ |
|---|

Select a template:

| Collaboration | Enterprise | Publishing | Custom |
|---|---|---|---|

Document Center
eDiscovery Center
Records Center
**Team Site - SharePoint Online configuration**
Business Intelligence Center
Compliance Policy Center
Enterprise Search Center
My Site Host
Community Portal
Basic Search Center

A Team Site configured to allow organization members to edit, create new sites, and share with external users.

*Figure 8-8. SharePoint Online prompting user to select a site collection template*

Remember that we're developers at heart, and so, to us, something is always missing in the default offering of site collections in SharePoint Online. The beauty of Office 365 is that it lets developers create their own sandbox to develop custom business apps and test them in the cloud. The online service offering gives the user the choice to create a developer's site collection, which is invaluable to any organization wanting to do testing for their SharePoint 2013 apps. The first thing we always do when registering a new Office 365 account is connect to its SharePoint Online portal and create such a site collection. The following few lines of PowerShell show how you can get started and automatically create such a site collection using PowerShell. The code shown here will automatically create a new developer site collection in your PowerShell SharePoint Online account. Figure 8-9 shows the new site collection being created in the SharePoint Online admin center. It normally takes a minute or two after the creation process has been initiated by PowerShell for the SharePoint Online site collection to be entirely created.

```
New-SPOSite -URL https://PoShSP2016.sharepoint.com/sites/dev -Owner PoShSP2016@PoShSP2016.
OnMicrosoft.com -StorageQuota 500 -Template DEV#0
```

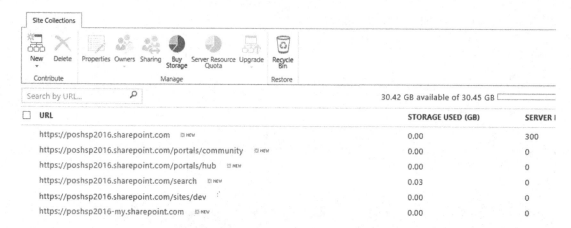

***Figure 8-9.*** *Developer site collection being created in SharePoint Online admin center*

## Remove-SPOSite

The `Remove-SPOSite` cmdlet is to be used when you wish to delete an existing SharePoint Online site collection. The only parameter required for this PowerShell cmdlet is the URL to the site collection that you wish to delete. The following PowerShell code will prompt you to delete the developer site collection that you've created in the previous section of this chapter:

```
Remove-SPOSite https://PoShSP2016.sharepoint.com/sites/dev
```

Once you confirm your choice to delete the site collection, it will automatically be removed from your Office 365 SharePoint Online account.

## Repair-SPOSite

This SharePoint Online cmdlet is a special one. You can call `Repair-SPOSite` against a single site collection or a group of them in your SharePoint Online account, and it will run all health analyzer rules against them. If it encounters any errors, it automatically attempts to fix them. This operation is not available through the web interface of the SharePoint Online admin center; you must use the SharePoint Online Management Shell to use it. Although there is no real need for Office 365 clients to use this cmdlet at the moment, it was probably one of the most widely used cmdlets by the Microsoft team when they had to upgrade millions of tenants from SharePoint 2010 to SharePoint 2013 back in the spring of 2013. When the next version of SharePoint Online appears, there may be some future need for this cmdlet. Figure 8-10 shows the result of running this cmdlet against your demo intranet site.

```
Repair-SPOSite https://PoShSP2016.sharepoint.com
```

```
                                                                                    Script ⊙
PS C:\> Repair-SPOSite https://PoShSP2016.sharepoint.com

SiteUrl            : https://PoShSP2016.sharepoint.com
Results            : {
                       SPSiteHealthResult Status=Passed RuleName="Conflicting Content Types"
                       RuleId=befe203b-a8c0-48c2-b5f0-27c10f9e1622,
                       SPSiteHealthResult Status=Passed RuleName="Customized Files" RuleId=cd839b0d-9707-4950-8fac-f306cb920f6c,
                       SPSiteHealthResult Status=Passed RuleName="Missing Galleries"
                       RuleId=ee967197-ccbe-4c00-88e4-e6fab81145e1,
                       SPSiteHealthResult Status=Passed RuleName="Missing Parent Content Types"
                       RuleId=a9a6769f-7289-4b9f-ae7f-5db4b997d284...}
PassedCount        : 7
FailedWarningCount : 0
FailedErrorCount   : 0


PS C:\> |
```

***Figure 8-10.*** *Running the repair site collection PowerShell cmdlet against a SharePoint Online site collection*

# Set-SPOSite

Suppose you want to use PowerShell to modify a property of an existing site collection, such as its title. Your normal reaction may be to use the Get-SPOSite PowerShell cmdlet to get a reference to the site collection, and then to set its Title property to whatever you wish. The big problem with this approach using SharePoint Online is that an SPOSite object does not expose the Update method that is normally used to commit changes on SharePoint artifacts back to the database. Therefore, simply getting a reference to the site collection and setting the value of one of its properties is not going to work. This is where the Set-SPOSite cmdlet comes to the rescue. This cmdlet lets you specify what property of a SPOSite object you wish to set, and in the background it secretly calls the Update method on the object. The following code shows how you can use PowerShell to set the title of your internal SharePoint Online site. Figure 8-11 shows the result of executing this line of PowerShell code.

```
Set-SPOSite https://PoShSP2016.sharepoint.com -Title "This is me showing the Set-SPOSite cmdlet"
```

***Figure 8-11.*** *Internal SharePoint Online site collection's root web title changed using PowerShell*

There are several other properties that can be modified using this method. Table 8-2 lists all of the properties of a SharePoint Online site collection that can be set using this PowerShell cmdlet.

**Table 8-2.** *SharePoint Online Site Collection Properties That Can Be Modified Using PowerShell*

| Property Name | Description |
|---|---|
| AllowSelfServiceUpgrade | True or false to specify if a site collection administrator is allowed to upgrade its site collection or not. |
| DenyAddAndCustomizePages | Enables or disables the option for users to customize pages on the site collection. |
| LocaleId | Specifies the locale ID of the language to use for the site collection. |
| LockState | Sets a lock on a site collection. Available values are:<br>NoAccess—Redirects user to a specific URL<br>Unlock—Users access the site normally. |
| Owner | Sets the owner of the specified site collection. |
| ResourceQuota | Specifies a resource quota in megabytes for the site collection. |
| ResourceQuotaWarningLevel | Specifies the warning level in megabytes that, when reached, notifies the site collection administrator that the site collection is approaching its maximum resource quota. |
| SandboxedCodeActivationCapability | Determines whether sandboxed solutions are enabled or disabled for the given site collection. |
| StorageQuota | Specifies a storage quota in megabytes for the site collection. |
| StorageQuotaWarningLevel | Specifies the warning level in megabytes that, when reached, notifies the site collection administrator that the site collection is approaching its maximum storage quota. |
| Title | Specifies the title of the site collection. |

## Test-SPOSite

The Test-SPOSite cmdlet does the same thing as the Repair-SPOSite cmdlet, but it doesn't actually commit the changes. Using it has the same result as calling the Repair-SPOSite using the -WhatIf switch, which also won't commit the results of the operation.

## Upgrade-SPOSite

Just as was the case for the test and repair functions, the upgrade cmdlet for SharePoint Online site collections has already served its purpose, and tenants won't have to use it anymore. It was heavily used by the Microsoft team when upgrading tenant site collections from SharePoint 2010 to SharePoint 2013. If you try to call this PowerShell cmdlet against any of your existing site collections, you will simply get a notification message saying that the site has already been updated and that it does not need to be updated (see Figure 8-12).

```
PS C:\> Upgrade-SPOSite https://PoShSP2016.sharepoint.com
WARNING: Site [Microsoft.SharePoint.Client.Site] does not need to be upgraded.

PS C:\> |
```

*Figure 8-12.* *SharePoint Online Management Shell printing notification on screen that site collection is not upgradable*

## Request-SPOUpgradeEvaluationSite

The Request-SPOUpgradeEvaluationSite PowerShell cmdlet lets a user request a temporary Upgrade Evaluation site collection in Office 365. This method was mostly used when Office 365 tenants were given the option to upgrade from their original SharePoint 2010 site collections to the new SharePoint 2013 collections. Now that every new tenant is automatically given a 2013 environment, the use for this cmdlet is slowing disappearing. Making calls to this cmdlet doesn't do anything in our system (see Figure 8-13). No upgrade evaluation sites will ever be triggered for site collections that are already running in compatibility mode.

```
PS C:\> Request-SPOUpgradeEvaluationSite https://PoShSP2016.sharepoint.com
Request-SPOUpgradeEvaluationSite :
        Cannot create an upgrade evaluation site for site https://poshsp2016.sharepoint.com. It is on
version 15. Upgrade evaluation sites are only available for sites that are on version 14. Database
Schema major version: 16",

At line:1 char:1
+ Request-SPOUpgradeEvaluationSite https://PoShSP2016.sharepoint.com
+ ~~~~~~~~~~~~~~~~~~~~~~~~~~~~~~~~~~~~~~~~~~~~~~~~~~~~~~~~~~~~~~~~~~~~~
    + CategoryInfo          : NotSpecified: (:) [Request-SPOUpgradeEvaluationSite], ServerException
    + FullyQualifiedErrorId : Microsoft.SharePoint.Client.ServerException,Microsoft.Online.SharePoint.P
   owerShell.RequestUpgradeEvalSite

PS C:\>
```

*Figure 8-13.* *Error requesting a SharePoint Online Upgrade evaluation site collection using PowerShell*

## Get-SPODeletedSite

Just as with SharePoint on-premises, site collections that have been deleted through the web interface are given a second shot at life. One major difference in the online world, however, is that in Office 365, all SharePoint site collections that have been deleted through PowerShell are sent to the Recycle Bin. The SharePoint Online admin center allows you to view deleted site collections by clicking the Recycle Bin button in the management ribbon (see Figure 8-14).

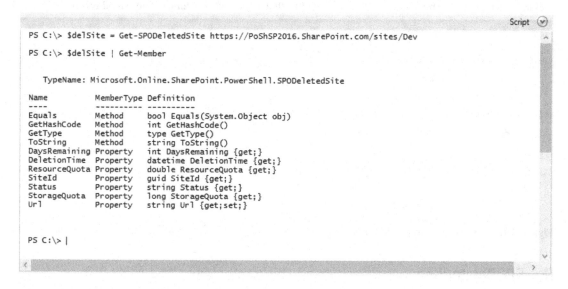

*Figure 8-14. Recycle bin in the SharePoint Online admin center*

The Get-SPODeletedSite PowerShell cmdlet takes a unique parameter, the URL of the deleted site collection to which you wish to obtain a reference. A deleted site collection in SharePoint Online is represented by the SPODeletedSite object. Figure 8-15 shows how you can obtain a reference to the developer site collection that you've deleted previously, and it displays all the methods and properties exposed by this object.

```
                                                                      Script ⌄
PS C:\> $delSite = Get-SPODeletedSite https://PoShSP2016.SharePoint.com/sites/Dev

PS C:\> $delSite | Get-Member


    TypeName: Microsoft.Online.SharePoint.PowerShell.SPODeletedSite

Name           MemberType Definition
----           ---------- ----------
Equals         Method     bool Equals(System.Object obj)
GetHashCode    Method     int GetHashCode()
GetType        Method     type GetType()
ToString       Method     string ToString()
DaysRemaining  Property   int DaysRemaining {get;}
DeletionTime   Property   datetime DeletionTime {get;}
ResourceQuota  Property   double ResourceQuota {get;}
SiteId         Property   guid SiteId {get;}
Status         Property   string Status {get;}
StorageQuota   Property   long StorageQuota {get;}
Url            Property   string Url {get;set;}


PS C:\> |
```

*Figure 8-15. Getting a reference to a deleted site collection in SharePoint Online and listing its available properties and methods using PowerShell*

## Restore-SPODeletedSite

The Restore-SPODeletedSite PowerShell cmdlet restores a deleted site collection to life. While they are in the Recycle Bin, site collections are no longer accessible through the browser. Restoring a deleted site collection puts it back in the list of available site collections in the SharePoint Online admin center. The Restore-SPODeletedSite cmdlet simply takes the URL of the site collection that you wish to restore from the Recycle Bin. The process of restoring a deleted site collection converts the SPODeletedSite object back to a

SPOSite object. For example, if we wanted to restore our deleted Dev site collection, we would simply need to execute the following line of PowerShell.

```
Restore-SPODeletedSite https://PoShSP2016.SharePoint.com/sites/Dev
```

## Remove-SPODeletedSite

Remove-SPODeletedSite takes a site collection that has been previously deleted and that is patiently waiting in the Recycle Bin, and makes it disappear permanently. Once a site collection has been removed from the Recycle Bin, it is no longer restorable; it's gone. One very interesting fact is that in SharePoint Online, there is no way for an administrator using the web interface to force the deletion of a site collection from the Recycle Bin. Site collections that have been deleted in Office 365 are given a 30-day grace period during which administrators can reverse their decision and restore them. If after these 30 days the site collections are still in the Recycle Bin, SharePoint Online will automatically remove them permanently. Using PowerShell is the only way for an administrator to force an immediate permanent deletion of a site collection. The following line of PowerShell will take the developer site that you've deleted previously and permanently delete it from this world. Figure 8-16 shows the permanent removal of your developer site using PowerShell.

```
Remove-SPODeletedSite https://PoShSP2016.sharepoint.com/sites/dev
```

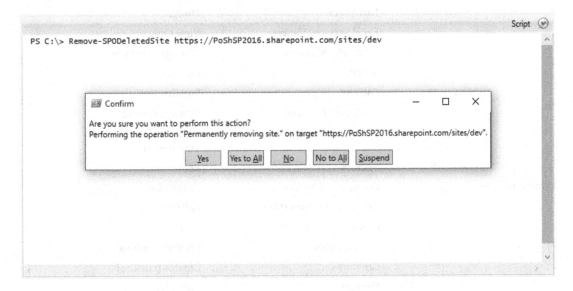

***Figure 8-16.*** *Permanently deleting a site collection from SharePoint Online using PowerShell*

## SPOSiteGroup

This section covers the various PowerShell cmdlets that are available in the SharePoint Online Management Shell console to manage site collection security groups. SharePoint Online includes default security groups that vary from the default ones that you have on-premises.

# Get-SPOSiteGroup

The Get-SPOSiteGroup PowerShell cmdlet displays a list of all existing security groups for a specific site collection. The default security groups in each site collection vary. Table 8-3 lists the various default security groups in each, along with their default permissions.

***Table 8-3.*** *Default Security Groups and Their Permissions in Office 365*

| Site Collection | Security Group | Permissions |
|---|---|---|
| Intranet | Excel Services Viewers | View Only |
| | Team Site Members | Edit |
| | Team Site Owners | Full Control |
| | Team Site Visitors | Read |
| My Site | Members | Contribute |
| | Owners | Full Control |
| | Visitors | Read |
| Search Center | Approvers | Approve |
| | Designers | Design |
| | Excel Services Viewer | View Only |
| | Hierarchy Managers | Manage Hierarchy |
| | Members | Contribute |
| | Owners | Full Control |
| | Restricted Readers | Restricted Read |
| | Translation Managers | Restricted Interfaces for Translation |
| | Visitors | Read |
| Community Portal | Community Members | Contribute |
| | Community Owners | Full Control |
| | Community Visitors | Read |
| | Contributors | Contributor (custom) |
| | Creators | Creator (custom) |
| | Viewers | Viewer (custom) |
| Community Hub | PointPublishing Hub Site Members | Contribute |
| | PointPublishing Hub Site Owners | Full Control |
| | PointPublishing Hub Site Visitors | Read |
| | Contributors | Contributor (custom) |
| | Creators | Creator (custom) |
| | Viewers | Viewers (custom) |

You can obtain the permission level associated with each site collection security group by accessing the Roles property of a group. The following example shows how you can determine the permission level associated with the Translation Managers group of our default Search Center site collection (see Figure 8-17).

```
$groups = Get-SPOSiteGroup https://PoShSP2016.sharepoint.com/Search
$translationMgt = $groups | Where{$_.Title -eq "Translation Managers"}
$translationMgt.Roles
```

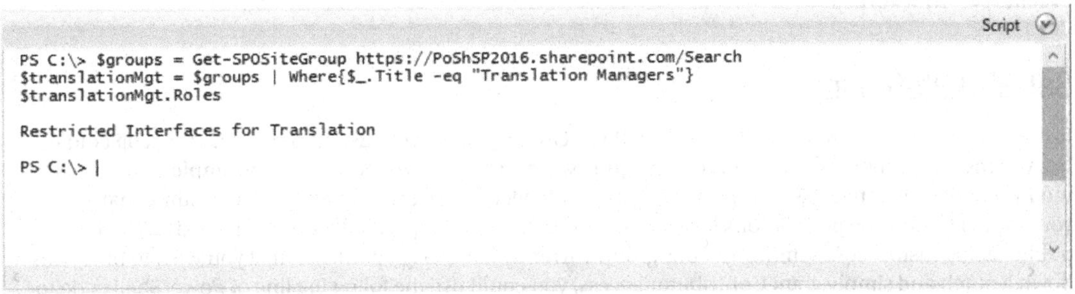

*Figure 8-17. Getting the permission level of a site collection security group in Office 365 using PowerShell*

## New-SPOSiteGroup

The New-SPOSiteGroup PowerShell cmdlet lets you create a new SharePoint Online site collection security group. It requires you to pass in the site collection's URL where you wish to create this new security group, the name of the new group, and the permission level that you want to assign to it. Figure 8-18 shows how you can use this cmdlet to create a new security group on your public site called MyNewGroup that has both Contribute and Design rights.

```
New-SPOSiteGroup https://PoShSP2016.sharepoint.com
-Group "MyNewGroup" -PermissionLevels "Contribute", "Design"
```

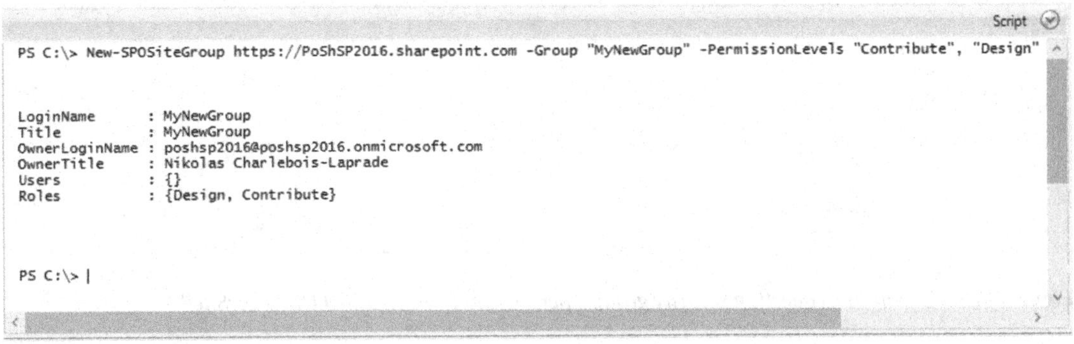

*Figure 8-18. Creating a new site collection security group in Office 365 using PowerShell*

## Remove-SPOSiteGroup

Starting to figure out a pattern in the available methods? Yes, you've guessed it; the Remove-SPOSiteGroup cmdlet lets you delete an existing site collection security group. It simply requires you to pass it the URL of the site collection, as well as the name of the security group to delete. For example, to delete the security group that you created in the previous section, you could run the following line of PowerShell:

```
Remove-SPOSiteGroup https://PoShSP2016.sharepoint.com
-Identity "MyNewGroup"
```

## Set-SPOSiteGroup

Just as was the case when we dealt with SharePoint Online site collections, the Set-SPOSiteGroup cmdlet lets you modify properties related to security groups in existing site collections. For example, if you wish to modify the permission levels of a specific group, you'll need to use this cmdlet to do it. Assume that you want to modify the permissions level of a custom security group called Partners that exists on your public-facing instance. Assuming that this group currently has Design permission, if you wish to bring this down a notch and simply grant Contributor access, you could use the following line of PowerShell code to make the change shown in Figure 8-19:

```
Set-SPOSiteGroup https://PoShSP2016.sharepoint.com -Identity "Team Site Visitors"
-PermissionLevelsToRemove "Read" -PermissionLevelsToAdd "Contribute"
```

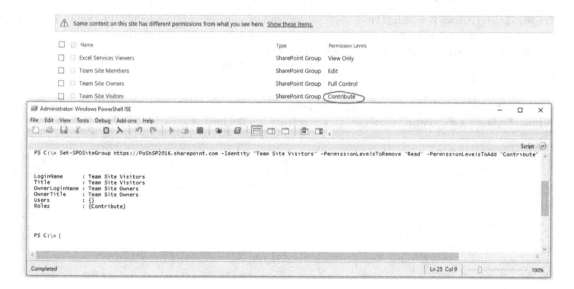

*Figure 8-19. Custom site collection security group's permission level modified by PowerShell*

## Users

This section covers the various PowerShell cmdlets that are available to interact with SharePoint user objects. In Office 365, there are two types of users with whom you can interact. The first type, internal users, typically works for your company. They have been assigned an Office 365 license and have a user name on the company's domain in the cloud. External users are those who are not employees of the company but need to be granted some level of access to SharePoint sites in order to consult on or contribute to documents or items stored in SharePoint Online. These users are identified by their personal or external organization's email (for example, @gmail.com, @hotmail.com, @contoso.com, and so on). In this section you will learn how to use PowerShell to interact with both types of users in the SharePoint Online context.

## Get-SPOUser

The Get-SPOUser cmdlet lets you obtain a list of all users (internal and external) on a specific SharePoint Online site collection. The only required parameter is the site collection's URL. Figure 8-20 shows the result of executing this PowerShell cmdlet against our internal site collection.

```
$users = Get-SPOUser https://PoShSP2016.sharepoint.com
```

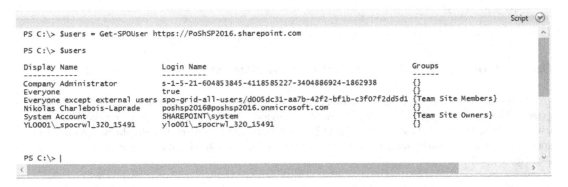

*Figure 8-20.* *Listing all users on an internal SharePoint Online site collection using PowerShell*

You can see from this example that there are some abstract users being returned. Those are simply what we would consider "maintenance" accounts. They are required accounts that the SharePoint farm needs in order to operate properly. What we are really interested in are the two accounts right in the middle of the list. You can easily see one author's personal account on his domain (nik@powershellbook.onmicrosoft.com), but what about the live.com#powershellbook@outlook.com user? This is an external user we invited to join our SharePoint site. We put him in the Owners group, giving him complete access over the site collection. This user can log in to our Office 365 environment by using his personal @Outlook.com email account, and interact with the environment as if he was a company's user.

## Get-SPOExternalUser

The Get-SPOExternalUser cmdlet displays a list of all external users specified in your current Office 365 tenant account. For an external user to be listed using this PowerShell cmdlet, they need to have accepted the invitation to the SharePoint Online environment, and have logged in at least once. The last point is key to understanding how external users are managed in SharePoint Online. They are not managed at the site-collection level directly but are instead generic to all of your SharePoint environments. Just like the internal users, they are stored at the account level. When you add an external user to a site collection, however, it gets registered against the collection, and the site collection keeps a footprint of its login name. This makes sense when you think that even external users have a My Site page created in your environment; SharePoint needs to know who they are, no matter what site collection you are in. Get-SPOExternalUser doesn't require any parameters. It simply connects to your tenant store and returns all of the external users it finds, no matter where in the-site collection architecture they were granted access. Figure 8-21 shows the result of executing this cmdlet against our demo Office 365 tenant account.

```
Get-SPOExternalUser
```

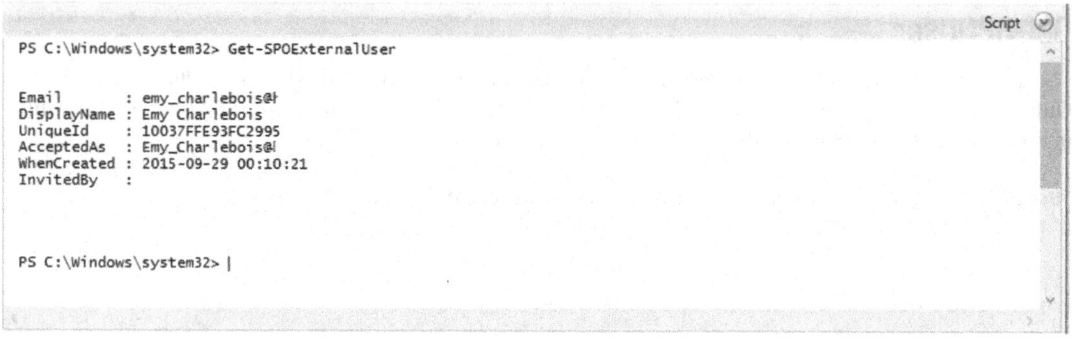

```
PS C:\Windows\system32> Get-SPOExternalUser


Email       : emy_charlebois@
DisplayName : Emy Charlebois
UniqueId    : 10037FFE93FC2995
AcceptedAs  : Emy_Charlebois@
WhenCreated : 2015-09-29 00:10:21
InvitedBy   :



PS C:\Windows\system32> |
```

*Figure 8-21.* *Getting a list of all external users for an Office 365 tenant account using PowerShell*

Note that there is no way with this cmdlet to identify where in the site collection architecture a specific external user has been granted access. You would have to loop through each collection and check for that user's presence in the list of users. The following PowerShell script allows you to enter the user name of a specific external user and to figure out what site collections he or she has been granted access to (see Figure 8-22):

```
# Prompts for the external user's login name;
$extUserName = Read-Host "External User Name?"

# Gets a list of all available site collections in the current tenant;
$sites = Get-SPOSite

# Loops through all site collections
for($i = 0; $i -lt $sites.Count; $i++)
{
    # Query the list of users for the current site collection to see if external user is in
    # there;
    $user = Get-SPOUser $sites[$i].Url | Where{$_.LoginName -like "*$extUserName"}
    if($user -ne $null)
    {
        # If the user has been found, print the site's Url he has been found in;
        Write-Host $sites[$i].Url
    }
}
```

```
                                                                              Script ⊗
PS C:\> # Prompts for the external user's login name;
$extUserName = Read-Host "External User Name?"

# Gets a list of all available site collections in the current tenant;
$sites = Get-SPOSite

# Loops through all site collections
for($i = 0; $i -lt $sites.Count; $i++)
{
    # Query the list of users for the current site collection to see if external user is in
    # there;
    $user = Get-SPOUser $sites[$i].Url | Where{$_.LoginName -like "*$extUserName"}
    if($user -ne $null)
    {
        # If the user has been found, print the site's Url he has been found in;
        Write-Host $sites[$i].Url
    }
}

External User Name?: emy_charlebois_'          #ext#@poshsp2016.onmicrosoft.com
https://poshsp2016.sharepoint.com/

PS C:\> |
```

*Figure 8-22.* *Finding site collections in which a specific external user has access to using PowerShell*

## Add-SPOUser

The Add-SPOUser cmdlet lets you add an existing user to a SharePoint Online security group. This PowerShell method takes three required parameters: the URL of the site collection, the name of the group to add the user in, and the login name for the user to add. This cmdlet allows you to add both internal and external users to security group. For example, you could try to add an internal user by passing its user name in the form Domain\Username or add an external user using the default user ID provided with Office 365 that includes its email address (such as powershellbook_outlook.com#ext#@poshsp2016.onmicrosoft.com). However, an external user name needs to have been registered against the site collection before attempting to add it to a security group; otherwise, Office 365 won't recognize its login name. Figure 8-23 shows the use of this cmdlet when trying to add the same external user to two different site collections. In the first case, the external user had not been registered with the site collection, but in the second case, the user had properly been registered. Note that there is currently no way to use the SharePoint Online Management Shell to automatically register an external user against a site collection.

```
                                                                              Script ⊗
PS C:\> Add-SPOUser https://PoShSP2016.sharepoint.com/search -Group "Members" -LoginName "powershellbook_outlook.com#ext#@poshsp2016.onmicrosoft.com"
Add-SPOUser : The specified user powershellbook_outlook.com#ext#@poshsp2016.onmicrosoft.com could not be found.
At line:1 char:1
+ Add-SPOUser https://PoShSP2016.sharepoint.com/search -Group "Members" ...
+ _____
    + CategoryInfo          : NotSpecified: (:) [Add-SPOUser], ServerException
    + FullyQualifiedErrorId : Microsoft.SharePoint.Client.ServerException,Microsoft.Online.SharePoint.PowerShell.AddSPOUser

PS C:\> Add-SPOUser https://PoShSP2016.sharepoint.com/ -Group "Team Site Members" -LoginName "powershellbook_outlook.com#ext#@poshsp2016.onmicrosoft.com"

Display Name   Login Name                                               Groups
------------   ----------                                               ------
Nik Charlebois powershellbook_outlook.com#ext#@poshsp2016.onmicrosoft.com {Team Site Members}

PS C:\> |
```

*Figure 8-23.* *Trying to add an external user against two different site collections using PowerShell*

# Remove-SPOUser

The Remove-SPOUser cmdlet lets you remove both an internal and an external user from a SharePoint site collection. It requires you to pass it both the site collection's URL and the login name for the user to remove. Remember that when dealing with external users, when you are at the site collection level, login names take the form of <Email Address>#ext#@<Domain> (for example, powershellbook_outlook.com#ext#@ poshsp2016.onmicrosoft.com). The following line of PowerShell will remove the external user you've added to our internal site collection:

```
Remove-SPOUser https://PoShSP2016.sharepoint.com
-LoginName powershellbook_outlook_com#ext#@poshsp2016.onmicrosoft.com
```

# Remove-SPOExternalUser

You are probably wondering why you might need a separate remove method to get rid of external users, when the method we've just covered takes care of both internal and external users. Remember that when we talk about external users, you must think of this in the tenant context, meaning that external users are registered against your entire Office 365 account. When an external user is registered against a specific site collection, it becomes what we'd call a "semi-internal" user, meaning that you can interact with it as if it was just a regular internal SharePoint user. The concept of external user only really makes sense when you're talking about the higher level of SharePoint management: the entire SharePoint environment. This method deals exactly with this. It gets rid of an external user at the tenant level, meaning that the user will no longer be registered at the account level.

In order to use the Remove-SPOExternalUser cmdlet, you'll need to obtain the external user's unique ID. An important thing to note as well is that by simply removing the entry to the external user at the tenant level, you are not revoking the user's access to the site collections to which he has been granted access previously. The following PowerShell script will come in handy if you ever need to get rid of an external user and want to ensure that all registered instances are also removed from the site collections. Therefore, the script makes sure that the specified external user is no longer able to access any SharePoint site collection in your Office 365 environment:

```
# Get the external user login name;
$extUser = Read-Host "External User Login Name?"

# Get a list of all site collection;
$sites = Get-SPOSite

for($i = 0; $i -lt $sites.Count; $i++)
{
    $user = Get-SPOUser $sites[$i].Url | Where{$_.LoginName -like "*$extUser"}
    if($user -ne $null)
    {
        # Remove the user from the site collection;
        Remove-SPOUser $sites[$i] -LoginName $user.LoginName
    }
}

# Gets the external user's unique ID and remove it from the tenant account;
$userRec = Get-SPOExternalUser | Where{$_.LoginName -eq $extUser}
Remove-SPOExternalUser $userRec.UniqueIds -Confirm:$false
```

This could also be easily achieved by simply calling Get-SPOExternalUser, obtaining the UniqueID of an external user, and then calling the Remove-SPOExternalUser cmdlet directly (see Figure 8-24).

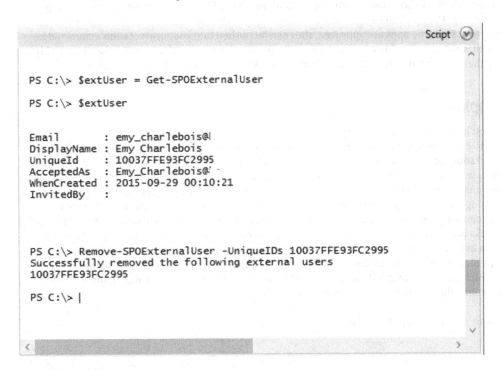

*Figure 8-24.* *Removing a SharePoint Online external user using PowerShell*

## Set-SPOUser

The Set-SPOUser cmdlet lets you specify whether a specific user should be granted site collection administrator rights or not. For example, the following PowerShell code could be used to revoke one user's SharePoint site collection administrator rights from your internal SharePoint environment. Just make sure that you don't accidentally remove administrative rights from your unique administrator account when using this cmdlet (see Figure 8-25).

```
Set-SPOUser https:// PoShSP2016.sharepoint.com -LoginName PoShSP2016@ PoShSP2016.
OnMicrosoft.com -IsSiteCollectionAdmin $false
```

```
PS C:\> Set-SPOUser https://PoShSP2016.sharepoint.com -LoginName PoShSP2016@PoShSP2016.OnMicrosoft.com -IsSiteCollectionAdmin $false

Display Name            Login Name                              Groups
------------            ----------                              ------
Nikolas Charlebois-Laprade  poshsp2016@poshsp2016.onmicrosoft.com  {Team Site Members}


PS C:\> |
```

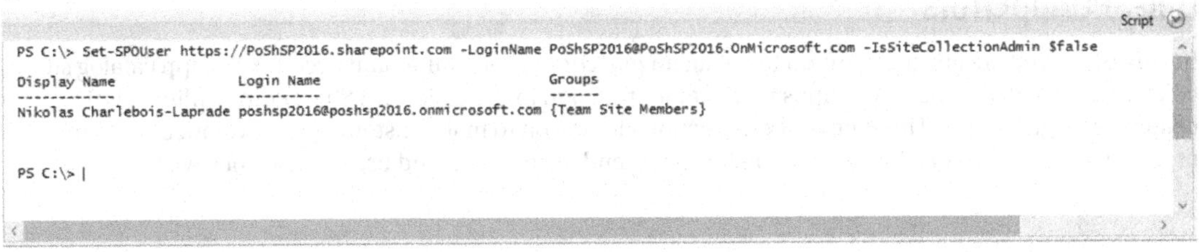

*Figure 8-25.* *Removing a SharePoint Online site collection administrator's rights using PowerShell*

# Apps

Just like the on-premises version, SharePoint in the cloud on Office 365 also lets you install and develop custom SharePoint 2013 apps. You can create a developer's site collection and let your developers publish apps in testing to it. Once the apps are approved, they can be pushed into your organization's store and be consumed by all your site collections. This section will give you an overview of what can be achieved with PowerShell to maintain and monitor your apps in an Office 365 SharePoint Online environment.

## Get-SPOAppInfo

Assume that you have installed a custom app from the Office marketplace on one of your sites. The Get-SPOAppInfo cmdlet lets you get a reference to this app instance by simply passing it the name of the app you've installed somewhere in any of your site collections. Because this is tough to explain, we'll show you a concrete example. Assume that a user went in the Office app marketplace and installed an app, called Timer Clock, on our internal SharePoint Online site collection. You now want to go and get a reference to this app instance. By using the Get-SPOAppInfo cmdlet and passing it the name of your app instance, you can get easily get a reference to that object. Notice that in this example, you're simply passing it part of the actual app's name. This works fine because PowerShell treats this parameter as a wildcard and gets any app that has the word "timer" in its name. Using this method gives you an overview of all of the apps that have been installed throughout the SharePoint Online environment and provides important information about them, such as the source from which they were installed (organizational catalog, marketplace, and so on). Figure 8-26 shows the result of running this line of PowerShell code:

```
$timerClockApp = Get-SPOAppInfo -Name "Timer"
```

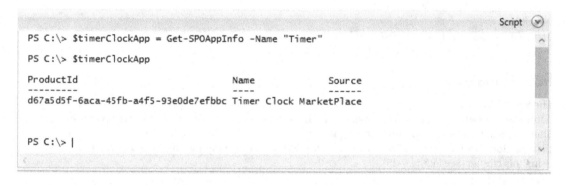

*Figure 8-26.* *Getting information related to installed apps in an Office 365 environment using PowerShell*

## Get-SPOAppErrors

In Office 365, you are given the option to create an *app catalog* for your tenant account. An app catalog site collection is created by using the Apps management section in the Office 365 SharePoint Online admin center (see Figure 8-27). This type of site collection allows you to make custom apps developed by your organization available to all site collections, and lets end users install and use them as they wish.

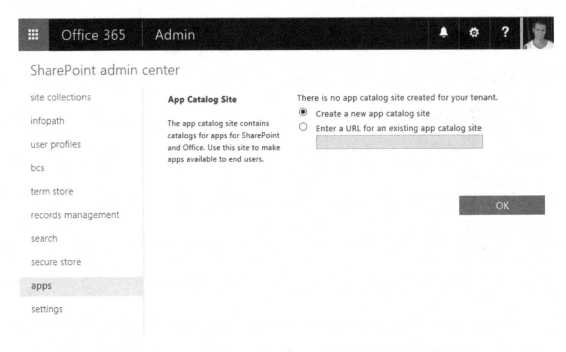

***Figure 8-27.*** *Creating a new App Catalog site collection using the web interface in Office 365*

The question now becomes, how do you monitor errors related to these custom apps that your development team produces? The Get-SPOAppErrors cmdlet lets you access information related to errors due to installation, upgrade, and execution errors. It requires you to pass the app's product ID as a parameter. This data is updated only every 24 hours by Office 365 timer jobs, so don't worry if you don't see stats appear right after your users start calling you about errors. The following example shows a scenario in which a faulty app has been deployed to the organization. Users trying to access the app in question are getting an error page. Calling the following lines of PowerShell code would return a list of all errors associated with the MyCrashingapp instance:

```
$myCrashingApp = Get-SPOAppInfo -Name "MyCrashingApp"
Get-SPOAppErrors $myCrashingApp.ProductId
```

# Tenant

As mentioned previously, SharePoint Online in Office 365 runs in a multitenant mode, meaning that there are multiple users/organizations on the same SharePoint farm. PowerShell provides various ways of viewing information about the tenant's account. This section will give an overview of the various options available to you with the SharePoint Online Management Shell.

# Get-SPOTenant

The Get-SPOTenant cmdlet returns information about the current tenant account. Figure 8-28 shows the result of running this cmdlet against our demo environment:

```
Get-SPOTenant
```

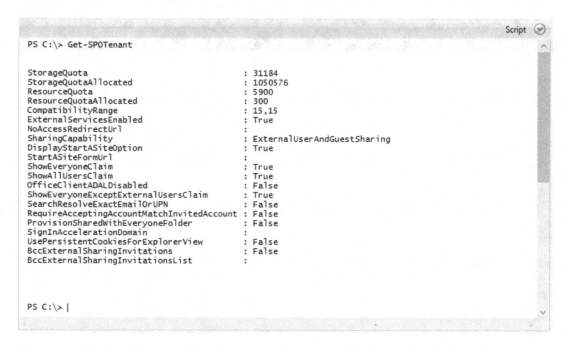

*Figure 8-28.* *Getting information about the current Office 365 tenant account using PowerShell*

## Set-SPOTenant

You can use this cmdlet to set properties of the current tenant account. One example of a property you can set is NoAccessRedirectUrl, which specifies a URL to redirect a user if the site they are trying to access has been locked. A locked site means it can't be accessed by users. In real life, you want to lock a site while it is in development or while it is undergoing maintenance. It is a temporary state that freezes a site collection into its current state. To illustrate this, assume that you need to lock down the developer's site collection in your environment because you want to prevent users from submitting new apps in testing (a harsh example). You want users trying to access the developer site while it is locked down to be redirected to a user-friendly page that will explain to them what is going on, and tell them when to expect that the site will be back up. This PowerShell script will start by locking the developer site and then set the NoAccessRedirectUrl property of your tenant account to contain the URL of the temporary page to which you want to redirect users:

```
Set-SPOSite https://PoShSP2016.sharepoint.com/sites/dev -LockState NoAccess
Set-SPOTenant -NoAccessRedirectUrl https://NikCharlebois.com
```

In this example, any user trying to access the dev site (https://poshsp2016.sharepoint.com/sites/dev) will automatically be redirected to the author's personal blog at http://nikcharlebois.com.

## Get-SPOTenantLogEntry

You probably got very excited when you first read the name of this PowerShell cmdlet. Let us burst your bubble right away; it doesn't do what you think it does, at least not exactly. The biggest downside of SharePoint Online is that we don't have direct access to our servers and therefore can't directly get access to the SharePoint logs. The cmdlet gives you access to certain information pertaining to your tenant account logged in the SharePoint logs. It will contain information about any component failures (BCS, User Profile Service, and so on). It also contains information related to important events that happened in the environment. Figure 8-29 shows the result of running the method against our demo environment. You can see that two events have been logged, one for every developer's site that we created. This could be important information for you to monitor, because developer sites allow users to side-load SharePoint apps. You probably don't want anybody creating such sites and loading their own applications in them.

```
$logs = Get-SPOTenantLogEntry
$logs[0].Message
```

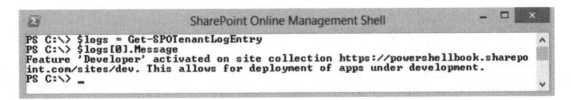

Figure 8-29. Displaying the latest log entry from our SharePoint Online environment using PowerShell

## Get-SPOTenantLogLastAvailableTimeInUtc

Yes, somebody at Microsoft ought to be fired for coming up with such a long name for this PowerShell cmdlet. On the good side, the Get-SPOTenantLogLastAvailableTimeInUtc cmdlet does exactly what its name says it does: it returns the date of the latest log entry in UTC time. This cmdlet could prove useful if you are automating a script that regularly checks on the cloud server to see if any new errors have been logged, and then notify the user. Figure 8-30 shows the result of running this cmdlet against our demo environment.

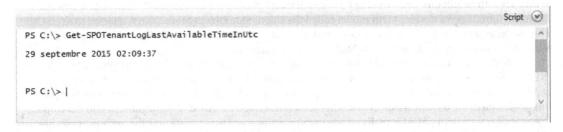

Figure 8-30. Getting the last log entry time from SharePoint Online using PowerShell

## Web

We have mentioned previously that there is no way through the SharePoint Online Management Shell to create new webs in SharePoint Online. When you create a new site collection, however, you are also creating a root web, which is assigned a web template type. There is only one PowerShell cmdlet in SharePoint Online that interacts with web objects. However, as you'll learn in the next section, there are many more options available to you to deal with webs in Office 365.

## Get-SPOWebTemplate

The Get-SPOWebTemplate cmdlet returns a list of all available web templates in SharePoint Online. Figure 8-31 shows the resulting list produced by this cmdlet.

```
                                                                         Script ⌄
PS C:\> Get-SPOWebTemplate

Name                        Title                                   LocaleId CompatibilityLevel
----                        -----                                   -------- ------------------
STS#0                       Team Site                                   1033                 15
BLOG#0                      Blog                                        1033                 15
BDR#0                       Document Center                             1033                 15
DEV#0                       Developer Site                              1033                 15
OFFILE#1                    Records Center                              1033                 15
EHS#1                       Team Site - SharePoint Online configuration 1033                 15
BICenterSite#0              Business Intelligence Center                1033                 15
SRCHCEN#0                   Enterprise Search Center                    1033                 15
BLANKINTERNETCONTAINER#0    Publishing Portal                           1033                 15
ENTERWIKI#0                 Enterprise Wiki                             1033                 15
PROJECTSITE#0               Project Site                                1033                 15
PRODUCTCATALOG#0            Product Catalog                             1033                 15
COMMUNITY#0                 Community Site                              1033                 15
COMMUNITYPORTAL#0           Community Portal                            1033                 15
SRCHCENTERLITE#0            Basic Search Center                         1033                 15
visprus#0                   Visio Process Repository                    1033                 15


PS C:\> |
```

*Figure 8-31.* *Listing all available web templates in SharePoint Online using PowerShell*

# Doing More with the Client Context

We're sure that a lot of people were disappointed when they learned that there were only 30 PowerShell cmdlets made available to manage SharePoint Online. Let us bring some good news: there are other ways to interact with SharePoint Online using PowerShell than by using the default cmdlets. In SharePoint 2010, Microsoft introduced a development model called the Client Side Object Model, often referred to as CSOM. This model allows developers to build applications running remotely outside the SharePoint server and allows them to interact with the remote SharePoint environment.

Microsoft released three flavors of this new model: the JavaScript model, the Silverlight model, and the .NET model. If you've never heard of Silverlight, don't worry about it; it was never good enough to get two capitalized letters like the other good Microsoft products (just joking). We will not be covering this topic in this book, due to the technical aspect of it. This book is intended for PowerShell beginners, and developing PowerShell scripts with CSOM is really an advanced development topic. Just know that whatever you are able to do using this model, it is possible to automate with PowerShell; for example, it's now possible to create webs and sub-webs under a site collection and dynamically change themes for sites with this new approach.

# Summary

In this chapter, you've learned that you can use PowerShell for more than just managing SharePoint on-premises environments. With the SharePoint Online Management Shell, you now have the option to automate operations on your cloud environments residing in Office 365. The next chapter will show how you can use PowerShell to manage add-ins and solutions.

# CHAPTER 9

■ ■ ■

# Managing Add-ins and Solutions using PowerShell

Those of you who are SharePoint administrators are probably starting to feel a little dirty doing all these examples of scripts that are normally the job of developers and end users. Now's the time go take a shower and to start back fresh. What you will learn in this chapter is what SharePoint administrators normally do in their daily jobs. This chapter builds on the concepts learned in the previous chapters and will enable you to understand how certain configuration changes made to a SharePoint farm can affect artifacts that business users use daily.

In this chapter, you will learn how to deploy and manage custom code solutions developed by developers in your organization or by external companies. You will also be introduced to the development model, known as the Add-in model, that was introduced in SharePoint 2013 and will learn how, as an administrator, you can leverage PowerShell to manage these custom solutions. By the end of this chapter, you will have a complete understanding of the differences between a farm solution and a SharePoint app and will have all the tools to help you manage them in your day-to-day work.

## Solutions

This section shows how you, as a SharePoint administrator, can use PowerShell to manage solutions in your SharePoint environment. SharePoint solutions are contained in a Windows SharePoint (.wsp) file, and contain pieces of functional logic that will be installed in your environment. Solutions can contain different SharePoint features, list definitions and instances, documents, and so on.

### Types of Solutions

In SharePoint 2016, there are three types of solutions that are officially supported by Microsoft: farm solutions, sandboxed solutions, and SharePoint add-ins. Table 9-1 details the differences between each type of solution.

© Nikolas Charlebois-Laprade and John Edward Naguib 2017
N. Charlebois-Laprade and J. E. Naguib, *Beginning PowerShell for SharePoint 2016*,
DOI 10.1007/978-1-4842-2884-5_9

***Table 9-1.*** *Types of Solutions in SharePoint 2016*

| Solution Type | Description |
| --- | --- |
| Farm Solutions | When installed, these can interact with the entire farm. Their contents can be used across various site collections. |
| Sandboxed Solutions | These are limited to the site collection in which they have been uploaded. That's right, sandboxed solutions can be uploaded, which means that anyone who has the site collection administration role in a site collection can build their own sandboxed solutions and deploy them themselves. However, their contents can't affect other site collections. When Office 365 originally launched back in July 2011, sandboxed solutions were the only way of deploying reusable customization to your cloud environment. Currently they are removed from Office 365 and actually not preferred for development. |
| SharePoint Add-ins | This is a new type of solution that was introduced in SharePoint 2013 as *apps*; then the name was changed to *add-ins*. These can be executed outside the SharePoint environment and are allowed to interact with its artifacts using calls to the various SharePoint 2016 web services and REST APIs. |

Our word of advice about building new solutions in SharePoint is the following: If the solution that you are trying to build serves solely an administrative function, use farm solutions. If all you need to do is to package a set of SharePoint artifacts that you would like to make reusable, then see if sandboxed solutions are appropriate depending on the scope of accessibility you want. For example, if you need your artifacts to be accessible across an entire SharePoint farm with over 50 site collections, a sandboxed solution may not be the best fit because it would require you to activate its features on every site collection manually. Remember that sandboxed solutions cannot include code in them. If your solution needs to be accessed throughout the farm, in every site collection, then go with farm solutions. For anything else, you should consider building an app.

Because of the uncertain future of sandboxed solutions, the focus of this section will remain on farm solutions. You will learn how to use PowerShell to deploy, install, uninstall, remove, and upgrade farm solutions in your SharePoint environment. One thing to note is that the process of adding or removing a farm solution in SharePoint automatically recycles the application pools associated with your SharePoint environment in the Internet Information Service manager, causing interruption for the end users. This is not the case when deploying sandboxed solutions.

## Adding a New Farm Solution

Before you can install a SharePoint farm solution in your environment, you need to add it to the solutions store by calling the Add-SPSolution PowerShell cmdlet and passing it the full path to the solution file you're trying to add (see Figure 9-1). Doing so will automatically add an entry to the list of available farm solutions under Central Administration ➤ System Settings ➤ Manage Farm Solutions (see Figure 9-2).

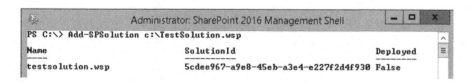

```
Administrator: SharePoint 2016 Management Shell          _ □ x
PS C:\> Add-SPSolution c:\TestSolution.wsp

Name                         SolutionId                          Deployed

testsolution.wsp             5cdee967-a9e8-45eb-a3e4-e227f2d4f930 False
```

***Figure 9-1.*** *Adding a new SharePoint farm solution*

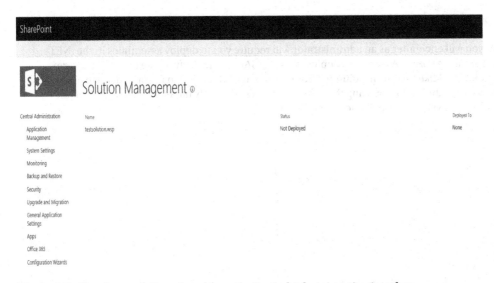

Figure 9-2. *New farm solution viewed from the Central Administration interface*

## Installing a Farm Solution

At this point, the solution has been added to your farm. In reality, all that you've done so far is to upload the .wsp file as a BLOB in your SQL database. You can find information about the solutions that have been added to SharePoint in the configuration database in the Objects table, as shown in Figure 9-3.

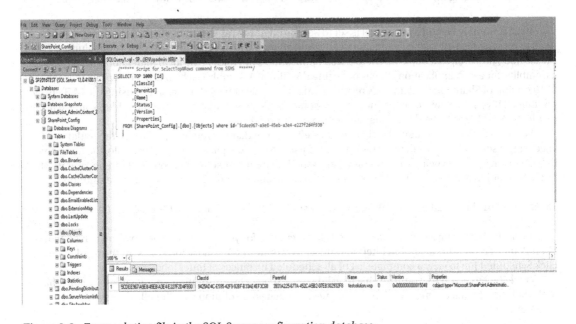

Figure 9-3. *Farm solution file in the SQL Server configuration database*

Before you can use the content of your solution, you need to have it installed on your farm. The PowerShell cmdlet to use to install a specific farm solution in a SharePoint environment is `Install-SPSolution`. Most solutions that you will encounter as an administrator will require you to deploy assemblies in the .NET Global Assembly Cache (GAC). Assemblies deployed in the GAC are made available to the entire farm by default. If you would like to prevent solutions from having to be deployed to it, you'll need to ask your developers to package their solution using the `WebApplication` assembly target instead of the default `GlobalAssemblyCache` value in Visual Studio (see Figure 9-4).

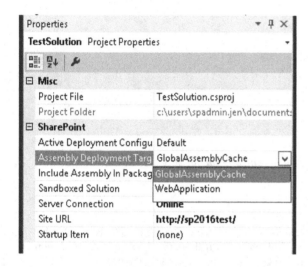

***Figure 9-4.*** *Changing the Assembly Deployment Target Type of a SharePoint solution in Visual Studio*

If the Assembly Deployment Target is set to `WebApplication` (as shown in Figure 9-4), then you will need to provide the URL of the destination web application to which you wish to deploy your solution. Please note, however, that deployment to a web application's bin folder (the local folder containing assemblies for a web application) that is not using the Global Assembly Cache has been deprecated since the 2010 version of SharePoint. Microsoft's recommendation is that you deploy it globally, using the `GACDeploy` parameter. If you do, however, need for some reason to deploy your solution in the bin folder, you will need to add the `FullTrustBinDeploment` parameter to your method call.

When you install a solution, the changes take effect immediately. You have, however, the option of specifying a schedule for the deployments to occur using the `-Time` parameter. For example, the following line of PowerShell code will create a deployment schedule for our custom solution at 12 PM on January 18, 2017. A timer job will be scheduled to execute at that time and will take care of installing the solution.

```
Install-SPSolution –Identity testsolution.wsp -GACDeploy -Time "2017-1-18 12:00:00"
```

To verify that a scheduled job has correctly been created for your solution to deploy, you can open the SharePoint Central Administration interface and go to Monitoring ➤ Check job status. In the top-left menu, click Scheduled Job to view a complete list of all scheduled instances of timer jobs.

Once the job executes, you'll be able to validate the status of your solution's deployment by going back to the Solution Management page. You should now see that your solution was globally deployed (see Figure 9-5).

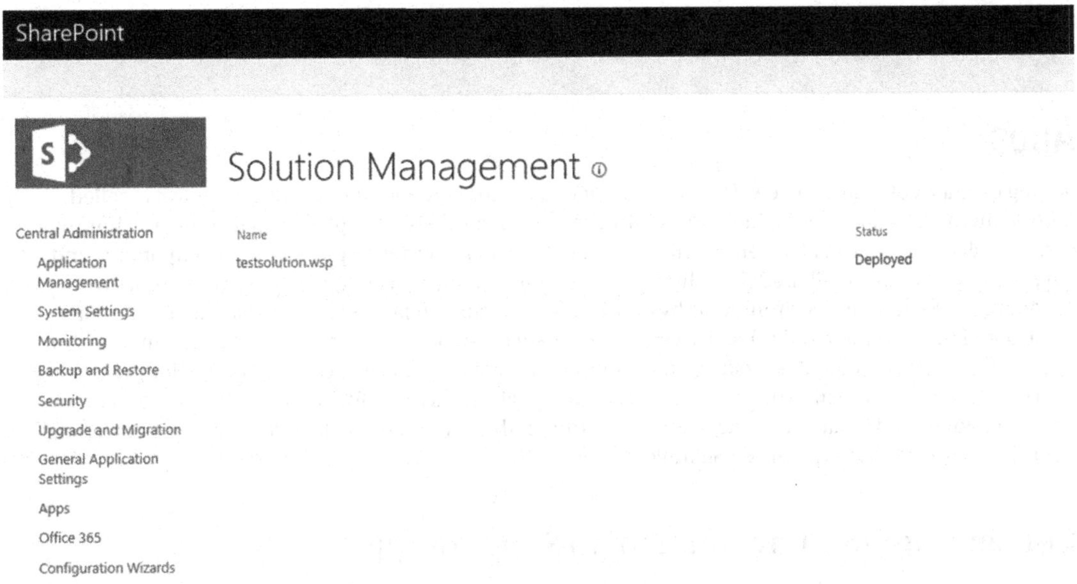

SharePoint

## Solution Management ⓘ

| Central Administration | Name | | Status |
|---|---|---|---|
| Application Management | testsolution.wsp | | Deployed |
| System Settings | | | |
| Monitoring | | | |
| Backup and Restore | | | |
| Security | | | |
| Upgrade and Migration | | | |
| General Application Settings | | | |
| Apps | | | |
| Office 365 | | | |
| Configuration Wizards | | | |

*Figure 9-5.* *Deployed farm solution viewed in Central Administration*

## Uninstalling a Farm Solution

Uninstalling a farm solution is the process of unbinding its logical components from the farm. It doesn't remove the solution file from the database; it simply deactivates it. To uninstall a solution from the farm, you'll need to use the Uninstall-SPSolution PowerShell cmdlet and pass it the name of the solution to uninstall. You can use the -Confirm parameter to prevent PowerShell from prompting you to confirm before uninstalling your farm solution, as shown here:

```
Uninstall-SPSolution -Identity TestSolution.wsp -Confirm:$false
```

## Removing a Farm Solution

Removing a farm solution from your SharePoint environment deletes the solution from the Config database. The PowerShell cmdlet that allows you to remove a solution from your SharePoint farm is Remove-SPSolution. If you no longer need a farm solution in your environment, the recommendation is to uninstall and then remove it from your farm using the PowerShell cmdlets. Once again, you can use the -Confirm parameter to prevent PowerShell from prompting you to confirm your changes before committing them to your environment:

```
Remove-SPSolution -Identity TestSolution.wsp -Confirm:$false
```

## Updating a Farm Solution

You can update an existing farm solution only if the set of files and features contained in the new version of the solution is the same as the set contained in the old one. Otherwise, you will need to uninstall/remove the existing solution and reinstall the new version:

```
Update-SPSolution -Identity TestSolution.wsp -LiteralPath "C:\Solutions\Solutionv2.wsp"
-GACDeploy
```

If the new version of the solution has the same GUID as the previous one, then the latter is removed completely from the Config database.

# Apps

Staring in SharePoint 2013, a new development model, the *app* model, was introduced; now it is called *add-ins*. In the new SharePoint lingo, every entity that is not a web is an app: custom lists, picture libraries, contacts, all are apps. The idea behind this new model was to allow developers to build components and have them run outside of SharePoint. This new paradigm was introduced to help minimize problems introduced in SharePoint environments by poorly designed custom farm solutions that did not properly make use of the resources and caused several performance issues. At the same time, this new model also helped Microsoft build their new Office Store component that allows users to "shop" online for preexisting SharePoint solutions meeting their needs. Add-ins are packaged as .app files and, just like solutions, they can be deployed and installed on the SharePoint farm. In this section you will learn how to use PowerShell to interact with these new apps within SharePoint.

## Configuring your Environment to Support Apps

Before we begin playing with SharePoint add-ins, we need to get the environment configured. In order to be able to install apps within your farm, you'll need to create an instance of two essential components: the App Management Service and Microsoft SharePoint Foundation Subscription Settings Service applications.

# App Management Service Application

The App Management Service application is responsible for storing information about app licenses and permissions. It acts as the police between the server that serves the app and the end users to determine whether they are authorized to use the app in question. It is accessed every time an app is requested in your SharePoint environment. It is this component that allows you to purchase apps straight from the SharePoint store.

To create a new instance of this component using PowerShell, you should start by creating a new application pool in IIS that will be dedicated to serving requests to the service application. To create a new IIS application pool, you can use the following lines of PowerShell. This will create a new IIS application pool named AppMgmtServiceAppPool that will use the identity of our administrator's account to run (see Figure 9-6).

```
$adminAcc = Get-SPManagedAccount "jen\spadmin"
$appMgmtPool = New-SPServiceApplicationPool -Name AppMgmtServiceAppPool -Account $adminAcc
```

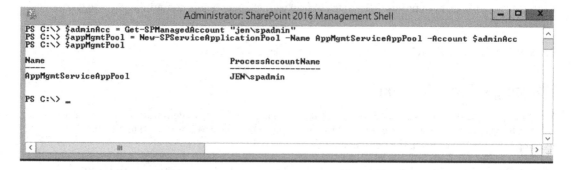

***Figure 9-6.*** *Creating a new IIS application pool using PowerShell*

Once your new application pool has been created, you can create a new instance of our App Management Service application by calling the following cmdlet. This will create a new instance of the service application named `AppManagementServiceApp` and will also create an associated database named `AppManagementDB`.

```
$appMgmtSvc = New-SPAppManagementServiceApplication –ApplicationPool $appMgmtPool –Name
AppManagementServiceApp –DatabaseName AppManagementDB
```

To verify that the creation was successful, open Central Administration and browse to the list of service applications on the server (in the Application Management section). You should see an entry for the instance that you just created, as shown in Figure 9-7.

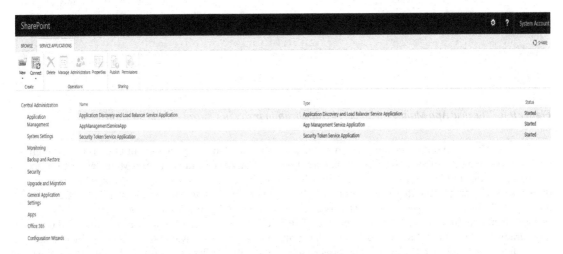

***Figure 9-7.*** *The new App Management Service application in Central Administration*

You're almost done! The next step is to create the associated proxy for the instance of the service application just created. This will allow your Web application to communicate with the instance itself:

```
$appMgmtProxy = New-SPAppManagementServiceApplicationProxy -ServiceApplication $appMgmtSvc
-Name AppManagementProxy
```

Once that code is executed, you should see a new entry under the previously created AppManagementServiceApp instance, as shown in Figure 9-8.

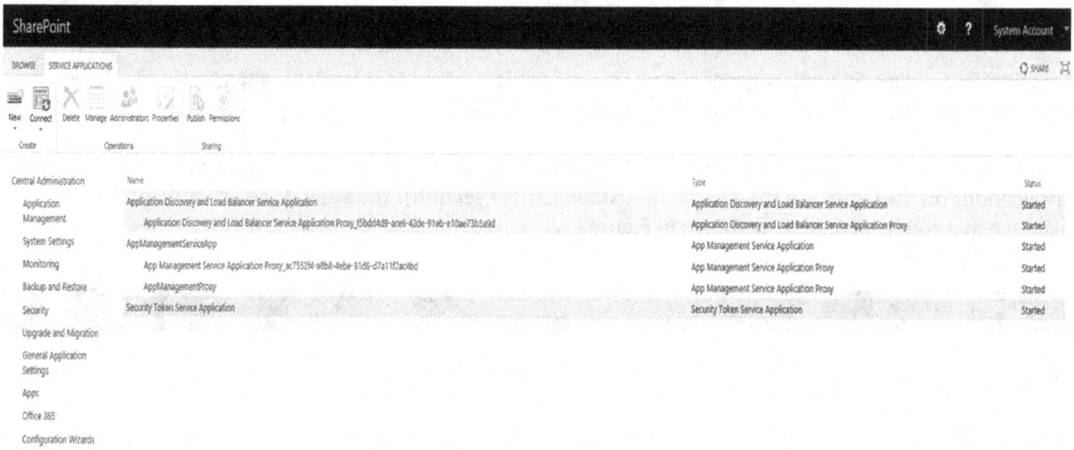

**Figure 9-8.** *The new App Management Service application proxy in Central Administration*

You now have the service application instance and its associated proxy created, but that is not enough for the App Management Service to be enabled on the farm. You need to turn the App Management Service on. To do so, you could navigate to Central Administration, choose System Settings ➤ Manage Services on Server, and then activate the service manually, but you're on your way to being a PowerShell expert, aren't you? To begin, you need to get a reference to the instance of the App Management Service. This service's instance can be obtained using the Get-SPServiceInstance cmdlet. This cmdlet doesn't take any parameters by default. Calling it directly will simply return a list of all available services on the current server. To get the reference to our specific service (see Figure 9-9), you'll need to query the returned dataset containing all the services by specifying the type name of the service instance you're trying to get.

```
$service = Get-SPServiceInstance | Where{$_.TypeName -eq "App Management Service"}
```

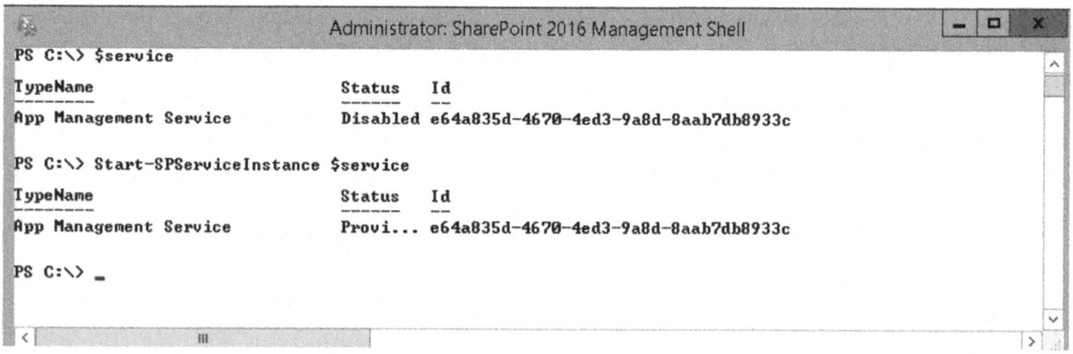

**Figure 9-9.** *Obtaining a reference to the App Management Service on a SharePoint 2016 server using PowerShell*

You can see from the figure that the status of the service instance is set to Disabled, meaning that it is not activated on the server. To start the service instance, you have two choices: you can either manually set the Status property of our service instance to Online or use the `Start-SPServiceInstance` PowerShell cmdlet and pass it the reference to your service instance. Either would work in this situation.

**Option A:**

```
$service.Status = [Microsoft.SharePoint.Administration.SPObjectStatus]::Online
$service.Update()
```

**Option B:**

```
Start-SPServiceInstance $service
```

To confirm that the App Management Service has been properly started, navigate to the Services on Server page in Central Administration and verify that the service is set to Started (see Figure 9-10).

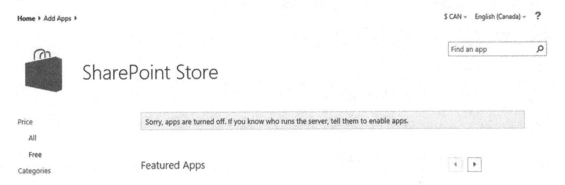

***Figure 9-10.*** *The App Management Service entry marked as Started through the Central Administration interface*

You now have the App Management component of your SharePoint farm up and running. Unfortunately, that is not enough to allow your users to use the app model and install apps in the environment. Still another service application needs to be installed before that. At this point, if users try to install an app from the SharePoint Store, they'll get a notice like the one in Figure 9-11 that apps are turned off in their environment, and that they should contact their administrator.

**Home** ▸ Add Apps ▸    $ CAN ⌄    English (Canada) ⌄    **?**

Find an app    🔍

🏪 SharePoint Store

Price
All
Free
Categories

Sorry, apps are turned off. If you know who runs the server, tell them to enable apps.

Featured Apps    ◀ ▶

***Figure 9-11.*** *Notification that the apps are turned off in the SharePoint Store*

# The Microsoft SharePoint Foundation Subscription Settings Service Application

The second SharePoint service application that is required to enable the use of add-ins (apps) in your environment is called the Microsoft SharePoint Foundation Subscription Settings Service application. This service application is used to manage subdomains for your add-ins. Basically, every add-in that you install

175

in your farm, with the exception of the default apps such as lists and document library, will each have its own subdomain. By default, app URLs will take the following structure:

```
http://[app prefix]-[app ID].[domain name]
```

where the app prefix is a value you specify in your farm's configuration (we'll get to that shortly), and the app ID is a random unique identifier for your app. It's interesting that unlike other service applications in the farm, this type is not available to be created through the Central Administration interface. You must use PowerShell to create an instance of it. Figure 9-12 shows you the available service applications from the interface. The Subscription Settings Service is not one of them.

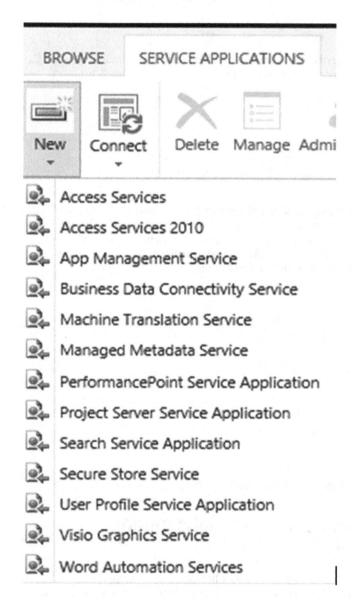

*Figure 9-12.* *List of available service applications in the Central Administration interface*

Just as it does for the App Management Service application, PowerShell provides us with a prebuilt cmdlet for creating an instance of the Subscription Settings Service application. The cmdlet in question is New-SPSubscriptionSettingsServiceApplication. (Is it just us or do these names keep getting longer and longer?) This cmdlet, just like the one for the App Management Service, take three parameters: a name, a database name, and an application pool to use.

```
$adminAcc = Get-SPManagedAccount "contoso\administrator"
$subSettingsPool = New-SPServiceApplicationPool -Name
SubSettingsServiceAppPool -Account $adminAcc

$subSettingsService = New-SPSubscriptionSettingsServiceApplication -Name
SubSettingsService -DatabaseName SubSettingsDB -ApplicationPool
$subSettingsPool
```

As with the previous application service, you need to create an associated proxy instance. Just when you thought cmdlet names couldn't get any longer, along comes New-SPSubscriptionSettingsServiceApplica tionProxy! If you can place this on a Scrabble board, victory is yours for sure. This cmdlet takes a reference to your service application and a name as parameters:

```
$subSettingsProxy = New-SPSubscriptionSettingsServiceApplicationProxy
-ServiceApplication $subSettingsService
```

Again, to verify that both your service application and its associated proxy have been created properly, open Central Administration and navigate to the Service Applications page. You should see the two entries shown in Figure 9-13.

| | |
|---|---|
| Security Token Service Application | Started |
| State Service | Started |
| State Service Proxy | Started |
| Microsoft SharePoint Foundation Subscription Settings Service Application | Started |
| Microsoft SharePoint Foundation Subscription Settings Service Application Proxy | Started |

***Figure 9-13.*** *Microsoft SharePoint Foundation Subscription Settings Service application and its proxy viewed in Central Administration*

As explained in the previous section, it is not enough to just create the service application and proxy instances. You also need to enable the associated service on the server. The name of the associated service is Microsoft SharePoint Foundation Subscription Settings Service. Use the piping method shown in Chapter 3 to obtain a reference to the instance of the service, and to turn it on:

```
$subSettingsSvc = Get-SPServiceInstance | Where{$_.TypeName -eq "Microsoft SharePoint
Foundation Subscription Settings Service"}

Start-SPServiceInstance $subSettingsSvc
```

# Final Configuration Steps

You are now down to the last step of configuring SharePoint apps for your environment. As mentioned earlier in this section, apps in the context of SharePoint 2016 are accessed using a very specific URL. The first part of that URL is the app prefix, which can be any identifier you want to specify. By default, we tend to simply use the word "Apps" as a prefix. It helps us quickly identify whether what we're looking at is an app or a SharePoint page by simply looking at the URL in the browser.

Before configuring the app prefix using PowerShell, let's take a brief look at how one would normally do it using the web interface. Notice that when you open Central Administration in SharePoint 2016, the interface looks very similar to what you were accustomed to in the 2010 version of the product. However, one big difference jumps out at us right from the start: the introduction of a totally new section called Apps, which is represented by two white octagons on a blue background. This is a brand new management section that Microsoft introduced in 2013 and in 2016 to allow administrators to easily manage settings related to the configuration and the licensing of apps. To configure the app's prefix through the interface, navigate to the Apps section by clicking on the header, and then choose Configure App URLs. This will bring a page up that will allow you to specify the app domain to use, as well as the app prefix.

We will now do it the PowerShell way. Start by configuring the app domain using the Set-SPAppDomain cmdlet. This cmdlet takes a single parameter, appdomain, which lets you identify the DNS of the domain your SharePoint farm is on. In our case, we will use the following line of PowerShell to get it configured properly within our environment:

```
Set-SPAppDomain -AppDomain "app.jen.com"
```

The next step is to configure the app prefix. The cmdlet's name for this is less intuitive; it is Set-SPAppSiteSubscriptionName. The cmdlet takes a single parameter, Name, which represents the app prefix that you wish to use across your farm. The following line of PowerShell will configure our farm to use the prefix "apps" for all of its SharePoint apps' URLs.

```
Set-SPAppSiteSubscriptionName -Name "apps" -Confirm:$false
```

To verify that everything has been configured properly, you can navigate to the Configure App URLs page in Central Administration. You should now see both the app domain and app prefix values specified in the text boxes, as shown in Figure 9-14.

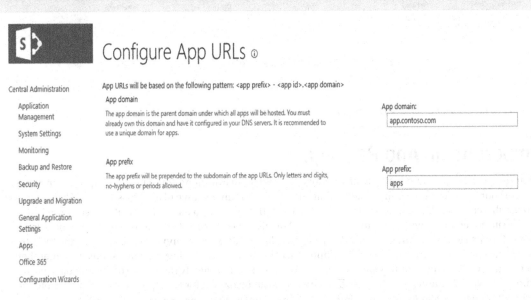

*Figure 9-14. App domain and prefix viewed through the Central Administration interface*

At this point, you are now ready to deploy and install apps within your SharePoint 2016 environment. If you navigate back to the SharePoint Store page, you should see that the yellow notification banner is now gone, indicating that apps are configured properly. In the next section, you will learn how to use PowerShell to interact with app instances and have them automatically deployed within your environment.

Only one problem remains: the app URLs are not being resolved by our DNS service. In order to allow your DNS service to resolve them, you need to create a new subdomain on your main contoso.com domain. Before PowerShell version 3, interacting with DNS entry using PowerShell required you to do all sorts of gymnastics using obscure Windows Management namespaces. Starting with version 3, you now have a full set of extremely useful PowerShell cmdlets that allow you to interact directly with DNS entries. You need to create a new alias for the apps prefix in your DNS server. The following line of PowerShell will take care of it for you:

```
Add-DnsServerResourceRecordCName -Name "*.app" -HostNameAlias "jen.com" -ZoneName "jen.com"
```

---

■ **Note** This command needs to run on the server that contains DNS or configure remoting.

---

To verify that the entry was properly created, run the DNS manager console, by typing **dnsmgmt.msc** in the Run console of windows (Windows key + R). When the console opens, expands the node representing your server, expand the Forward Lookup Zone folder, and click the contoso.com node. You should see the entry shown in Figure 9-15.

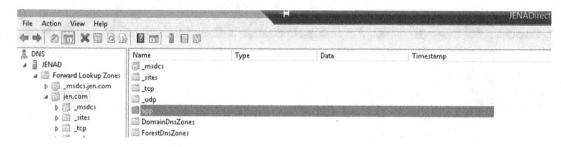

***Figure 9-15.*** *New entry in the DNS manager console for app management*

# Importing an App Package

Before you can deploy and install a SharePoint app in your environment, you'll need to import an instance of it in your farm. The PowerShell cmdlet that lets you import an instance of an app is Import-SPAppPackage. To use this command, you'll need to pass it the local path to your .app package, and also specify the URL of the site collection in which it is to be imported. You also need to specify the source of the app package to import. To use this command, you need to pass it the local path to your .app package and specify the URL of the site collection into which it will be imported. (The user who is calling the cmdlet must be a member of the site owners' group for this site collection.) You also need to specify the source of the app package to import. Table 9-2 enumerates the possible values that can be passed for an app package's source. Note there is a sixth value—InvalidSource—that indicates an error and can be seen only as a return value.

***Table 9-2.*** *Valid Value Options for an App Package Source*

| Value | Description |
| --- | --- |
| Marketplace | Indicates that the app is taken from the Office Marketplace. |
| CorporateCatalog | Indicates that the app is taken from the Corporate Catalog. This means that the application has been made available to all employees by the farm administrator. |
| DeveloperSite | Indicates that the app is taken from a developer's site. Normally developers will push their development apps onto a special type of site called a Developers' site. |
| ObjectModel | Indicates that the app has been compiled onto a local package and that it is that local app package that we are trying to import. |
| RemoteObjectModel | Indicates that the app that you're trying to import was uploaded using the Client Object Model. |

The following example will import a custom local SharePoint app into our root site collection (see Figure 9-16):

```
$app = Import-SPAppPackage -Path C:\test.app -Site http://localhost/
-Source ([Microsoft.SharePoint.Administration.SPAppSource]::ObjectModel)
```

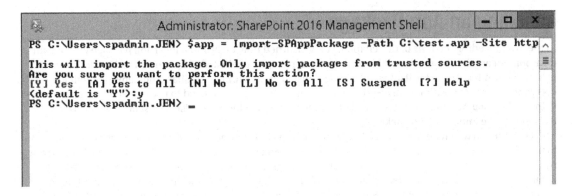

***Figure 9-16.*** *Importing a SharePoint 2016 app package using PowerShell*

As mentioned earlier, Microsoft made a big push with the 2016 release of SharePoint to help developers make their apps available to the largest number of users, by enabling the Office Store. Most organizations will probably start their SharePoint 2016 app journey by browsing the Office Store and installing from that source.

# Exporting App Packages

It is important here to note the difference between an app package and an app instance. The term package represents the actual .app file that is produced once SharePoint code is compiled. An instance, by contrast, represents an installed entity of a specific app. An instance is associated with a particular web onto which it has been deployed. Assuming that for some reason you have lost the original .app package of a custom app in your organization, if there is still an instance of that app existing in your SharePoint environment, PowerShell provides you with a mechanism to extract the .app package that is associated with your instance. The Export-SPAppPackage cmdlet expects two parameters: an app instance, and a path that specified where to store the extracted app package.

The following example describes how you can get an app package from the SharePoint store. First you have to install an app from the store manually in your farm, and then retrieve its related information using the Get-SPAppInstance cmdlet. We won't cover the details of how you can install an app from the SharePoint Store using the web interface. It is a very straightforward process that we're sure you'll be able to figure out easily. Calling the cmdlet will give you an app instance object. To retrieve its associated package, you need to look at its App property (one important point to note is that an administrator account is not allowed to install apps on a SharePoint web):

```
$app = Get-SPAppInstance -Web http://localhost | Where {$_.Title -like "appname*"}
```

With this information in hand, you can now call the Export method, specifying the app package object, as well as a local path to extract the app package to:

```
Export-SPAppPackage -App $app.App -Path "C:\appname.app"
```

Navigate to the specified path, and verify that the local .app package has been created as expected. You are now ready to move forward and install an app package within our SharePoint environment.

# Installing an App Package

In the two preceding sections of this chapter, you've learned how to import a local app package within your environment and how to produce a local package from an already installed app instance. Now let's look at how you can take those local app packages and install them within your SharePoint environment for everyone in the organization to use and consume. The cmdlet that you need to use to install an app package is `Install-SPApp`. You need to pass it the URL of the web onto which you wish to install it, as well as a reference to the imported app package.

One thing to watch out for here is that for security reasons, the administrator account is never allowed to install apps in a SharePoint farm. Therefore, you will need to launch PowerShell as a separate user before running the scripts that follow. This user will need to be granted special permissions against the content databases associated with the web where you're trying to install the app package. In order to grant these permissions, you can run the `Add-SPShellAdmin` cmdlet and specify the user name and the GUID of the content database in question:

```
$contentDB = Get-SPContentDatabase -WebApplication http://localhost
Add-SPShellAdmin -UserName jen\testuser -Database $contentDB
```

This code example assumes that there is only one database returned for the web application; otherwise, the variable DB will represent an array of content databases, and you will need to specify the one to which you wish to grant permissions.

The following example will import and install the test app that you extracted locally in the previous section. Note if that this app package was taken from the online store, it will require you to specify two additional parameters when importing it: the `AssetId`, and the `ContentMarket`, both of which you obtained in the preceding section of this chapter:

```
$testApp = Import-SPAppPackage -Path "C:\test.app" -Site http://localhost
Install-SPApp -Web http://localhost -Identity $testapp
```

Once executed, an installation process for the specified app will be initiated. The app instance status is set to installing. Give it a few seconds and navigate to the All Site Contents page of your root web (`http://localhost`). If everything went as expected, you should see your test app installed in the list of available SharePoint apps.

# Uninstalling a SharePoint App

To uninstall an app instance, the cmdlet to use is `Uninstall-SPAppInstance`, and as a parameter, it simply takes a reference to the app instance to uninstall. Note that what you are doing here is simply removing a specific instance of an app on a particular web. You are not removing the app entirely from our farm. As was the case for installing an app, the default administrator account is prohibited from uninstalling apps. You will have to run PowerShell using another administrator account. The following example shows how to uninstall the instance of the test app we've just installed at the root of our main site collection:

```
$testApp = Get-SPAppInstance -Web http://localhost | Where{$_.Title -like "test*"}
Uninstall-SPAppInstance -Identity $testApp
```

One very important piece of information you'll probably want to obtain as an administrator is a list of webs on which a specific app is installed on. You can easily create a short PowerShell script using everything that you've learned so far and get the result printed out on screen. Our script would need to begin by obtaining a reference to the Web Application instance in which you want to check for instances of your apps. You would then loop through each site collection and each web to determine if the specified app is installed or not. The following lines of PowerShell would allow you to create such a useful script:

```
# Prompt the user to enter the name of the app to check for instances of
$appTitle = Read-Host "What is the name of your app?"

# Get a reference to the Web Application on port 80
$webApp = Get-SPWebApplication http://localhost

# Loop through all site collections in the Web Aplication
foreach($site in $webApp.Sites)
{
    # Loop through each Web in the current site collection
    foreach($web in $site.AllWebs)
    {
        # Query the current site for an instance of our app
        $appInstance = Get-SPAppInstance -Web $web.Url |
            Where {$_.Title -like "*$appTitle*"}

        # If the appInstance variable is not null, then an instance was found
        if($appInstance -ne $null)
        {
            Write-Host $web.Url -BackgroundColor "green"
        }

        $web.Dispose()
    }
    $site.Dispose()
}
```

# The App Catalog

SharePoint 2013 introduced a new site collection template called the App Catalog. An app catalog is a site that makes custom apps available to your organization. It lets administrators control apps for Office and SharePoint, and it also allows users to request apps from the Office Store. App requests can then be approved or rejected by the administrator. An app catalog is an essential piece of any SharePoint 2016 farm in which apps are enabled to end users.

# Creating an App Catalog

By default, the new App Catalog template is not made available via the New Site Collection page. To create an app catalog through the web interface, go to Central Administration and navigate to the Apps ➤ Manage App Catalog page using the option shown in Figure 9-17. This page will let you create a new app catalog and specify the primary and secondary administrators, as if you were just creating a normal site collection.

# Apps

SharePoint and Office Store
Purchase Apps | Manage App Licenses | Configure Store Settings

App Management
Manage App Catalog | Monitor Apps | Configure App URLs | App Permissions

***Figure 9-17.*** *The Manage App Catalog link in Central Administration*

Using PowerShell, things are almost as easy. We simply call the New-SPSite cmdlet as if we were creating a new site collection, and we specify the custom APPCATALOG#0 template name. The following line of PowerShell shows how to create a new app catalog for our environment (shown in Figure 9-18). The app catalog will be created at

```
$catalogSite = New-SPSite -Url http://localhost/sites/appcatalog -OwnerAlias
"contoso\administrator" -Name "App Catalog" -Template "APPCATALOG#0"
```

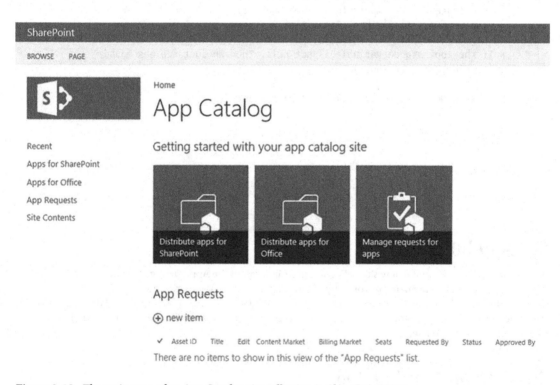

***Figure 9-18.*** *The main page of an App Catalog site collection in SharePoint 2016*

At this point, your app catalog site collection has been properly created, but it is not yet associated with your current Web application. Even if you were to add new applications at this point, they would not be discoverable by users on other sites. What you need to do now is associate the site collection with your current web application. Each web application in a SharePoint environment can have an instance of an app catalog associated with it. You cannot have more than one catalog per web application, however. To associate your catalog, you need to execute the following line of PowerShell:

```
Update-SPAppCatalogConfiguration -Site http://localhost/sites/appcatalog
```

To verify that the app catalog has been properly associated with your web application, you can navigate back to the Manage App Catalog page in Central Administration (Figure 9-19), and ensure that the site collection is configured properly.

*Figure 9-19.* *The Manage App Catalog screen in Central Administration*

# Adding an App to the Catalog

Once your app catalog is up and running, one of the first things you'll probably want to do is add authorized apps for your end users to start consuming. Although it is very easy to upload custom app packages through the catalog's web interface, there might be scenarios in which you will want to use PowerShell to achieve this instead. In fact, in many organizations the process of adding apps to the corporate catalog is controlled by the administration team, which uses PowerShell scripts to add, remove, and modify app packages from the catalog. Unfortunately for us, there are no "shortcut" cmdlets that will let us do this in an easy way. You need to treat the app catalog site as if it was just any other site, and upload our local .app package in the appropriate document library.

Each app catalog site has three main document libraries that are made available to SharePoint administrators: Apps for SharePoint, Apps for Office, and App Requests. The first one is the one that we are interested in. It contains a list of all apps that have been made available by the administrators to users in the organization. The following lines of PowerShell will allow you to get a reference to it and to upload a custom .app file in it. Assume this app file (`ChapterRestrictedApp.app`) was provided to us by developers within our organization:

```
$web = Get-SPWeb http://localhost/sites/appcatalog

#Gets a reference to the AppCatalog library
$appCatalog = $web.GetFolder("AppCatalog")
$appFiles = $appCatalog.Files
```

```
$myAppPackage = Get-ChildItem C:\Apps\ChapterRestrictedApp.App
$appFiles.Add("AppCatalog/ChapterRestrictedApp.App",
$myAppPackage.OpenRead(), $false);
```

Executing these lines of PowerShell will automatically make the uploaded app package available to everyone in the organization. To confirm that the upload process worked as expected, simply navigate to the Apps for SharePoint library of your app catalog. You should now see an entry in there for your new app package (see Figure 9-20).

## Apps for SharePoint

⊕ new app or drag files here

| | | | | | | | | | |
|---|---|---|---|---|---|---|---|---|---|
| All Apps | Featured Apps | Unavailable Apps | ··· | Find a file | 🔎 | | | | |
| ✓ | 🗋 | Title | | Name | App Version | Edit | Product ID | Metadata Language | Default Metadata Language | Modified |

◢ Product ID : {4BC57D8C-3AE9-4A79-8A5C-3D071679F5E6} (1)

| | 🗋 | Chapter RestrictedApp | Chapter RestrictedApp ☒ | ··· | 1.0.0.1 | 🗔 | {4BC57D8C-3AE9-4A79-8A5C-3D071679F5E6} | English - 1033 | Yes | 13 minutes ago |

***Figure 9-20.*** *A SharePoint 2016 app uploaded into the app catalog*

With this package deployed, users who try to add a new app to their sites will now see the newly added app as an available choice (see Figure 9-21).

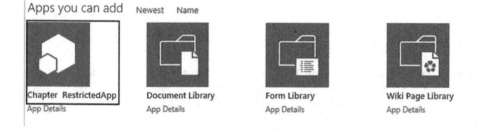

Apps you can add   Newest   Name

Chapter RestrictedApp
App Details

Document Library
App Details

Form Library
App Details

Wiki Page Library
App Details

***Figure 9-21.*** *Available apps on a SharePoint 2016 web*

# Managing App Permissions

As a SharePoint administrator, you may decide to prevent users from installing apps on certain sites in your environment. PowerShell provides you with various cmdlets that will give you better control over how you want apps to be automatically deployed throughout your organization. However, with PowerShell there is no way to specify granular permissions for end users on specific apps. That is, you need to start by defining how permissions work within the context of SharePoint 2016 apps.

In SharePoint 2016, every app package contains an XML declaration file known as the *manifest*. An app manifest file contains information about its associated resources such as its app's title, product ID, and version. It also contains very important information about the set of permissions it needs in order to be installed. When installing an app, the installation process looks at the permissions of the user who's trying to install the app to determine whether the minimum set of permissions required is attained. A user trying to install an app needs to be able to meet every single permission requirement for the app in order to be granted rights to install it. Once the app is installed, every user trying to use the app will also need to meet the minimum permission requirement. Because the minimal installation permissions are set in the app package directly, there is no way with PowerShell to block specific users from installing apps. If you need to prevent a certain group of users from being able to install and use a specific app using PowerShell, you will need to lower their permissions, making sure they don't meet the minimum required set of permissions to use the app.

To illustrate this, let's take a look at the `ChapterRestrictedApp` app. When first developed in Visual Studio, the app had the permissions shown in Figure 9-22 applied to it.

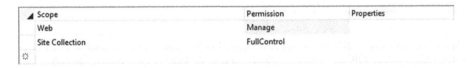

***Figure 9-22.*** *SharePoint 2016 custom app permissions viewed in Visual Studio*

This basically means that in order for a user to be able to install and use this app, they'll need to be granted permissions to manage the web on which the app is to be installed, and be an administrator of its site collection. Now, let's assume a new user named Bob Houle has the Full Control role on the web on which he wants to install your app, but he is not a site collection administrator, which is a requirement for the app to install. He also does not have any access whatsoever on the app catalog site on which your custom app has been deployed. When this user goes to the Add an App page and looks at the apps that are available to him, he won't see the `ChapterRestrictedApp` listed (see Figure 9-23).

***Figure 9-23.*** *Custom app not listed on available apps page*

To even be made aware that this app is available to his organization, Bob needs to be granted at least Read access to the app catalog site. We can use what we've learned before and grant the user read access to the site using PowerShell. Once the access has been granted, the user will see the app appear on the From Your Organization page but won't be given the option to install it. Clicking on the app details will display the message shown in Figure 9-24 to the user.

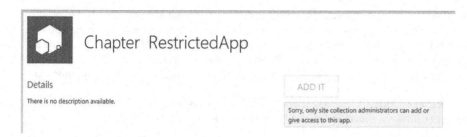

*Figure 9-24.* *Denied permission to install a custom app*

In order to allow the user to install your custom app, you'll need to make him a site collection administrator. Doing so will automatically allow the user to install and trust the application for the current site (see Figure 9-25).

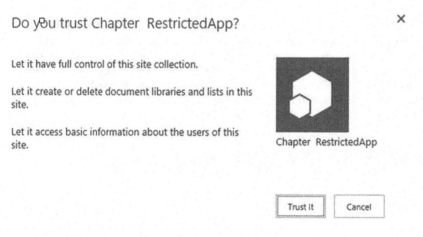

*Figure 9-25.* *The Trust dialog for a custom SharePoint 2016 app*

# Updating an Existing App

The new app model allows different versions of a single app to run across various webs. For example, the Finance division in our organization could have deployed version 1.0.0.4 of our ChapterRestrictedApp, while the Human Resources division can have the 1.0.0.5 version deployed. As a SharePoint administrator, this is something you need to be aware of and is something you should pay close attention to. From an app catalog perspective, a different version of an app is simply another version of an app package you need to upload to your Apps for SharePoint library.

You may argue that running several versions of the same app is good for your organization because it offers backward compatibility, but personally we smell nothing but trouble coming out of this. As a SharePoint administrator, you'll probably want to be able to tell, when deploying a new version of an app, what sites are using the previous version of your app. This would allow you to figure out who the client for the site is, and try to see if there's a way for them to upgrade to the latest version. Out-of-the-box, this is not something that is easily feasible, but with PowerShell, the sky is the limit! Every app package object in SharePoint exposes a property called VersionString that contains the version of the current app package installed on a specific web. Given our example, Figure 9-26 shows the result of obtaining our app instance on both the Finance and Human Resource sites.

```
PS C:\Users\charln> $financeInstance = Get-SPAppInstance -Web http://localhost/sites/finance | where ($_.Title -Eq "Chap
ter RestrictedApp")
PS C:\Users\charln> $financeInstance.App.VersionString
1.0.0.3
PS C:\Users\charln>
PS C:\Users\charln>
PS C:\Users\charln>
PS C:\Users\charln> $hrInstance = Get-SPAppInstance -Web "http://localhost/sites/human resources" | where ($_.Title -Eq
"Chapter RestrictedApp")
PS C:\Users\charln> $hrInstance.App.VersionString
1.0.0.4
PS C:\Users\charln> _
```

***Figure 9-26.*** *Displaying two versions of the same app on different sites using PowerShell*

All right, so you now know that the Finance site needs some upgrading of its `ChapterRestrictedApp` app. How do you make sure that you upgrade to the latest version of the app using PowerShell? Fear not; `Update-SPAppInstance` is coming to your rescue. This cmdlet takes two parameters: `App`, a reference to the newest version of the app package; and `Identity`, a reference to the app instance to upgrade. Normally, you would get a reference to the newest app package using the `.app` file on disk. Assume the newest package of your app is located on disk at `C:\temp\ChapterRestrictedApp-1.0.0.4.app`. You should get a reference to this package using `Get-SPAppInstance`:

```
$financeAppInstance = Get-SPAppInstance -Web http://localhost/sites/Finance |
Where {$_.Title -eq "ChapterRestrictedApp"}

$newestPackage = Import-SPAppPackage -Path C:\Temp\ChapterRestrictedApp-1.0.0.4.app
-Site http://localhost/sites/Finance
-Source ([Microsoft.SharePoint.Administration.SPAppSource]::CorporateCatalog)

Update-SPAppInstance -Identity $financeAppInstance -App $newestPackage
```

To recap, in order to update an app to its latest version, you need to begin by importing the newest version of the app package onto the web where the outdated app is located. Then, once the package has been imported, you can simply get a reference to the outdated app instance, and then call the `Update-SPAppInstance` cmdlet, passing both values as parameters.

# Summary

In this chapter, you've learned how, as a SharePoint administrator, to control custom solutions and apps produced by your developers using PowerShell. We've also gone through the process of creating new service application instances using scripts.

■ ■ ■

# CHAPTER 10

# Extending PowerShell for SharePoint

We are approaching the end of the book and we have discussed various topics about PowerShell for SharePoint 2016 and how to control many SharePoint 2016 functionalities using PowerShell. What if you found that there are some commands missing or you need to create your own commands to manage your farms? Is there a way to do that?

The answer is yes, you can extend PowerShell. In this chapter we will go through creating modules, cmdlets, and functions. First let us differentiate between a module and a snap-in:

> **Snap-In:** This is the model from the first version of PowerShell. To deploy a snap-in, an installer would have to hack the registry, which would require elevated privileges. Currently SharePoint functionality is in snap-ins.

> **Module:** This model was introduced in PowerShell 2.0, and the functionality is defined in assemblies or scripts. To load a module, you simply use the `Import-Module` command.

## Creating Modules and Cmdlets

The module is going to be the DLL that contains the cmdlet we are going to create. We will name the module that we create in this chapter `GetSitesModule`, and will create a cmdlet to get sites. (Although a similar cmdlet is available, it was created to demonstrate how to create a module and cmdlet and import the created module and use the newly defined cmdlet.)

Let us start by opening Visual Studio. We are using Visual Studio 2015 and will choose the Class Library project as in Figure 10-1. You can download and install the community edition of Visual Studio 2015, which is free.

© Nikolas Charlebois-Laprade and John Edward Naguib 2017
N. Charlebois-Laprade and J. E. Naguib, *Beginning PowerShell for SharePoint 2016*,
DOI 10.1007/978-1-4842-2884-5_10

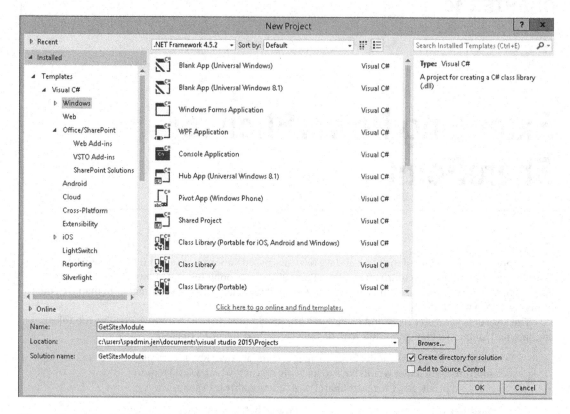

*Figure 10-1. The Class Library project*

Clicking OK will create the project. We can then rename the class to GetAllSites, and the project screen will look like Figure 10-2.

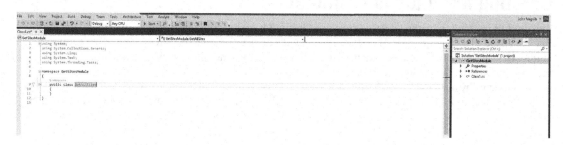

*Figure 10-2. The project after creation*

Then we need to add a reference to `system.management.Automation`. To do so, we need to right-click Add Reference and browse. We will find the DLL for this namespace in the path `C:\Windows\assembly\ GAC_MSIL\System.Management.Automation\1.0.0.0__31bf3856ad364e35`, as shown in Figure 10-3.

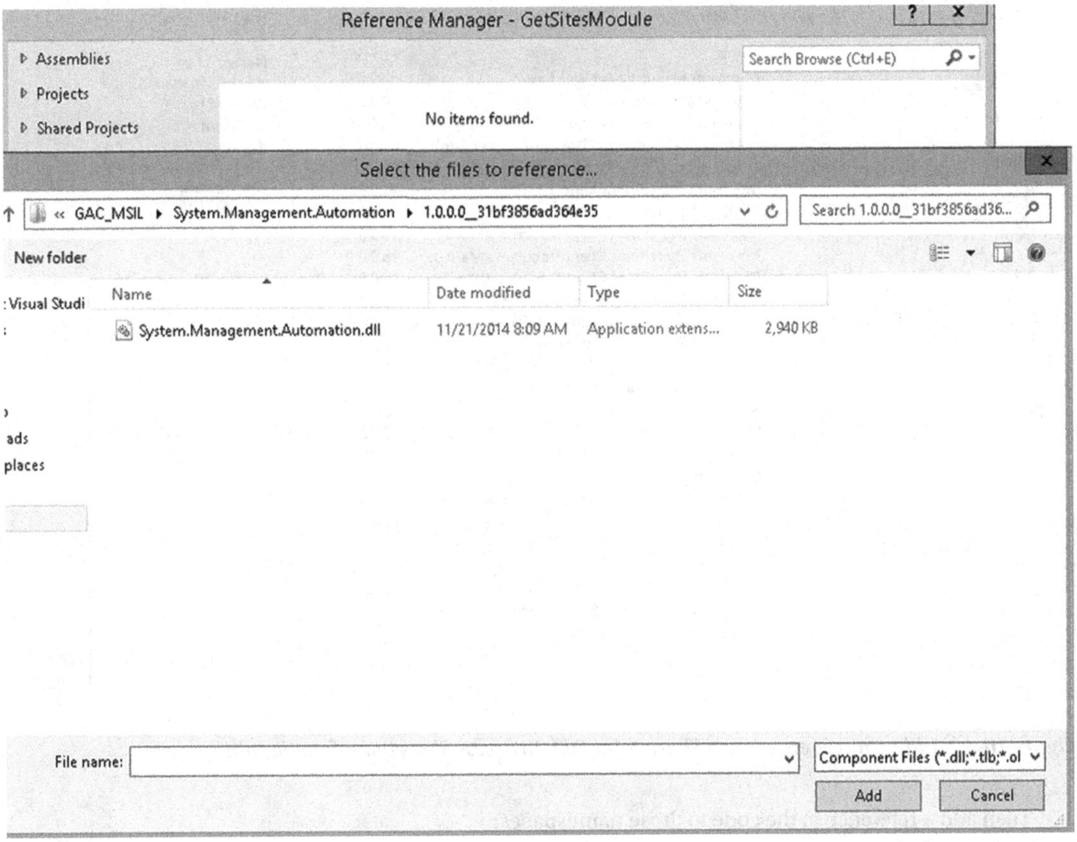

*Figure 10-3.* *Adding a reference to the Automation DLL used to access PowerShell*

Then we need to add a reference to the SharePoint DLL, as in Figure 10-4.

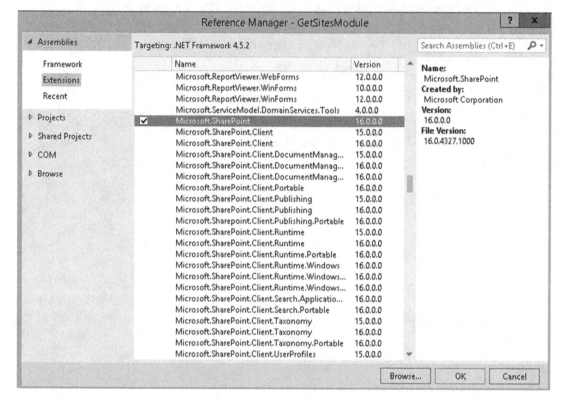

***Figure 10-4.*** *Adding a reference to the SharePoint DLL to access SharePoint functionality*

Then add a reference in the code to those namespaces:

```
using System.Management.Automation;
using Microsoft.SharePoint;
```

Then, before the top of the class definition, add this line:

```
[System.Management.Automation.Cmdlet(System.Management.Automation.VerbsCommon.Get,
"SPAllSites")]
```

This line declares the class as a cmdlet by specifying the verb to use, and the noun. In this example, our verb is "Get" and our noun "SPAllSites, meaning that our cmdlet will be accessed using the Get-SPAllSites method.

Then we need our class to inherit from the Cmdlet class in the System.Management.Automation namespace:

```
public class GetAllSites: Cmdlet
```

If we need to define parameters, then we will need to declare class variables, like the following:

```
[System.Management.Automation.Parameter(Position = 0, Mandatory = true)]
    public string WebApplicationName;
```

This code defines the input order and whether it is mandatory.

Then we will need to override the ProcessRecord function; in this function we are going to put the logic for our cmdlet. In the example we will retrieve all site collections by passing as a parameter the web application name where we want to get all the site collections.

The complete code will look like this:

```
using System;
using System.Collections.Generic;
using System.Linq;
using System.Text;
using System.Threading.Tasks;
using System.Management;
using System.Management.Automation;
using Microsoft.SharePoint;
using Microsoft.SharePoint.Administration;

namespace GetSitesModule
{

[System.Management.Automation.Cmdlet(System.Management.Automation.VerbsCommon.Get, "SPAllSites")]
    public class GetAllSites : Cmdlet
    {
        [System.Management.Automation.Parameter(Position = 0, Mandatory = true)]
        public string WebApplicationName;

        protected override void ProcessRecord()
        {
            SPFarm farm = SPFarm.Local;
            SPWebService service = farm.Services.GetValue<SPWebService>("");
            foreach(SPSite site in service.WebApplications[WebApplicationName].Sites)

            {
                //Site collections
                this.WriteObject(site.RootWeb.Url);
            }

        }
    }
}
```

Then we will need to compile the code (in the Build menu, select Build) and once it is compiled we will get the generated DLL and will put in a path or copy it to the server where we will run the cmdlet. It needs to be a SharePoint server.

Then we will need to import the module:

```
Import-Module c:\GetSitesModule.dll
```

Then we will call the cmdlet:

```
Get-SPAllSites -WebApplicationName "Root"
```

The output will be the site collections in this web application, as shown in Figure 10-5.

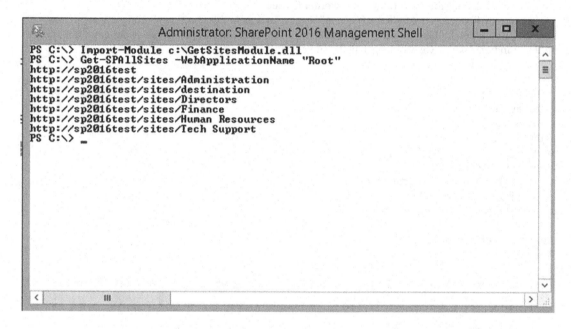

*Figure 10-5.* *Output of the cmdlet we created*

We can get the name of the web application parameter from Central Administration as shown in Figure 10-6.

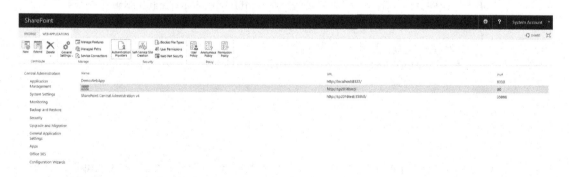

*Figure 10-6.* *Web application names*

## Creating a Function

In this section we will go through creating a PowerShell function in a PowerShell file (.ps1 extension).

The following example code is a function that has no parameter and returns all the databases. It is called from outside the function by calling the function name and setting it to a variable:

```
"$Outputreport= ContentReport"

Function ContentReport (){

$f1 = Get-SPDatabase
$result  = $f1 | Select-Object DisplayName,WebApplication,CurrentSiteCount,disksizerequired,
WarningSiteCount,MaximumSiteCount
if($result -ne $null)
{

return $result
}

}

$Outputreport= ContentReport
```

To create a function with parameters we can do the following, which specifies the parameter as a string:

```
Function FunctionName
{
param(
        [string]$computerName

)

# put the function logic here
}
```

PowerShell also provide other ways to define parameters. For example, to specify a parameter as mandatory, we can do the following:

```
Param(
  [Parameter(Mandatory=$True,Position=1)]
  [string]$computerName,

  [Parameter(Mandatory=$True)]
  [string]$filePath
)
```

# Summary

In this chapter you learned how to create your own modules, cmdlets, and functions that can extend or tailor SharePoint 2016 to the requirements or environment we are working on, and we have now reached the end of this book.

# APPENDIX

# Common Cmdlets

This appendix gives a brief overview of the various PowerShell cmdlets we covered in this book and some other useful cmdlets, along with examples of how to use them.

## Set-SPServer

Sets the role in the SharePoint 2016 farm:

```
Set-SPServer -Identity <server name> -Role <server role>
```

## Get-SPFarmConfig

Returns a global property or a collection of global properties for the local farm:

```
Get-SPFarmConfig [-AssignmentCollection <SPAssignmentCollection>] [-ServiceConnectionPoint
<SwitchParameter>]
```

## Set-SPPassPhrase

Sets the passphrase to a new value:

```
Set-SPPassPhrase -ConfirmPassPhrase <SecureString> -PassPhrase <SecureString>
[-AssignmentCollection <SPAssignmentCollection>] [-Confirm [<SwitchParameter>]] [-WhatIf
[<SwitchParameter>]]
```

## Add-SPSolution

Adds a SharePoint solution to the farm. Needs to reference the local .wsp solution file:

```
Add-SPSolution -LiteralPath c:\solution.wsp
   [UNCPath to the local .wsp file]
```

© Nikolas Charlebois-Laprade and John Edward Naguib 2017
N. Charlebois-Laprade and J. E. Naguib, *Beginning PowerShell for SharePoint 2016*,
DOI 10.1007/978-1-4842-2884-5

# Backup-SPFarm

Creates a backup of a specific database, a web application, or the entire SharePoint farm:

```
Backup-SPFarm -Directory [Path to the backup directory] -BackupMethod Full
```

# Backup-SPSite

Creates a backup of a specific site collection:

```
Backup-SPSite -Identity [URL of the site collection to backup]
-Path [Path to where to store the resulting .bak file]
```

# Copy-SPSite

Creates a copy of an existing site collection at a different location in the same SharePoint web application:

```
Copy-SPSite -Identity http://contoso/sites/OldTeam
 [URL of the site collection to copy]
-TargetUrl http://contoso/sites/NewTeam

[URL of the destination to copy the site collection to]
```

# Disable-SPTimerJob

Disables a specific timer job, preventing its execution:

```
Disable-SPTimerJob -Identity [Reference to the timer job instance]
```

# Enable-SPTimerJob

Enables a specific timer job, allowing it to execute based on its established schedule:

```
Enable-SPTimerJob -Identity [Reference to the timer job instance]
```

# Export-SPAppPackage

Exports a specific app instance into a local .app package:

```
Export-SPAppPackage -App [Reference to the app instance]
-Path [Local path to the .app file to store]
```

# Export-SPWeb

Exports a SharePoint web into a local file:

```
Export-SPWeb -Identity[URL of the web to export] -Path [Local path of the .cmp export file
where to store the exported web]
```

# Get-SPAppInstance

Returns a collection of app instances installed on a specific web:

```
Get-SPAppInstance -Web [URL of the web to get the app instances from]
```

# Get-SPBackupHistory

Returns the history of all backup and restore operations that took place in a specific folder:

```
Get-SPBackupHistory -Directory [Path to backup folder]
```

# Get-SPFarm

Returns a reference to the local SharePoint farm:

```
Get-SPFarm
```

# Get-SPServiceApplication

Returns a collection of all instances of service applications in the SharePoint farm:

```
Get-SPServiceApplication
```

# Get-SPServiceApplicationPool

Returns a collection of all IIS application pools:

```
Get-SPServiceApplicationPool
```

# Get-SPServiceInstance

Returns a collection of all service instances for a specific server or for the entire SharePoint farm:

```
Get-SPServiceInstance
```

# Get-SPSite

Returns a collection of all site collections in the SharePoint farm:

```
Get-SPSite
```

# Get-SPTimerJob

Returns a collection of all timer jobs registered in the SharePoint farm:

```
Get-SPTimerJob
```

# Get-SPUser

Returns a collection of all users associated with a specific SharePoint web:

```
Get-SPUser -Web [URL of the web to get the user list from]
```

# Get-SPWeb

Returns a reference to a specific SharePoint web:

```
Get-SPWeb -Identity[URL of the web to get a reference to]
```

# Get-SPWebApplication

Returns a collection of all SharePoint web applications contained in the local farm:

```
Get-SPWebApplication
```

# Get-SPWebTemplate

Returns a collection of all web templates contained in the local SharePoint farm:

```
Get-SPWebTemplate
```

# Import-SPAppPackage

Imports a local app package into a specified site collection. It requires users to specify the source origin of the package. This value can be Marketplace, CorporateCatalog, DeveloperSite, ObjectModel, or RemoteObjectModel:

```
Import-SPAppPackage
-Path [Local path to the .app package to import]
-Site [URL of the site collection in which to import the app package]
-Source ([Microsoft.SharePoint.Administration.SPAppSource]::ObjectModel)
```

# Import-SPWeb

Imports a SharePoint web, a list, or a library based on an exported .cmp SharePoint artifact from a local file:

```
Import-SPWeb -Identity [URL of where to restore the web]
-Path [Local path to the .cmp exported web file]
```

# Install-SPApp

Installs an app on a specific SharePoint web:

```
Install-SPApp
-Web [URL of the web on which to install the app instance]
-Identity [Reference to app instance]
```

# Install-SPSolution

Installs a SharePoint farm solution that has been previously added to the farm:

```
Install-SPSolution -Identity [Name of the solution]
```

# Mount-SPContentDatabase

Attaches a SharePoint database to the current farm:

```
Mount-SPContentDatabase —Name [Name of the content database on the SQL Server]
-WebApplication [URL of the web application to link the database to]
```

# Move-SPSite

Moves a site collection from one content database to another:

```
Move-SPSite -Identity [URL of the site collection to move]
-DestinationDatabase [Name of the destination database on the SQL Server]
```

# New-SPAppManagementServiceApplication

Creates a new instance of the App Management Service application:

```
New-SPAppManagementServiceApplication
-ApplicationPool [Reference to the associated application pool]
-Name [Name to give to the service application instance]
-DatabaseName [Name to give to the associated SQL Server database]
```

# New-SPAppManagementServiceApplicationProxy

Creates an App Management Service application proxy and associates it with its service application instance:

```
New-SPAppManagementServiceApplicationProxy
-ServiceApplication [Reference to the service application instance]
-Name [Name you wish to give to the service application proxy]
```

# New-SPConfigurationDatabase

Creates a new SharePoint configuration database for the local farm:

```
New-SPConfigurationDatabase
-DatabaseServer [Name of the SQL Server]
-DatabaseName [Name you wish to give to the new database]
-AdministrationContentDatabaseName [Reference to the SharePoint Administrative Database]
-Passphrase [Secret passphrase to configure the farm]
-FarmCredentials [Secure credentials to run the farm account]
```

# New-SPContentDatabase

Creates a new SharePoint content database in the farm's SQL Server:

```
New-SPContentDatbase —Name [Name of the new content database]
-DatabaseServer [Name of the farm's SQL Server]
-WebApplication [URL of the SharePoint web application to associate the content database
with]
```

# New-SPServiceApplicationPool

Creates a new IIS application pool:

```
New-SPServiceApplicationPool —Name [Name to give]
-Account [Username of the account to use to run this application pool]
```

# New-SPSite

Creates a new site collection:

```
New-SPSite -Url [URL of the new site collection]
-OwnerAlias [Username of the account to use as farm administrator]
```

# New-SPSubscriptionSettingsServiceApplication

Creates a new instance of the Subscription Settings Service application:

```
New-SPSubscriptionSettingsServiceApplication
-Name [Name to give the service application instance]
-DatabaseName [Name of the database associated to the service application instance]
-ApplicationPool [Reference to the application pool to use to run the service application]
```

# New-SPSubscriptionSettingsServiceApplicationProxy

Creates a new service application proxy for a Subscription Settings Service application instance:

```
New-SPSubscriptionSettingsServiceApplicationProxy
-ServiceApplication [Reference to the associated service application]
```

# New-SPWeb

Creates a new SharePoint web:
```
New-SPWeb -Url [URL of the new web]
```

# New-SPWebApplication

Creates a new SharePoint web application:

```
New-SPWebApplication
-Name [Name of the new Web Application]
-ApplicationPool [Name of an existing application pool to associate the web application
with]
```

# Remove-SPConfigurationDatabase

Permanently deletes the SharePoint farm's configuration database that has been previously dismounted:

```
Remove-SPConfigurationDatabase
```

# Remove-SPContentDatabase

Permanently deletes an instance of a SharePoint content database from SQL Server:

```
Remove-SPContentDatabase -Identity [Reference to the SharePoint content database]
```

# Remove-SPServiceApplication

Permanently deletes an instance of a SharePoint service application:

```
Remove-SPServiceApplication -Identity [GUID of the service application to delete]
```

# Remove-SPServiceApplicationPool

Permanently deletes an IIS web service application pool:

```
Remove-SPServiceApplicationPool -Identity [Reference to the IIS web service application pool
to delete]
```

# Remove-SPSite

Deletes a SharePoint site collection:

```
Remove-SPSite -Identity [URL of the site collection to delete]
```

# Remove-SPSolution

Deletes a SharePoint farm solution from the farm:

```
Remove-SPSolution -Identity [Name of the .wsp package to remove]
```

# Remove-SPWeb

Deletes a SharePoint web:

```
Remove-SPWeb -Identity [URL to the web to delete]
```

# Remove-SPWebApplication

Deletes a SharePoint web application:

```
Remove-SPWebApplication -Identity [URL or name of the web application to delete]
```

# Request-SPUpgradeEvaluationSite

Makes a request to have an upgrade evaluation site collection created in a queue. The daily timer job will then take care of creating it:

```
Request-SPUpgradeEvaluationSite -Identity [Reference to the original site collection]
```

# Set-SPServiceApplicationPool

Changes the account used to run a SharePoint IIS web service application pool:

```
Set-SPServiceApplicationPool –Identity [Reference to the IIS web service application pool]
-Account [Username to use to run the application pool]
```

# Set-SPTimerJob

Sets a new schedule for a running SharePoint timer job:

```
Set-SPTimerJob
-Identity [Reference to the timer job]
-Schedule "Hourly between 5 and 10"
```

# Set-SPWeb

Configures various properties of a specific SharePoint web:

```
Set-SPWeb -Identity[URL to the SharePoint Web]
-RelativeUrl [New relative URL of SharePoint web]
```

# Start-SPServiceInstance

Enables a specific SharePoint service instance on a specific server or on the entire farm:

```
Start-SPServiceInstance –Identity [GUID of the service instance to start]
```

# Start-SPTimerJob

Immediately executes a specific SharePoint timer job; then its normal execution schedule resumes:

```
Start-SPTimerJob -Identity[Reference to the timer job to execute]
```

# Stop-SPServiceInstance

Stops a service instance for a specific SharePoint service:

```
Stop-SPServiceInstance Identity [GUID of the service instance to stop]
```

# Test-SPContentDatabase

Tests a SharePoint content database against its associated web application to ensure that all customized components are installed:

```
Test-SPContentDatabase -Name[Name of the content database to test]
-WebApplication [URL of the web application to test the database against]
```

# Uninstall-SPAppInstance

Uninstalls a specific SharePoint app instance:

```
Uninstall-SPAppInstance -Identity[Reference to the app instance to uninstall]
```

# Uninstall-SPSolution

Uninstalls a specific SharePoint farm solution from the environment. Uninstalling it doesn't remove the .wsp from the server. You will need to use the Remove-SPSolution cmdlet to do so.

```
Uninstall-SPSolution -Identity [Name of the wsp solution to remove with its .wsp extension]
```

# Update-SPAppCatalogConfiguration

Updates the location of the app catalog:

```
Update-SPAppCatalogConfiguration -Site [URL of the new location of the app catalog]
```

# Update-SPAppInstance

Updates an app instance to a newer version:

```
Update-SPAppInstance -Identity[Reference to the old version of the app instance]
-App [Reference to the newest app instance]
```

# Update-SPSolution

Updates an already deployed SharePoint farm solution to its newest version:

```
Update-SPSolution -Identity [Name of the farm solution to update including the .wsp
extension]
-LiteralPath [Local path to the newest .wsp solution package]
-GACDeploy
```

# Index

## A

Add-ins, 172
Add-SPOUser cmdlet, 159
Add-SPSolution, 199
App catalog
    creation, 183–184
    document libraries, 185
    SharePoint 2016 app uploaded, 186
Application server role, 48
App Management Service application
    central administration, 173
    central administration interface, 175
    IIS application pool creation, 172
    notification, turned off, 175
    proxy, 174
    service instance status, 175
    SharePoint 2016 server, 174

## B

Backup-SPFarm, 200
Backup-SPSite, 200
Business Productivity Online Services (BPOS), 139

## C

Central Administration, 58
Client Side Object Model, 166
Cmdlets
    Add-SPSolution, 199
    Backup-SPFarm, 200
    Backup-SPSite, 200
    Copy-SPSite, 200
    Disable-SPTimerJob, 200
    Enable-SPTimerJob, 200
    Export-SPAppPackage, 200
    Export-SPWeb, 201
    Get-SPAppInstance, 201
    Get-SPBackupHistory, 201
    Get-SPFarm, 201

Get-SPFarmConfig, 199
Get-SPServiceApplication, 201
Get-SPServiceApplicationPool, 201
Get-SPServiceInstance, 201
Get-SPSite, 202
Get-SPTimerJob, 202
Get-SPUser, 202
Get-SPWeb, 202
Get-SPWebApplication, 202
Get-SPWebTemplate, 202
Import-SPAppPackage, 202
Import-SPWeb, 203
Install-SPApp, 203
Install-SPSolution, 203
Mount-SPContentDatabase, 203
Move-SPSite, 203
New-SPAppManagementServiceApplication, 203
New-SPAppManagementService
    ApplicationProxy, 204
New-SPConfigurationDatabase, 204
New-SPContentDatabase, 204
New-SPServiceApplicationPool, 204
New-SPSite, 204
New-SPSubscriptionSettingsService
    Application, 205
New-SPSubscriptionSettingsServiceApplication
    Proxy, 205
New-SPWeb, 205
New-SPWebApplication, 205
Remove-SPConfigurationDatabase, 205
Remove-SPContentDatabase, 205
Remove-SPServiceApplication, 206
Remove-SPServiceApplicationPool, 206
Remove-SPSite, 206
Remove-SPSolution, 206
Remove-SPWeb, 206
Remove-SPWebApplication, 206
Request-SPUpgradeEvaluationSite, 206
Set-SPPassPhrase, 199
Set-SPServer, 199
Set-SPServiceApplicationPool, 207

# Get the eBook for only $5!

Why limit yourself?

With most of our titles available in both PDF and ePUB format, you can access your content wherever and however you wish—on your PC, phone, tablet, or reader.

Since you've purchased this print book, we are happy to offer you the eBook for just $5.

To learn more, go to http://www.apress.com/companion or contact support@apress.com.

# Apress®

Printed in the United States
By Bookmasters